Studies in English and European Historical Dialectology

Linguistic Insights

Studies in Language and Communication

Edited by Maurizio Gotti,
University of Bergamo

Volume 98

PETER LANG
Bern · Berlin · Bruxelles · Frankfurt am Main · New York · Oxford · Wien

Marina Dossena & Roger Lass (eds)

Studies in English and European Historical Dialectology

PETER LANG

Bern · Berlin · Bruxelles · Frankfurt am Main · New York · Oxford · Wien

Bibliographic information published by Die Deutsche Bibliothek
Die Deutsche Bibliothek lists this publication in the Deutsche National-
bibliografie; detailed bibliographic data is available on the Internet at
‹http://dnb.ddb.de›.

British Library and Library of Congress Cataloguing-in-Publication Data:
A catalogue record for this book is available from *The British Library*,
Great Britain.

Library of Congress Cataloging-in-Publication Data

Studies in English and European historical dialectology / Marina Dossena &
Roger Lass (eds.).
p. cm. – (Linguistic insights, ISSN 1424-8689 ; v. 98)
Includes bibliographical references.
ISBN 978-3-0343-0024-7 (alk. paper)
1. Dialectology. 2. Language and languages–Variation. 3. English language–
Dialectology. 4. English language–Variation. 5. Historical linguistics.
I. Dossena, Marina, 1961- II. Lass, Roger.
P367.S88 2009
417'.2–dc22

          2009007258

Published with a grant from Università degli Studi di Bergamo (Italy),
Dip. di Lingue, Letterature e Culture Comparate.

ISSN 1424-8689
ISBN 978-3-0343-0024-7

© Peter Lang AG, International Academic Publishers, Bern 2009
Hochfeldstrasse 32, Postfach 746, CH-3000 Bern 9, Switzerland
info@peterlang.com, www.peterlang.com, www.peterlang.net

Printed in Germany

Contents

Marina Dossena / Roger Lass

Introduction

Historical dialectology provides an interesting, though at first sight a somewhat contradictory, contrast between its seemingly static object of study and its constantly dynamic methodological approaches. This is because the study of variation in past stages of the language must of necessity rely on crystallized images of forms that may have died out centuries ago, but that have been preserved in documents, whether originals or copies, and that therefore stand as eloquent witnesses of a linguistic situation beyond current usage. At the same time, scholars have always had a very dynamic approach to the study of such forms, adapting and indeed creating state-of-the-art new tools giving rise to significant methodological developments.

The discipline has therefore been an important laboratory for the achievement of increasingly reliable findings. Already the development of the so-called 'fit'-technique to localize data was a ground-breaking point in the history of dialect atlases (see Benskin 1991), and the *Linguistic Atlas of Late Medieval English* (*LALME*), designed and compiled by the team in which this technique had been developed, became a cornerstone for subsequent dialectological investigations. In more recent years, the intersection between dialectology and typology has shed new light on what information may be gleaned from the combination of theoretical approaches that encompass both the analysis of language-specific data and the attempt to derive general rules applicable to different contexts and features (see Nevalainen/Klemola/Laitinen 2006). Indeed, this approach has shown the usefulness of moving from approaches that centred on one language to others in which cross-linguistic analyses may be performed and discussed critically. As a result, scholarly interest in historical dialectology appears to have increased to a considerable extent. As far as English is concerned, various projects are in progress, and the ones currently under way at the University of Edinburgh – for the creation of the *Linguistic Atlas of Early Middle English* (*LAEME*) and of the *Linguistic Atlas of Older Scots* (*LAOS*), in addition to the project aiming to make *LALME* available in electronic format[1] – are especially noteworthy and promising.

Such new developments are normally discussed at international conferences; the most relevant ones addressing cross-linguistic interests, mainly in a synchronic perspective, are of course those in the series on 'Methods in Dialectology', started in 1972. The much more recent series on 'English Historical Dialectology' (started in 2003) has instead a much more defined focus on English and centres on diachronic studies. It is however undeniable that increasing convergence between a more general approach and a more specific one may lead to fruitful results.

For this reason, this volume aims to go beyond an English-only approach, and to step into an idea of dialectology that may inform analyses of language varieties more in general. As pointed out by Laing/Lass (2006: 417), "a dialect does not exist as a discrete entity"; this means that linguistic realizations, no matter how restricted from the point of view of their social, historical or geographical distribution, always interact with other forms, making it necessary to study them in the awareness that they may be construed as regional, social, or genre-specific dialects, depending on the facet that appears to be most relevant for their users or indeed the scholars analyzing them. As a result, for instance, the use of geographically-restricted forms in argumentative discourse may prove a tool of propaganda conveyed by means of linguistic stereotypes, whereas the analyses of social dialects in courtroom discourse may shed light on pragmatic dynamics; in both cases, historical sociolinguistics and historical pragmatics may profit from the contribution of historical dialectology, and vice versa – concrete examples are indeed provided in this collection.

The papers in this volume were selected among those first presented at the 2nd International Conference on English Historical Dialectology (2 ICEHD), held in Bergamo in late August 2007, four

---

1   See e-LALME: <www.ling.ed.ac.uk/research/ihd/projects.shtml>.

years after the first one (for the Proceedings of which see Dossena/ Lass 2004). As we mentioned above, the innovative research presented here extends from its main (and original) focus on English to encompass methodological issues, the discussion of which relies on data pertaining to Dutch historical dialectology. Indeed, the history of English is such that approaching it in a wider European perspective is practically inevitable, if important and very relevant points are not to be missed or at least overlooked, and it is hoped that this may prove a useful starting point for more extensive explorations in this field. The Conference was very successful in its cohesiveness, a trait reflected in the contributions collected here. Throughout the event the debate was constantly fruitful, and it is indeed this continuing exchange of views that has allowed authors to present their findings in ways that now ensure the presentation of a coherent sequence of contributions in this volume.

The book opens with two papers on important methodological issues. The first one, by PIETER VAN REENEN, MARGIT REM and EVERT WATTEL, discusses problems concerning the localization of medieval texts of unknown provenance, paying special attention to the distribution of quantitative findings and the way in which this may be 'normalized' in order to ensure reliable assessments. As will be recalled, Lass (2004) had outlined a metaphorical similarity between archaeology and historical linguistics; in a similar vein, the authors of this paper compare the possibly uneven distribution of archaeological finds with unevenly distributed features in dialectal texts, and propose a model for the application of information theory to the study of such features, so that (advancing from the 'fit'-technique mentioned above) texts whose provenance cannot be established by means of language-external criteria may be attributed to a certain area with greater confidence.

The next contribution, by HERMANN MOISL, also addresses a methodological problem concerning quantitative findings, as it deals with varying document length and the impact this may have on the identification of clusters and patterns in the texts under discussion. While corpus linguists have long been aware of the importance of figure normalization, this contribution takes a step forward, in that it does not only consider snatches of texts, but actually full texts, the length of which is uneven, and indicates the usefulness of multivariate analysis, in order to ensure the reliability of findings.

At the intersection between the discussion of methodological issues and the investigation of data, the paper by ROGER LASS and MARGARET LAING analyzes the case of dental consonants in Early Middle English manuscripts; relying on the corpus of tagged texts created in the making of *LAEME*, they discuss the issue of litteral alternations (a typical problem in historical dialectology *stricto sensu*) using the tools of corpus linguistics. In addition, corpora, dictionaries and atlases are shown to be able to interact thanks to their availability as electronic tools – a scenario enabling both new types of searches and more accurate studies of earlier findings.

Indeed, the usefulness of external sources in the study of Middle English word geography is the object of the contribution by MARÍA JOSÉ CARRILLO-LINARES and EDURNE GARRIDO-ANES, who discuss dictionaries, atlases and corpora currently available to scholars, in order to highlight their increasing attention to the needs of present-day research. State-of-the-art approaches, such as those presented in *LAEME* and *LAOS*, allow the authors to show that even previously difficult investigations, such as those in word geography, can now be based on more reliable and extensively annotated material than in the past.

Along these lines, JULIA FERNÁNDEZ CUESTA and Mª NIEVES RODRÍGUEZ LEDESMA introduce a series of papers on specific geo-historical varieties; in particular, they discuss the links existing between present-day Northern English and its historical roots. Taking into consideration both phonological and morphosyntactic features, the authors discuss the persistence of such traits in documents pertaining to different time periods and different genres, but of the same provenance, in order to assess their continuing validity as markers of Northern texts.

Moving much further north, ROBERT MCCOLL MILLAR con-centrates on the origins of the Northern Scots dialects, in order to assess the extent to which the specificity of such dialects may be attributed to contact with Gaelic, as opposed to mechanisms of new dialect formation. The conclusions of the author show that both Scots and Gaelic appear to have contributed, though of course traits derived from contacts with Norse were also meaningful; in addition, the author stresses the difficulty of reaching clear-cut conclusions when much older stages of the language are concerned.

The last two papers approach geo-historical variation from the point of view of perceptual and pragmatic considerations. NICHOLAS BROWNLEES discusses uses of Welsh English in English Civil War pamphlets, showing the forcefulness and indeed the animosity with which phonological, lexical and syntactic divergence could be used for argumentative purposes. Linguistic and cultural stereotypes are shown to have been exploited for the achievement of perlocutionary effects designed to obtain the readers' support for the encoders, regardless of (in)accuracy in the presentation of phonological and morphosyntactic traits.

Finally, ADRIAN PABLÉ analyzes uses of two terms of address, *Goodman* and *Goodwife*, in New England at the time of the Salem Witchcraft Trials. These documents, a new scholarly edition of which is in preparation at the University of Helsinki (see <www.helsinki.fi/varieng/domains/salem.html>), have always proved of great interest to both scholars and lay people on account of their subject matter. In this paper, however, attention is given to the sociolinguistic framework in which the forms of address under discussion were used, and comparisons are made between uses in Britain and in the colonies.

The range of (both traditional and computerized) tools and sources employed in the studies presented here, together with the depth of the investigations conducted by the individual authors, highlights the importance of approaching such complex data as dialectological ones from a variety of angles. While it is useful to stress one aspect in relation to others, when specific studies are conducted, it is nonetheless true that all aspects of any given text (whether phonological, graphological, lexical, syntactic or pragmatic) always interact with and influence one another, giving rise to an intriguingly complex object of study – an object that only a superficial approach might cause to be dismissed as fixed and static.

Acknowledgements and dedication

We thank the Faculty of Foreign Languages and Literatures and the Department of Comparative Literature, Languages and Cultures of the University of Bergamo for the support granted to the conference. We also acknowledge the invaluable help of the Linguistic Insights series editor, Prof. Maurizio Gotti, of the anonymous reviewers who provided always useful comments on earlier drafts of the papers, and of the editorial staff at Peter Lang, in the preparation of this volume. Clearly, any remaining faults are the editors' responsibility.

Still concerning the conference, this publication allows us to express our gratitude to the Scientific and the Organizing Committees, and to all the colleagues who presented papers, chaired sessions and took part in the debate. Among these, we greatly miss Richard Hogg, whose sudden and untimely death just a few days after the Conference was a shock for all those who had known him, whether in person or through his numerous publications. Richard was a very distinguished and enthusiastic contributor to both editions of ICEHD: the following essay, by ROGER LASS, remembers his high academic and human profile, and it is to his memory that this volume is dedicated.

Bergamo / Cape Town, November 2008.

References

Benskin, Michael 1991. The 'Fit'-technique Explained. In Riddy, Felicity (ed.), *Regionalism in Late Medieval Manuscripts and Texts*. Cambridge: Brewer, 9-26
Dossena, Marina / Lass, Roger (eds) 2004. *Methods and Data in English Historical Dialectology*. Bern: Peter Lang.

LAEME = Laing, Margaret / Lass, Roger 2008. *A Linguistic Atlas of Early Middle English, 1150-1325*. At <www.lel.ed.ac.uk/ihd/laeme1/laeme1.html>. Edinburgh: The University of Edinburgh.

LALME = McIntosh, Angus / Samuels, Michael / Benskin, Michael [with the assistance of Margaret Laing and Keith Williamson] 1986. *A Linguistic Atlas of Late Mediaeval English*. Aberdeen: Aberdeen University Press.

Laing, Margaret / Lass, Roger 2006. Early Middle English Dialectology: Problems and Prospects. In Kemenade, Ans van / Los, Bettelou (eds). *The Handbook of the History of English*. Malden: Blackwell, 417-451.

LAOS = Williamson, Keith 2008. *A Linguistic Atlas of Older Scots. Phase 1: 1380-1500*. At <www.lel.ed.ac.uk/ihd/laos1/laos1.html>. Edinburgh: The University of Edinburgh.

Lass, Roger 2004. Ut Custodiant Litteras: Editions, Corpora and Witnesshood. In Dossena, Marina / Lass, Roger (eds) *Methods and Data in English Historical Dialectology*. Bern: Peter Lang, 21-48.

Nevalainen, Terttu / Klemola, Juhani / Laitinen, Mikko (eds) 2006. *Types of Variation: Diachronic, Dialectal and Typological Interfaces*. Amsterdam: Benjamins.

Roger Lass

Richard M. Hogg: *In memoriam*

This volume is dedicated to the memory of a man who once asked whether Old English dialectology was possible, and did not give an entirely sanguine answer (Hogg 1988). But he also kept working at the problem, and many others in Old English as well as phonology and other aspects of the language, past and present. In 1992 he produced the first volume of an alas uncompleted grammar of Old English, which became a classic as soon as it appeared. Campbell, Brunner and Hogg sit on my bookshelves, but it is to Hogg that I turn when I need to be reminded about anything serious to do with Old English phonology. In that same year he edited and wrote a chapter on Old English phonology and morphology in the first volume of the indispensable *Cambridge History of the English Language*. He was also the general editor of the series until its completion in 2006. To add a personal note, this volume is also dedicated to a fellow cat-person, cricket-lover and fan of the music of Emmy Lou Harris.

I will not detail Richard's biography or bibliography; a survey of his work and academic life is available in Nigel Vincent's fine obituary in the *Guardian* (20 September 2007), and a full list of his publications can be found on the website of the University of Manchester, where he was Smith Professor of English Language and Medieval Literature from 1980. I will rather, as seems more fitting in a dedication, comment briefly on his intellectual style, on what made him unique. The most salient feature of his work was an informed, insightful and controlled eclecticism. It is not customary these days, at least in many linguistic circles, to praise eclecticism: what is usually taken as worthy is strict adherence to a 'paradigm' or theory, so that one can be recognised as belonging to a particular 'school' or academic sub-community. This was never possible with Richard: even when he worked in a given modern and currently fashionable paradigm, as in his collaborative textbook on metrical phonology with Chris McCully (1987), or recent papers on optimality theory, the theoretical allegiance never dominated his whole body of work. So above all he was not a fundamentalist, but knew about and used what was available in good theory from the Prague School through American structuralism through classical generative phonology and beyond. His *Old English Grammar* is a fine example of what you can get from intertwined approaches without commitment to a particular theory: when phonemic status is at issue he is a structuralist, when deep/surface relations or problems of derivation are at issue he is a generativist; but his eclecticism is always tailored to the task at hand, not spineless or undirected.

Unfashionable as the term is (though I use it as a compliment), Richard was first and foremost a philologist. He delighted in the intricacy and detail of his data, in 'Old Englishness' in general, and in elaborate and involved argumentation based on hard-won and difficult materials. This love of data, and along with it a certain caution, partly based I suspect on his philologist's knowledge of how complicated things really are when you get right down to details, often made his 'positions' apparently somewhat ambivalent. He was quite capable of marshalling the evidence for both sides of an approach to a question, and then leaving it without an answer, but with the material available for anyone who might want to attempt one. He was of course equally capable of coming down in favour of a particular answer, if the data and his argument seemed to warrant it. So he was a model of care and conscientiousness, which are not minor virtues.

Our discipline in the widest sense, not dialectology alone but English historical studies, has sustained a great loss. And all of us who knew Richard, however slightly, whether as an enthusiastic and insightful conference participant, a colleague, teacher, friend – or some or all of these – find a gap in the landscape. His death was premature and shocking; he was in top intellectual form, not subsiding into the living-on-laurels kind of life that many academics, sadly, seem to at his age. He went in his prime, still full of plans for writing and teaching. And this is the way we will remember him, in the midst of ceaseless activity. This makes it even harder to accept that we will never encounter him again, except as he lives in the work and memories he left to us.

References

Hogg, Richard M. 1988. On the Impossibility of Old English Dialectology. In Kastovsky, Dieter / Bauer, Gero (eds) *Luick Revisited*. Tübingen: Narr, 183-203.

Hogg, Richard M. 1992a. *A Grammar of Old English. Volume 1: Phonology*. Oxford: Blackwell.

Hogg, Richard M. 1992b. Phonology and Morphology. In Hogg, Richard M. (ed.) *The Cambridge History of the English Language. I: The Beginnings to 1066*. Cambridge: Cambridge University Press, 67-167.

Hogg, Richard M. / McCully, Chris 1987. *Metrical Phonology. A Coursebook*. Cambridge: Cambridge University Press.

PIETER VAN REENEN / MARGIT REM / EVERT WATTEL[1]

The Localization of Medieval Texts of Unknown Provenance

1. Introduction

Research in medieval dialectology has to be based on texts. For lack of standard languages these texts were written in dialect, or mixtures of dialects, the dialects often being of unknown geographical provenance. Questions such as how to determine in what dialect, or mixture of dialects, a text has been written, and whether a text has been written in pure dialect or in a mixture of dialects, are basic for research in medieval dialectology. This study proposes an answer to these questions by presenting a localization procedure for texts of unknown geographical provenance, a 'fit'-technique in the sense of Benskin (1991a).[2]

In our localization procedure we distinguish texts which are localized, usually original charters, and texts to be localized. It is assumed that a localized charter represents the dialect of the settlement where it comes from. It follows that the dialect of a settlement is characterized by the dialect features, the locators, of the charters which are localized in that settlement. Ideally, great numbers of localized charters are equally spread over many settlements of the linguistic area.

The dialect features, the locators, of a text to be localized are compared to those (of the charters) of the settlements. The text of unknown provenance is localized in the settlement of which the locators show the highest degree of similarity with the locators of the text. In

---

1   Thanks to Chris De Wulf for providing data from the region of Courtrai.

2   This study is a revised version of Rem/Wattel/van Reenen (2003).

short, our localization procedure localizes texts of unknown provenance by comparing locators of such texts to the locators (of the charters) of the settlements.

Our localization procedure has been developed for Middle Dutch. It includes at this moment 101 locators or locator oppositions. Although the higher the number of locators the better fit, 20 well chosen locators might be already enough to localize most of the texts. Although it has been developed for Middle Dutch, localization procedures can be developed for other languages along the same lines, as long as sufficient quantities of localized texts are available, as is the case in, for instance, medieval English, French and German.

Our localization procedure contains a series of design choices, on the basis of which the dialect data are quantified. In this study we will focus on what these design choices are and why we have made them. Students of medieval dialectology may agree or disagree with these design choices. In the latter case, they might replace them with others of their own. However, once a design choice has been accepted, it should be kept as it is during the application of the localization procedure: design choices should not be varied during the quantification process.

In order to use locators in such a way that they would yield as much information as possible about the probability that a particular settlement is the origin of an unlocalized text, they are conceived of as witnesses to which we assign a weight. It will appear that determining the ratios of the individual locators for any settlement on the basis of the charters we have for that settlement is itself a fairly complicated operation.

To clarify some of these complications we will start in Section 2 with the introduction of some basic notions and a first illustration of our method. In Section 3 we will provide a hypothetical example from archaeology. Sections 4 and 5 are central in that they contain the description of our method of how to determine the significance of the frequency of a locator. They also contain the design choices we have made in order to arrive at our results. Section 4 determines the weight factor of a settlement on the basis of the charter factors, and the locator percentage of a settlement on the basis of the charter percentages. Section 5 deals with the problem of how to weigh related locators, i.e. locators which witness (almost) the same, the problem of ensuring that geographically infrequent locators receive more weight, and the problem of ensuring that missing information for lack of locator oppositions does not affect the results of the localization. It also contains the localization formula in its final shape. In Section 6 we will show and discuss some test results, while Section 7 presents some results of the localization procedure. We draw our conclusions in Section 8.

2. Some basic notions and a provisional illustration

The following notions are basic in this study: charters and texts (discussed in Section 2.1) and dialect forms or locator oppositions (see Section 2.2). In Section 2.3 we present an example illustrating our localization procedure.

2.1. Charters and texts

A text which is localized is localized by means of extralinguistic criteria. A text to be localized cannot be localized by means of extra-linguistic criteria. As observed, localized texts are usually original charters. We consider as extralinguistic criteria:

- names of settlement(s) mentioned in the charters;
- local authorities or inhabitants in the name of which they are written;
- local authorities or inhabitants to which they are destined;
- local topics dealt with in the charters.

If all extralinguistic criteria in a charter point to the same settlement, we consider the language of that charter representing the dialect of that settlement. Throughout this study charters which are not localizable by means of extralinguistic criteria are texts to be localized, just as the great majority of other texts.[3] In addition, although charters are usually dated, which is very important for diachronic research in medieval dialectology, in this study we will not focus on this property.

Texts are of very different kinds. They may have been transcribed from older texts, written in other rather different dialects and remnants of these dialects may still be present. A text composed of more than one dialect represents a *Mischsprache*: an arbitrary mixture of different dialects (see Benskin/Laing 1981). In this study we will not focus on this problem either. How to solve cases in which charters are not always available, see Benskin (1991b).

In what follows we adopt the following terminology, unless the context suggests otherwise: a 'charter' is a localized text; a 'text' is of unknown provenance and has to be localized.

In this study we use for illustration the charters from the van Reenen-Mulder Corpus (CRM), a corpus of fourteenth-century Middle Dutch. This corpus consists at this moment (end 2007) of about 3,000 charters, about 1,000,000 words, all localized in settlements in Flanders and the Netherlands, but excluding Frisia.[4]

2.2. Dialect forms or locator oppositions and locators

The dialect features we use as benchmarks in the charters and the texts are referred to as 'locators'. A locator occurs in a 'locator opposition'. A locator opposition is a variable which consists of two variants: locators and their opposites. A locator has at least one opposite. We refer to locators and their opposites as (dialect) forms. We have opted for a dichotomic distribution of the dialect data as the most adequate method to handle them.

Locator oppositions playing a part in this study are:

---

3   For more about the criteria used to distinguish localized charters from other texts, see Dees *et al.* (1980).
4   See Rem (2003: 307-310) for the list of most of the settlements.

1.   *Of* versus *Af* 'off', *Of* being the locator and *Af* its opposite
2.   *sInt* 'saint' versus the opposites *sEnt, sAnt, sUnt/sOnt*
3.   *sEnt* versus *sInt, sAnt, sUnt/sOnt*
4.   *sAnt* versus *sInt, sEnt, sUnt/sOnt*
5.   *sOnt/sUnt* versus *sInt, sEnt, sAnt*
6.   *viCHtich* 'fifty' versus forms such as *viFtech* and *viFtich*
7.   *viftEch* versus forms such as *vichtIch* and *viftIch*

2.3. Provisional illustration of our localization procedure

Ideally, one word may be enough to localize a text. Suppose a medieval text contains the word 'fifty', written as *vichtech*, for instance Genesis 18:26: "If I find at Sodom fifty (*vichtech*) righteous in the city, I will spare the whole place for their sake."

As observed above, in Middle Dutch this word can be written in several ways, for instance: *viftich, vichtich, vichtech*. We select the following two locator oppositions, *-ch-* and *-e-* being the locators, see locator 6: *-ch-* versus *-f-* and locator 7: *-e-* versus *-i-* above. The result, based on the locators in our charters, is shown on Maps 1 and 2.[5] Map 1 shows that *-ch-* occurs in West-Flanders and Zeeland, Map 2 that *-e-* occurs more to the east, essentially in Brabant, Antwerp province and East-Flanders. A comparison of Maps 1 and 2 shows that there is only one settlement where both locators occur abundantly: Courtrai, in Flemish: Kortrijk. This settlement and the area around is shown on Map 3.

In this case, one word, 'fifty', based upon two locators, is enough to localize the text. In our localization procedure we assign much geographical weight to such extremely informative locators. However, such locators are exceptional, and the localization procedure should contain many more locators in order to function appropriately.[6]

---

5   All the maps to which reference is made in this study are provided in the Appendix.

6   It has also to be assumed that the text does not consist of a *Mischsprache* in the sense of Benskin/Laing (1981).

3. Gold coins, finds and settlements

In this section we introduce a hypothetical example from archaeology in order to clarify and to illustrate the logarithmic function $\log_2(n+1)$, which plays a central part in our linguistic localization procedure, but that has an extra dimension making it more complicated.

During an archaeological survey gold coins were found in Paris, Moscow, Madrid and Rome: see Table 1. The coins were lost either as hoards or individually. In Moscow one hoard was found with 100 gold coins, in Madrid four hoards with 10, 20, 30, 40 gold coins respectively. Apparently, the finds represent one former owner in Paris and in Moscow, four former owners in Madrid and 100 former owners in Rome. What do these gold coins and finds tell us about the wealth of these cities in the past? For a satisfactory answer, do we have to count coins or do we have to count finds? Or both? Or perhaps just settlements?

Settlements	Gold coins	Finds
Paris	1	1
Moscow	100	1 (hoard with 100 coins)
Madrid	100	4 (hoards with 10+20+30+40 coins)
Rome	100	100
Total	301	106

Table 1. Number of finds, gold coins and hoards in four cities.

Archaeological finds are historical accidents in several respects. They might have been lost at the wrong place. They might have disappeared in the course of history. Or they might have been overlooked. Suppose that the hoard with 100 coins has been lost by an inhabitant of Saint Petersburg and does not belong in Moscow at all. In that case Moscow was in reality even less wealthy than Paris. However, if one or two of the coins found in Rome have been lost there by chance, without belonging there, it would make Rome hardly less rich. The 100 gold coins in Rome are considerably more solid evidence of the wealth of that city than the 100 gold coins of Moscow. What makes a dramatic difference in Moscow, is hardly perceived in Rome.

We cannot trust the data to be fully representative of the settlements in which they are found. This is the problem of the impact of the reliability of information. There is also the problem of the distribution of the finds: one find (owner) in Moscow and in Paris, four finds in Madrid and 100 finds in Rome. Does one very rich find (owner) make a city as rich as 100 modestly rich finds do? In historical research such situations are very common, and scholars have provided rather divergent answers to deal with this issue.

3.1. Three traditional choices

Choice 1. One answer is that one gold coin weighs as one witness, i.e. all coins have the same weight. The 100 coins of the hoard from Moscow and the 100 coins of the four hoards from Madrid witness the same as the 100 golden coins in Rome. This choice makes Moscow with one former owner as rich as Rome with 100 former owners. This is not really satisfactorily, the distribution of the coins – over one hoard, over four hoards, over 100 small hoards – being so extremely different. We think that the distribution of the coins over the hoards should be taken into account in one way or the other as well.

Choice 2. Another answer is that one find, whether hoard or isolated coin, weighs as one witness with the same weight for all finds. The implication is that the 100 coins of the hoard from Moscow weigh as one witness, that the 100 coins of the four hoards from Madrid weigh as four witnesses, and that the 100 coins in Rome weigh as 100 witnesses. Although there is something to say for this choice from the point of view of the distribution of the wealth – well spread in Rome, but not in Paris and Moscow, Madrid situated in between – this answer is not really satisfactorily either. It makes Moscow with its one very rich owner not wealthier than Paris, since the frequency of the coins in Moscow (and Madrid) has no impact at all.

Choice 3. A third answer is that one settlement counts as one witness with the same weight for all settlements. This choice makes the four cities equally rich, whatever the number of coins or finds. This choice does not make much sense in the context of our archaeological example since, for instance, Paris is obviously less wealthy than the other three cities. The relevance of this choice will become clear in the linguistic example of Section 4.

All three choices would have given reasonable results under favorable historical conditions. However, since historical conditions in our example were far from favorable (as they usually are), the three choices imply extremely different answers, as different as chalk and cheese. Instead of attempting to find arguments to prefer one of these choices and to reject the other two, we prefer to adopt a strategy which avoids the problem of the chalk and the cheese, and integrates the strong points of the three choices by making them to some extent comparable. A satisfactory way to do this comes from information theory, first proposed by Shannon (1948).

3.2. Information theory: $log_2(n+1)$

The solution coming from information theory can be summarized as follows: weigh your data by means of $\log_2(n+1)$. In our case this implies: first determine the *find factor* by weighing the coins in the finds; second, determine the *settlement factor* by weighing the weighted finds in the settlement. In this way, the find of 100 coins in Moscow would no longer weigh as 100 or as 1, but as $\log_2(100+1) = 6.66$ (we usually round off on two decimals).

This is the list of results after the weighing of the coins in the finds by means of $\log_2(n+1)$; see also Table 2:

> Paris find 1: coin 1 has a weight (find factor) of 1.
> Moscow find 2: hoard 1 (100 coins) has a weight (find factor) of 6.66.
> Madrid find 3: hoard 2 (10 coins) has a weight (find factor) of 3.46.
> Madrid find 4: hoard 3 (20 coins) has a weight (find factor) of 4.39.
> Madrid find 5: hoard 4 (30 coins) has a weight (find factor) of 4.95.
> Madrid find 6: hoard 5 (40 coins) has a weight (find factor) of 5.36.
> Madrid finds 3-6: have a total weight of 3.46+4.39+4.95+5.36 = 18.16.
> Rome finds 7-106: coins 1-100 have a total weight of 100.

Settlements	Gold coins	Finds	Weight
Paris	1	1	1
Moscow	100	1	6.66
Madrid	100	4	18.16
Rome	100	100	100
Total	301	106	125.82

Table 2. Gold coins in finds and their weight after $\log_2(n+1)$.

Why does Paris still weigh 1? Because in Paris $n = 1$ (gold coin) and $\log_2(n+1) = \log_2 2 = 1$. Why does Rome still weigh 100? Because in Rome $n = 1$ (each of the 100 gold coins) and $100 \times \log_2(n+1) = 100 \times 1 = 100$. Why does Moscow weigh 6.66 (and no longer 1 or 100)? Because in Moscow $n = 100$ (gold coins in one find) and $\log_2(100+1) = \log_2 101 = 6.66$. And why does Madrid weigh 18.16 (and no longer 4 or 100)? Because in Madrid $n = 10, 20, 30, 40$ (gold coins in four finds) and $\log_2(10+1) + \log_2(20+1) + \log_2(30+1) + \log_2(40+1) = 3.46 + 4.39 + 4.95 + 5.36 = 18.16$.

These calculations can be checked by means of a calculator, although a calculator usually does not contain the function $\log_2$, but rather $\log_{10}$ (and $\log_e$). However, since $\log_{10}(n+1) \times 3.321928095 = \log_2(n+1)$, it follows that, for instance in the case of find 4 in Table 2, $\log_{10}(20+1) \times 3.32 = \log_2 21 = 4.39$.

Thanks to $\log_2(n+1)$ we have made gold coins and finds comparable by avoiding extreme answers. We can do the same with respect to (the now weighted) finds and the settlements, since not only the distribution of the *gold coins over the finds* is a historical accident, but also the distribution of the *finds over the settlements*. By applying $\log_2(n+1)$ over the weighted finds, we obtain the settlement factor – see Table 3:

Settlements	Weighted settlement	Factors
Paris	1	1
Moscow	6.66	2.94
Madrid	18.16	4.26
Rome	100	6.66
Total	125.82	14.86

Table 3. Weight of the weighted finds per settlement.

Thanks to information theory we have made Paris, Moscow, Madrid and Rome comparable in terms of wealth:

(a)   Moscow with its one find of 100 coins becomes wealthier than Paris with its one find of 1 coin;

(b)   Madrid with its four finds of respectively 10, 20, 30, 40 coins becomes wealthier than Moscow, and

(c)   Rome with its 100 finds of 1 coin each becomes wealthier than Madrid.

By combining the three choices of Section 3.1, we have reduced the weight of the finds for those who prefer choice 1 above and increased the weight of the finds for those who prefer choice 3 above. Comparable reductions or increases concern choice 2. Neither coins nor finds nor settlements should dominate too much or not enough in settlements.

4. A linguistic example: the locator opposition *Of-Af* 'off'

In Section 3 the basic units were the gold coin, the find and the settlement. We also introduced the 'find factor' and the 'settlement factor'. By replacing the gold coin by the *dialect form*, the find by the *charter* and the find factor by the *charter factor*, and keeping the *settlement* and the *settlement factor* as they are, we will now apply the same reasonings to a linguistic example. There is, however, an important difference between the archaeological example of Section 3 and the linguistic one in this section. Our dialect form is part of a locator opposition which consists of two variables: the locator and its opposite, whereas in our archaeological example coins were not split up into, for instance, gold coins and silver coins. This is a complication which has to be worked out carefully in this section.

The linguistic example we have chosen is the locator opposition 'off', with the dialect forms *Of*, the locator, and *Af*, its opposite, as found in the charters of Amsterdam, Diemen, a small village east of

Amsterdam, Utrecht and Sittard, in the province of Limburg in the south east of the Netherlands. In Amsterdam, Diemen, in and around Utrecht, *Of* occurs more frequently than *Af*; in and around Sittard we find mainly *Af*; in the whole area *Of* is the minority form.

In Diemen and Sittard the locator opposition *Of-Af* is represented with one dialect form in one charter. In Diemen this is the locator *Of*, in Sittard its opposite *Af*. If we have one form in one charter in one settlement, the application of all three choices in Section 3.1 above gives the same result: 1, as with the one gold coin in Paris. However, as we will see below, the locator percentage in Diemen is 100%, in Sittard 0%. Amsterdam is represented in the database by 99 charters, of which 42 contain the locator opposition *Of-Af* with 91 forms, the proportion between locator *Of* and its opposite *Af* being 75:16. Forms of *Of* occur in 37 charters, of *Af* in four charters, and only one charter contains both *Of* (1x) and *Af* (2x). Utrecht is represented in the data-base by 63 charters, of which 37 contain the locator opposition *Of-Af* with 79 forms, of which 78 are *Of*, the locator, and one *Af*, its opposite – see Table 4:

Amsterdam				*Utrecht*			
Ch	*Of+Af*	*Totals*	*n*	*Ch*	*Of+Af*	*Totals*	*n*
9 x	(1+0) =	9+ 0 =	9	13 x	(1+0) =	13+0 =	13
20 x	(2+0) =	40+ 0 =	40	16 x	(2+0) =	32+0 =	32
7 x	(3+0) =	21+ 0 =	21	2 x	(3+0) =	6+0 =	6
1 x	(4+0) =	4+ 0 =	4	3 x	(4+0) =	12+0 =	12
1 x	(1+2) =	1+ 2 =	3	1 x	(7+0) =	7+0 =	7
3 x	(0+3) =	0+ 9 =	9	1 x	(8+0) =	8+0 =	8
1 x	(0+5) =	0+ 5 =	5	1 x	(0+1) =	0+1 =	1
42		75+16 =	91	37		78+1 =	79

Table 4. Frequencies of the dialect forms of the locator opposition *Of-Af* in the charters of Amsterdam and Utrecht.

In Section 4.1 we discuss the implications for the choices:

- one (dialect) form one witness
- one charter one witness
- one settlement one witness.

In Section 4.2 we will implement our strategy based upon information theory.

4.1. Dialect forms, charters and settlements

Dialect forms consist of locators and their opposites in locator oppositions. We apply the three choices of Section 3.1 to our example *Of-Af.* The 91 forms in Amsterdam and 79 forms in Utrecht weigh, according to choice 1, each as one witness, whatever their distribution over the charters and settlements (see Table 5). This choice not only assigns too much weight to these cities, and not enough to Diemen and Sittard, but also takes it for granted that variation of locators and opposites within charters is equal to variation between charters. However, variation within charters is usually less than between charters (see van Reenen 1988), just as variation within settlements will be less than between settlements. As in Section 3.1, this is not the best choice.

Choice 2, one charter one witness, assigns the same weight, 1, to all charters (the one charter in Amsterdam with 1 x *Of* and 2 x *Af* scoring as 0.33 and 0.67). This has, for instance, the following implication. Suppose we have a settlement with 11 charters, 10 of them with each once the form *Of*, and the 11th with 100 x *Af.* Choice 1 would result in a score of 91% *Af.* Choice 2, however, would result in a score of 9% *Af.* From this point of view, neither choice 1 nor choice 2 is satisfactory.

Choice 3, one settlement one witness, assigns relatively too much weight to the minimal locator oppositions of Diemen and Sittard. An extra inconvenience is that the one form *Of* in Diemen represents necessarily 100%, the only alternative being 0%, and the other way around with Sittard, whereas in Amsterdam and Utrecht the proportions between locator *Of* and opposite *Af* can vary widely.

We have shown above the weak sides of the three choices. However, under certain conditions, they can be adequate. If locator oppositions are equally spread over charters, and charters over settlements, all three choices would have given essentially the same results. For instance, choice 3 would be less problematic if in all four settlements a considerable number of dialect forms, say 20 or 100, were to be found. Another relevant example is the method used in the Goeman/Taeldeman/van Reenen Project (GTRP). In this survey of modern dialects just one dialect form per settlement has been selected. Since in the GTRP one form one witness equals one settlement one witness, results based on choice 1 or choice 3 are not different.

Of + Af =		*n*	
Choice 1. One form one witness			
	75+16 =	91	Amsterdam
	78+1 =	79	Utrecht
	1+ 0 =	1	Diemen
	0+1 =	1	Sittard
Choice 2. One charter one witness			
	37.33+ 4.67 =	42	Amsterdam
	36+1 =	37	Utrecht
	1+0 =	1	Diemen
	0+1 =	1	Sittard
Choice 3. One settlement one witness			
	0.82+ 0.18 =	1	Amsterdam
	0.99+ 0.01 =	1	Utrecht
	1+ 0 =	1	Diemen
	0+1 =	1	Sittard

Table 5. Three choices to calculate the weight of the locator opposition *Of-Af.*

The three choices have been discussed with respect to data from Middle Dutch, Old French and older German in Berteloot (1980), Dees *et al.* (1980), van Reenen (1986-1987), Mooijaart (1992), Mooijaart/van der Heijden (1992), Marynissen (1995), Mihm (2002) and Rem (2003). What we can learn from these studies is that, since medieval dialect data are usually not well spread over settlements, some kind of balance has to be created, not by selecting one of the three choices discussed above, but by combining all three of them in the strategy offered to us by information theory.[7]

---

7   To complete the discussion a few other considerations on the use of $\log_2$, all of different nature, have to be mentioned:
    a.   Information usually contains noise of that order – see Shannon (1948).

4.2. The settlement factor and the settlement percentage

The most balanced answer to the question 'what is the weight of the locator opposition *Of-Af*, or 'what does a locator witness', is to choose as basic units the settlement factor n_{fs} of the locator opposition and the settlement percentage p_{ls} of the locator *Of*.

In order to determine the settlement factor n_{fs} we first have to calculate the charter factors n_{fi} of the locator opposition in the charters, and in order to determine the settlement percentage p_{ls} we first have to calculate the charter percentages p_{li} of the locator in the locator opposition.

The settlement factor n_{fs} of a locator opposition is derived from the charter factors n_{fi} of the locator opposition (just as in the archaeological example of Section 3, Tables 2 and 3, the settlement was derived from the find factor) by means of:

$$n_{fi} = \log_2 (n+1)$$
$$n_{fs} = \Sigma\, n_{fi}$$
$$\log_2 (n_{fs}+1)$$

The settlement percentage p_{ls} of a locator is derived from the charter percentages of the locator in the same way:[8]

$$p_{li} = (n_{Of} \times 100\%) / n$$
$$p_{ls} = (\Sigma\, n_{fi} \times p_{li}) / \Sigma\, n_{fi}$$

---

    b. It is more common to use $\log_{10}$ or $\log_e$ than $\log_2$ (as observed earlier, calculators usually do not provide $\log_2$). However, although $\log_{10}$ and $\log_e$ give the same result as $\log_2$ (see earlier in this section), $\log_2$ is conceptually the better choice, since it makes it easy to keep the weight of the minimal unit of information (in our examples the gold coin and the dialect form) 1 on all levels.

    c. Instead of $\log_2$ one might prefer the square root. This choice would reduce small quantities of data more than $\log_2$ does and large quantities would not be reduced as much as by $\log_2$. To choose the square root instead of $\log_2$ is to a large extent a question of preference: see Rem (2003, Appendix 3a) for more about this choice.

8    $_f$ in n_{fi}: form, i.e (dialect) form, the locator or its opposite, in a locator opposition; $_l$ in p_{li}: locator; $_s$: settlement.

We will also determine the area percentage p_{la}, for reasons that will become clear in Section 4:

$$p_{la} = (\Sigma\, (n_{fs} \times p_{ls})) / \Sigma\, n_{fs}$$

Here we introduce our first design choices.

Design choice 1
Determine the $\log_2$ of the settlement factor n_{fs} of a locator opposition as follows:
a. Calculate by means of $n_{fi} = \log_2(n+1)$ the charter factor of each charter, where:

   n is the number of dialect forms in a charter;
   n_{fi} is the n forms of charter i, which are weighted by $\log_2(n+1)$
b. Calculate $n_{fs} = \Sigma\, n_{fi}$ (the sum Σ of all n_{fi}'s).
c. Apply $\log_2(n_{fs}+1)$ on the result.

Design choice 2
Determine the settlement percentage of a locator as follows:
a. Calculate the charter percentage p_{li} of a locator in a locator opposition of each charter by means of $p_{li} = n_{Of}/\,n \times 100\%$.
b. Calculate the settlement percentage p_{ls} of a locator by means of $p_{ls} = \Sigma\, (n_{fi} \times p_{li}) / \Sigma\, n_{fi.}$

Tables 6 and 7 provide examples of calculations on the basis of data from Amsterdam and Utrecht. We do not have to calculate the values for Diemen and Sittard. Here too, if we have one form in one charter in one settlement, application of our design choice 1 gives the result 1, application of our design choice 2 (the locator percentage) gives 100%in Diemen and 0% in Sittard.

Amsterdam				Utrecht			
Ch	*Of+Af*	*n*	*np*$_{li}$	*Ch*	*Of+Af*	*n*	*Np*$_{li}$
9x(1+0) =	9+0 =	9	100%	13x(1+0) =	13+0 =	13	100%
20x(2+0) =	40+0 =	40	100%	16x(2+0) =	32+0 =	32	100%
7x(3+0) =	21+0 =	21	100%	2x(3+0) =	6+0 =	6	100%
1x(4+0) =	4+0 =	4	100%	3x(4+0) =	12+0 =	12	100%
1x(1+2) =	1+2 =	3	33%	1x(7+0) =	7+0 =	7	100%
3x(0+3) =	0+9 =	9	0%	1x(8+0) =	8+0 =	8	100%
1x(0+1) =	0+1 =	1	0%	1x(0+5) =	0+5 =	5	0%
ΣOf+Af =	*75+16 =*	*91*		*ΣOf+Af =*	*78+1 =*	*79*	
Ch	*log$_2$(n+1)*		*n*$_{fi}$	*Ch*	*log$_2$(n+1)*		*n*$_{fi}$
9x(1+1) =	9x1.00 =		9	13x(1+1) =	13x1.00 =		13
20x(2+1) =	20x1.59 =		31.80	16x(2+1) =	16x1.59 =		25.44
7x(3+1) =	7x2.00 =		14	2x(3+1) =	2x2.00 =		4
1x(4+1) =	1x2.32 =		2.32	3x(4+1) =	3x2.32 =		6.96
1x(3+1) =	1x2.00 =		2	1x(7+1) =	1x3.00 =		3
3x(3+1) =	3x2.00 =		6	1x(8+1) =	1x3.17 =		3.17
1x(1+1) =	1x1.00 =		1	1x(5+1) =	1x2.59 =		2.59
		Σn$_{fi}$	*66.12*			*Σn*$_{fi}$	*58.16*
n$_{fi}$x*p*$_{li}$				*n*$_{fi}$x*p*$_{li}$			
9x100 =			900	13x100 =			1300
31.80x100 =			3180	25.44x100 =			2544
14x100 =			1400	4x100 =			400
2.32x100 =			232	6.96x100 =			696
2x33 =			66	3x100 =			300
6x0 =			0	3.17x100 =			317
1x0 =			0	2.59x0 =			0
Σn$_{fi}$x*p*$_{li}$ =			*5778*	*Σn*$_{fi}$x*p*$_{li}$ =			*5557*
Settlement factor: n$_{fs}$ =log$_2$(Σn$_{fi}$+1)							
log$_2$(66.12+1) =6.09				log$_2$(58.16+1) =5.89			
Settlement percentage p$_{ls}$ =Σ(n$_{fi}$xp$_{li}$):Σn$_{fi}$							
5778/66.12 =87.39%				5557/58.16 =96.54%			

Table 6. Calculation of charter factors n$_{fi}$ and settlement factors n$_{fs}$ of locator opposition *Of-Af* and calculation of charter percentages p$_{li}$, settlement percentages p$_{ls}$ and area percentage p$_{la}$ of locator *Of*. Ch = number of charters. See Table 4 for raw data.

	n_{fs} X p_{ls}	
Amsterdam	6.09 x 87.39 % =	532.205
Utrecht	5.89 x 96.54 % =	568.62
Diemen	1 x 100 % =	100
Sittard	1 x 0 % =	0
Sum	13.98	1200.825
$p_{la} = \Sigma\ (n_{fs} \times p_{ls})\ /\ \Sigma\ n_{fs} = \Sigma 1188.925\ /\ 13.98 = 85.05\%$		

Table 7. Results in terms of settlement factors n_{fs} of the locator opposition *Of-Af* and of settlement percentages p_{ls} and area percentage p_{la} of locator *Of*: see Table 6.

It should be kept in mind that the results in Tables 6 and 7 concern only one locator opposition and four settlements. The 101 locator oppositions, settlement factors and settlement percentages in Rem (2003) were calculated for more than 200 settlements. Three of the four settlements are situated in the *Of*-area. It follows that the area percentage p_{la} is relatively high. In reality it is lower than 50%, *Of* being, as observed, the minority form in the locator opposition.

Maps such as 1 and 2 are based upon the percentages p_{ls} of the settlements. The weights of these settlements, expressed by n_{ls}, determine the influence around them: usually low around Diemen, high around Amsterdam: we refer to Wattel/van Reenen (forth.) for more about this subject.

We may conclude this section by observing that in our view the best answer to the questions 'What do the dialect forms of a locator opposition in the charters of a settlement weigh', and 'What does a locator in a settlement witness', is along the lines of the results in Tables 6 and 7 above. This answer is strictly parallel to the hypothetical example in Section 3, with the addition of the split of the locator opposition into two types of dialect forms: locators and their opposites. However, although it is right that the more the percentages p_{lt} of a text and p_{ls} of a settlement are alike the higher the chance that the language of this text corresponds to the language of that settlement, this is not the whole story.

5. The localization procedure completed

So far we have illustrated how to determine p_{ls}, the locator percentage of a settlement, and $\log_2(n+1)$ of the settlement factor n_{fs} of the locator opposition, i.e. $\log_2(n_{fs}+1)$. Although the settlement factors n_{fs} and settlement percentages p_{ls} are important elements in it, we think that our localization procedure has to take into account several other values to obtain its final value v_{ls} of a locator. This value v_{ls} (*v*alue of *l*ocator at *s*ettlement) is built up as follows:

$$v_{ls} = \log_2(n_{fs}+1) \times \lambda$$

In this formula λ introduces a geographical weighing factor, which is partly based on p_{ls}; this will be discussed in Section 5.1. In Section 5.2 we show how we solve the problem of lacking information, i.e. locator oppositions. Two other problems, referred to as 'complexity' and 'repetition', are treated in Section 5.3; perhaps it cannot always be avoided to integrate them into the localization procedure, but in this study we will. How a text to be localized is formalized and combined with the settlement locator is the subject of Section 5.4. In Section 5.5 we introduce a last refinement to complete our procedure.

5.1. Charter locators in geographical space: the λ factor

If a locator covers only a small geographical area, it contains highly revealing information, whereas its opposite, covering by definition a large area, does not. Such locators are important witnesses for localization, and for that reason we assign them special weight. Although this choice is conceptually easy to understand, its implementation is slightly more complicated. For example, if a locator in the area as a whole is rare, its area percentage p_{la} being low, for instance 18% (0.18), and if this locator at a specific settlement has a settlement percentage p_{ls} of 100%, we assign it a weight which is inversely proportional, i.e. 82% (0.82). If this locator at another settlement has a settlement percentage p_{ls} of 0%, it obtains a weight of 18% (0.18) – see Figure 1.

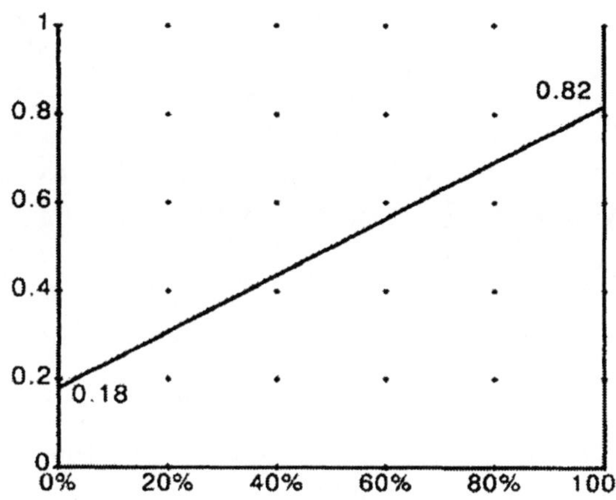

Figure 1. λ_{ls} as function of p_{ls}. Vertically: Distribution value λ_{ls}. Horizontally: settlement percentage p_{ls}.

Design choice 3

If for a locator l both the settlement percentage p_{ls} and the area percentage p_{la} have been determined, then the geographical distribution value λ_{ls} is defined as:

$$\lambda_{ls} = (p_{la} + 0.01 \times (100 - 2 \times p_{la}) \times p_{ls}) / 100$$

It follows that $0 < \lambda_{ls} < 1$.

Assuming that the locator *Of* has a $p_{la} = 18\%$, it follows that

$$\lambda_{ls} = (18 + 0.01 \times (100 - 2 \times 18) \times p_{ls}) / 100 = (18 + 0.64 \times p_{ls}) / 100$$

Diemen, with $p_{ls} = 100\%$ (see Table 7), has $\lambda_{ls} = 82\%$; Sittard, with $p_{ls} = 0\%$, has $\lambda_{ls} = 18\%$: see also our example above. For Amsterdam, with $p_{ls} = 88.43\%$, $\lambda_{ls} = (18 + 0.64 \times 88.43): 100 = 74.6\%$; Utrecht, with p_{ls} = 95.50%, λ_{ls} = 79.1%. Since a locator, ideally, has been chosen in such a way that it covers a relatively small area (with a relatively high information content), its area percentage p_{la} will tend to be <50%. As a consequence the λ_{ls} at a settlement will tend to be relatively high for a p_{ls} that is high, relatively low for a p_{ls} that is low.

In this manner locators such as *vi-CH-tich* and *vift-E-ch* 'fifty' (see Maps 1 and 2) receive relatively much geographical weight in and around Courtrai, since in that area both have a high percentage p_{ls} for locators with a relatively low area percentage p_{la}.

5.2. No information at a settlement

It frequently occurs that information for a locator at a settlement is lacking. In such cases this should be prevented from raising the total score of all locators at that settlement.

Design choice 4
If no information of a locator opposition at a settlement is available, bias in the total locator score at that settlement is avoided by assigning it a settlement factor of n_{fs} = 0.

The consequence of this design choice is that the total localization score at that settlement changes neither positively nor negatively, since we have built the localization formula around 0.[9] For example, if a locator factor has a weight n_{fs} = 0, the v_{ls} of the locator is also 0, since

$$v_{ls} = \log_2 (n_{fs}+1) \times \lambda = \log_2 (0+1) \times \lambda = 0 \times \lambda = 0$$

---

9   In order to avoid too many zeros, which are problematic for computer treatment, we take for instance the average percentage of all locators at that settlement in the formula of geographical weight λ.

5.3. Complexity and repetition

The choice of a locator might imply that it exhibits overlaps with one or more other locators. We consider two such cases, to which we refer as complexity c_{ls} (Section 5.3.1) and repetition r_{ls} (Section 5.3.2).

5.3.1. Complexity (c_{ls})

We call 'complexity' the case in which we split up a series of dialect forms in more than one locator opposition. An example is: *sint* (A), *sent* (B), *sant* (C), *sont/sunt* (D), four types of form to oppose, each locator (either A, or B, or C, or D) once versus the other three, all occurring in different areas (see Map 4). In such cases each locator weighs half, since A, B, C and D are each opposed to the others only twice: see for instance A and D in Table 8. Altogether the four locator oppositions weigh 4 x 0.5 = 2.

A = B, C, D
B = A, C, D
C = A, B, D
D = A, B, C

Table 8. Number of locator oppositions.

Design choice 5
If a series of dialect forms is split up into more than one locator opposition, each locator opposition weighs 0.5.

If the weight of a locator opposition is 0.5 instead of 1, our localization formula should be

$$v_{ls} = \log_2(n_{fs}+1) \times c_{ls} \times \lambda = v_{ls} = \log_2(n_{fs}+1) \times 0.5 \times \lambda$$

Since it is our experience that the influence of this factor is modest we will not take it into account in the following. By assigning to c_{ls} the value 1 we simplify our formula

$$v_{ls} = \log_2(n_{fs}+1) \times c_{ls} \times \lambda \rightarrow v_{ls} = \log_2(n_{fs}+1) \times \lambda$$

5.3.2. Repetition (r_{ls})

The *O-A* variation occurs in other words than *Of* and *Af*, for instance in *ambOcht* versus *ambAcht* 'trade'. It may be the case that by introducing the locator *ambOcht* (almost) the same information is measured as in *Of-Af*, *O* and *A* having (almost) the same distribution in the two locators. In such a case there is to some extent question of repetition r_{ls}. Such locators should weigh between 0.5 and 1, i.e. $0.5 < r_{ls} < 1$ and $v_{ls} = \log_2(n_{fs}+1) \times r_{ls} \times \lambda$.

If it appears that there is hardly any overlap in distribution between two locators, they are (almost) independent, and both should weigh close to 1, i.e. they can be considered as independent, so we do not need to introduce r_{ls}. By contrast, in case of considerable overlap between them, their weight approaches 0.5; in that case we might consider taking them together as one locator opposition: *Of/ambOcht* versus *Af/ambAcht*. In all cases the linguist has to make an assessment on the basis of his knowledge and intuition.

Our experience has shown that this factor does not have much influence on the localization result. In addition, since it can be avoided without many problems, we will not include repetition r_{ls} in our localization formula by assigning it a value 1[10] and we simplify our formula as follows:

$$v_{ls} = \log_2(n_{fs}+1) \times r_{ls} \times \lambda \rightarrow v_{ls} = \log_2(n_{fs}+1) \times \lambda$$

5.4. A provisional localization formula

What we aim at is, first, to compare the total locator score of a text (or series of texts) of unknown provenance to the total locator score of each settlement and, second, to select the settlement with the highest score as being the place to localize the text. To arrive at that goal we start with how to formalize a locator in a text.

The way the formula for texts is built is essentially the same as in the case of settlements, with one exception: the geographic factor λ

---

10   To know more about c_{ls} and r_{ls}, see Rem (2003: 142-143).

does not play a part in texts, since it is unknown by definition. If more texts together are considered as a unit for localization we establish the text factor n_{ft} and the text percentage p_{lt} exactly parallel to the settlement factor n_{fs} and the settlement percentage p_{ls}. If we handle one text only, it is not even necessary to apply the $\log_2$ twice. If for a settlement locator the final value is $v_{ls} = \log_2 (n_{fs}+1)$ x λ, for a text locator we only need its n_{ft} and p_{lt}.

The text percentage p_{lt} of a text locator can be compared to the p_{ls} of any settlement. It may happen to be higher than any corresponding settlement percentage p_{ls}, i.e. the degree of similarity is so to say higher than 100%. In such cases we cannot do better, we believe, than to consider this p_{lt} as equal to the p_{ls}. For such text locators, we decide

Design choice 6
If the percentage p_{lt} of a text locator is higher than the highest settlement percentage p_{ls}, i.e. $p_{lt} > p_{ls}$, then $p_{lt} = p_{ls}$.

Now we can compare each locator of a text and each locator of each settlement by means of w_{ls} (*w* of *weight* or *witness*):

$$w_{ls} = v_{ls} \text{ x } n_{ft} \text{ x } (2 \text{ x } 1/\exp(d^2) - 1)$$

This formula contains the new element distance *d*. The distance *d* between a text and a settlement is defined by[11]

$$d = 0.025 \text{ x } |(p_{ls}-p_{lt})|$$

Since the difference between p_{ls} and p_{lt} is a percentage, it is situated between 0 and 100. It follows that the values for *d* are situated between 0 and 2.5, for d^2 between 0 and 6.25. And since the value of *exp*, the base of the natural logarithm, is approximately 2.71828, the

---

11   Since p_{lt} by definition $=< p_{ls}$ the | | notation is in fact superfluous.

value of $exp(d^2)$, being minimally 0 and maximally $exp(6.25)$, varies between 1 and 500.[12]

Since for $|(p_{ls}-p_{lt}| = 0$ the value of $2 \times 1/exp(d^2) - 1 = 1$ and for $|(p_{ls}-p_{lt}| = 100$ the value of $2 \times 1/exp(d^2) - 1 = -1$, it follows that the value of $(2 \times 1/exp(d^2) - 1)$ ranges from $+1$ to -1.

Per locator comparison we obtain a positive value, a negative value or a zero (plus the zeros in case a locator is lacking in the text and/or in the settlement, see Section 4.2). Counting together the w_{ls} of all locators – maximally the 101 locators in the case of Rem (2003) – we obtain $\Sigma\ w_{ls} = w_s$ per settlement. We localize the text by selecting the settlement with the highest w_s.

5.5. The final localization formula

In testing the procedure of Section 5.4 we were surprised to find out that texts tend to localize at small settlements, i.e. settlements with only one charter containing only a few locators. We did not consider this result entirely satisfactory, since these settlements often have nothing to suggest that they have been centres of text production. For that reason we decided to add still another weighing factor, the final one, and to obtain a score S, instead of w_s, per settlement. This decision can be worded as:

Design choice 7
If a settlement contributes to the localization of a text only minimally – with one locator in one locator opposition – the settlement weighs half as compared to the settlement with the maximal score M of its locators, other settlements situated proportionately in between. The result is the final score S. In formula:

$$S = w_s \times 0.5 \times (\log(U_s+B) / \log B)$$

---

12   e^a is usually denoted as *exp(a)* and can be seen as an exponential function (i.e. the converse of the logarithm).

Design choice 7 contains three new variables: U_s, B and M; for w_s see Section 5.4. We determine the score U_s by calculating for each locator at each settlement its absolute value:

$$| v_{ls} \; x \; n_{ft} |$$

and add them all together per settlement. The sum per settlement of all locators is:

$$U_s = \Sigma \left(|v_{ls} \; x \; n_{ft}| \right)$$

All settlements having their own U_s, we select the settlement with the highest $U_s = M$. From this maximal score M B is derived by means of:

$$B = 0.5 + \sqrt{(0.25 + M)}$$

Now, suppose $M = 6400$, then $B = 80.50$ and

$$S = w_s \; x \; 0.5 \; x \; (\log(U_s + 80.50) : \log 80.50)^{13}$$

The following example shows some implications of design choice 7 for final score S. Suppose $w_s = 80$ and for four settlements:

U[low] = 1
U[mid] = 100
U[high]= 1000
U[max]= 6400

We obtain the following results:

S[low] = 80 x 0.5 x log (1 + 80.5) / log 80.5 = 80 x 0.5 = 40
S[mid] = 80 x 0.5 x log (100 + 80.5) / log 80.5= 80 x 0.59 = 47.2
S[high] = 80 x 0.5 x log (1000 + 80.5) / log 80.5= 80 x 0.79 = 63.2
S[max] = 80 x 0.5 x log (6400 + 80.5) / log 80.5 = 80 x 1 = 80

---

13   Since the base of the logarithm is not important, we use $\log_{10}$.

In other words: under otherwise equal conditions a small settlement, i.e. a settlement with the minimum amount of locators, obtains a score $S = 40$, whereas the best documented settlement still obtains a score $S = w_s = 80$.

6. Testing weights and reliability

In this section we test our localization procedure on two different points. A first test concerning the effects of weighing is discussed in Section 6.1. In Section 6.2 we test the reliability of series of localization results.

6.1. Varying weights

What is the difference between different kinds of weighing? Maps 5 and 6 present two different design choices on the basis of the same data. Map 5 presents the data on the basis of $\log_2 (n_{ls})$ x p_{ls} (see Section 4.2 design choice 1), whereas Map 6 presents the same data on the basis of one settlement one witness (see Section 4.1 choice 1). Several differences can be noted between the maps:

- differences between the maps are local; the global patterns are to a large extent the same;
- the shapes of Map 6 are capricious as compared to those of Map 5;
- settlements in the North seem to have relatively much weight on Map 6.

Since these settlements are usually small, this must be due to the fact that they have received relativily much weight. Map 5 represents what we think is a better balanced result.

6.2. Localizations of settlements

The test we present in this section is based upon all 101 locators used in Rem (2003). It concerns the question whether the localization procedure does what it is supposed to do: localize texts at the right settlement or at least in the right region. In the test we consider charters of a settlement as texts to be localized by making a copy of them. In addition, we either leave the copied charters in the database or take them out of the database.

For this experiment we have selected Utrecht city, Diemen, Amsterdam, Amstelveen and Dordrecht. In Diemen and Amstelveen, with one and four charters respectively, the difference between leaving or not leaving the copied charters in the database is negligible, and we leave them in.

The localization of the charters of Utrecht city, taken out of the database as copies, does not surprise. The charters of Utrecht city localize where they are expected to localize, in Utrecht city: see Map 7. The result is hardly different when we localize the charters of Utrecht city without the charters of Utrecht left in the database: see Map 8. Virtually all locators in Utrecht city also seem to occur at the – usually rather small – settlements around Utrecht. A very satisfactory result.

However, localizing the one charter from Diemen gives a result which is less satisfactory, at least at first sight: see Map 9. How is it possible that Diemen localizes in Utrecht city? One part of the answer may be that the locators of Diemen will tend to have less weight than the corresponding locators of Utrecht city.[14] Moreover, it must be the case that the language of (the one charter from) Diemen resembles to a large extent that of (the many charters from) Utrecht city, so that hardly any locator scores obtain negative values, since negative scores with relatively high weight could easily have prevented a localization at Utrecht city. We have seen already that the usually small settlements around Utrecht city point towards Utrecht city without its

---

14   That they are few in number does not make any difference, because by definition only those locators which are present play a part in the localization process.

charters being present in the database. Apparently Diemen still belongs to them. Finally, if we had assigned the same weight to the relevant locators both at Diemen and at Utrecht, not only might Diemen have scored on Diemen, but also Utrecht city might have scored on Diemen. That would have been an undesirable result. A small village such as Diemen with only a few locators is not expected to be a centre of text production.

When we localize Amsterdam texts, the Amsterdam charters still being in the database, they localize at Amsterdam as we expect them to do: see Map 10. However, without charters of Amsterdam in the database, Amsterdam as text does not localize entirely at the same place. The reason is that the language of Amsterdam resembles that of the southern part of Holland: Gouda, Schoonhoven, Leiden, but not that of Utrecht city, Haarlem (west of Amsterdam) or the dialects north of Amsterdam.

Amstelveen, with only four charters, has, just as Diemen, only a low number of locators with relatively small weight. These locators point towards Amsterdam, as shown on Map 11. What this map also tells us is that, although Amstelveen is close to Diemen, its language does not resemble that of Utrecht city as does the language of Diemen, but that its language is Hollandish, as that of Amsterdam.

A rather different case is Dordrecht, near the border with the Utrecht province, and perhaps still the most important city in Holland, at least during the first part of the fourteenth century. Map 13 shows that the charters of Dordrecht as text localize west of Dordrecht, even if the charters of Dordrecht are still in the database. The reason is that the language of Dordrecht resembles that of west Holland (Delft, 's-Gravenzande, The Hague, Leiden), and that east of Dordrecht no Hollandish dialects are found. This point becomes even more salient when we take the Dordrecht charters out of the database (see Map 14). Since the only Hollandish dialect in the region, that of Dordrecht, is no longer present, the dialect of Dordrecht as text is localized as if it came from Delft, 's-Gravenzande, The Hague and Leiden (or, perhaps more probably, the other way around).

These results suggest, we think, that our localization method functions satisfactorily. However, our results still need interpretation due to either insufficient data or sharp dialect borders. More Hollandish dialects east of Dordrecht, or more data in Diemen and Amstelveen, might lead to more satisfactory localization results in these areas.

7. Results: localizations of (the hands of) clerks

In this section we show two results of our localization procedure. We localize the charters of the clerks of the Count of Holland, Willem III, and his entourage, and the charters of a more isolated clerk, Johannes, who – to some extent – might also belong to Willem's circle.

Map 15 shows where the hands of eight clerks of the Count of Holland localize. The results point definitely towards Holland. This is not the case of the ninth clerk, Johannes: see Map 16. Although he sometimes carried out work for the Count, he was not one of his scribes.[15] The language of clerk Johannes does not show a very specific localization profile. It looks like a rather neutral *Mischsprache*: it contains, although weakly, elements from the north of Holland, and – to an even lesser extent – from Amsterdam and south east of it. This result shows that his charters are far from fit to serve as part of the basic documentation of localized charters. His language is to a large extent characterized by dialect features which are rather the opposites of our locators, since they are hardly specific for any region.

---

15   These charters are to be conceived as text to be localized, since the clerks of the Count of Holland may have very different, and often unknown provenances. As far as Johannes is concerned, he was probably a clerk of Willem van Duven-voorde, Chamberlain or Keeper of the Seal of the Count. For more on this subject we refer to Rem (2003: 70-80, 286).

8. Conclusion

In this study we have described how Middle Dutch texts of unknown provenance can be localized in settlements by comparing their dialect forms (locators) to those of the settlements. Even if the basics of our strategy are easy to understand, their implementation is far from trivial. The reason why we have chosen our strategy is that historical data tend to be highly irregular in spatial distribution and frequency. In order to cope with these problems we have made the data comparable by adopting a strategy based on information theory.

We have proposed a series of design choices, wording them as explicitly as possible. At all points where we made choices we asked ourselves: What do the data witness and what do they weigh? Or perhaps better: What do we want them to witness and to weigh? We have weighted frequencies of occurrence of locators, and of numbers of locators, at settlements and we have weighted geographical distribution. We have also considered the problem of complexity in locator oppositions and that of repetition of related data. And we have designed the localization formula around zero, in order to avoid biases as a consequence of lacking information.

Application of information theory asks for much inventivity in order to arrive at what we think the best possible results. To what extent we have succeeded is for the reader to judge, who might try out our approach not only on Middle Dutch, but also on other languages such as Middle English, Old French and variants of older German by accepting our design choices or by replacing them with perhaps better ones.

References

Benskin, Michael 1991a. The 'Fit'-technique Explained. In Riddy, Felicity (ed.) *Regionalism in Late Medieval Manuscripts and Texts*. Cambridge: Brewer, 9-26.

Benskin, Michael 1991b. In Reply to Dr Burton. *Leeds Studies in English*. NS 22, 209-262.

Benskin, Michael / Laing, Margaret 1981. Translations and *Mischsprachen* in Middle English Manuscripts. In Benskin, Michael and Samuels, M.L. (eds) *So meny people longages and tonges: Philological Essays in Scots and Mediaeval English Presented to Angus McIntosh*. Edinburgh: Edinburgh Middle English Dialect Project, 55-106.

Berteloot, Armand 1984. *Bijdrage tot een klankatlas van het dertiende-eeuwse Middelnederlands [Contribution to a Sound Atlas of 13th-Century Middle Dutch]*, 2 vols. Gent: KANTL.

Dees, Anthonij / van Reenen, Pieter Th. / de Vries, J.A. 1980. *Atlas des formes et des constructions des chartes françaises du 13e siècle*, Beihefte zur Zeitschrift für romanische Philologie Band 178. Tübingen: Niemeyer.

GTRP 2003: Goeman-Taeldeman-Van Reenen-Project 1980-1995. *Phonology and Morphology of Dutch and Frisian Dialects in 1.1 million transcriptions*, version 2.2 / J.L.van den Berg. Meertens Instituut Electronic Publications in Linguistics (MIEPiL III), (cd-rom).

Marynissen, Ann 1995. Een vergelijking van diverse telmethoden in het historisch-linguïstisch onderzoek [A Comparison of Different Methods of Counting in Historical-linguistic Research]. In Goossens, Jan / van Loon, Joseph / Niebaum, Hermann (eds) *Historische Dialectologie. Taal en Tongval*, themanummer 8, 124-138.

Mihm, Arend 2002. Graphematische Systemanalyse als Grundlage der historischen Prosodieforschung. In Mihm, Arend 2007. *Sprachwandel im Spiegel der Schriftlichkeit, Studien zum Zeugniswert der historischen Schreibsprachen des 11. bis 17. Jahrhunderts.* Frankfurt a.M.: Peter Lang, 147-172.

Mooijaart, Marijke 1992. *Atlas van vroegmiddelnederlandse taalvarianten [Atlas of Language Variants in Early Middle Dutch].* Utrecht: Led.

Mooijaart, Marijke / Heijden, Peter van der 1992. Linguïstische en geografische afstand in dertiende-eeuws Middelnederlands [Linguistic and Geographical Distance in 13th-Century Middle Dutch]. *Taal en Tongval* 44/2, 188-216.

Reenen, Pieter van 1986-1987. De lange weg naar een betrouwbare en systematische beschrijving van het Middelnederlands [The Long Road towards a Reliable and Systematic Description of Middle Dutch]. *Spektator* 16, 131-148.

Reenen, Pieter van 1988. Les variations des graphies *o/ou* et *en/an* en ancien français. In van Reenen, Pieter / van Reenen-Stein, Karin (eds) *Distributions spatiales et temporelles, constellations des manuscrits, Etudes de variation linguistique offertes à Anthonij Dees à l'occasion de son 60ième anniversaire.* Amsterdam: Benjamins, 163-176.

Rem, Margit 2003. *De taal van de klerken uit de Hollandse grafelijke kanselarij (1300-1340), Naar een lokaliserings-procedure voor het veertiende-eeuws Middelnederlands [The Language of the Clerks of the Chancellery of the Count of Holland (1300-1340), Towards a Localization Procedure for 14th-Century Middle Dutch].* Amsterdam: Stichting Neerlandistiek VU.

Rem, Margit / Wattel, Evert / van Reenen, Pieter 2003. De taalkundige lokaliseringsmethode. In Rem, 129-150, 303-306.

Shannon, Claude E. 1948. A Mathematical Theory of Communication. *The Bell System Technical Journal* 27, 379-423, 623-656.

Wattel, Evert / van Reenen, Pieter forthcoming. Probabilistic Maps. In Lameri, Alfred / Kehrein, Roland / Rabanus, Stefan (eds) *Handbook of Language Mapping.* Berlin: Mouton.

Appendix

Map 1. *-ch-* versus *-f-* in *vichtich* etc. versus *viftich* etc. 'fifty'.

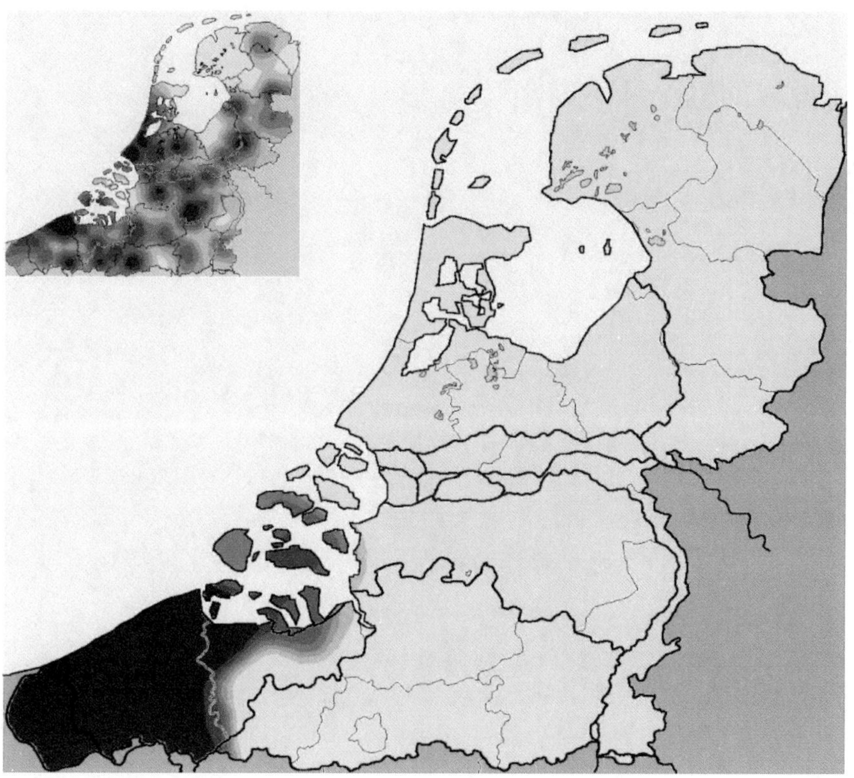

                                    Pieter van Reenen / Margit Rem / Evert Wattel

Map 2. *-e-* versus *-i-* in *viftech* etc. versus *viftich* etc. 'fifty'

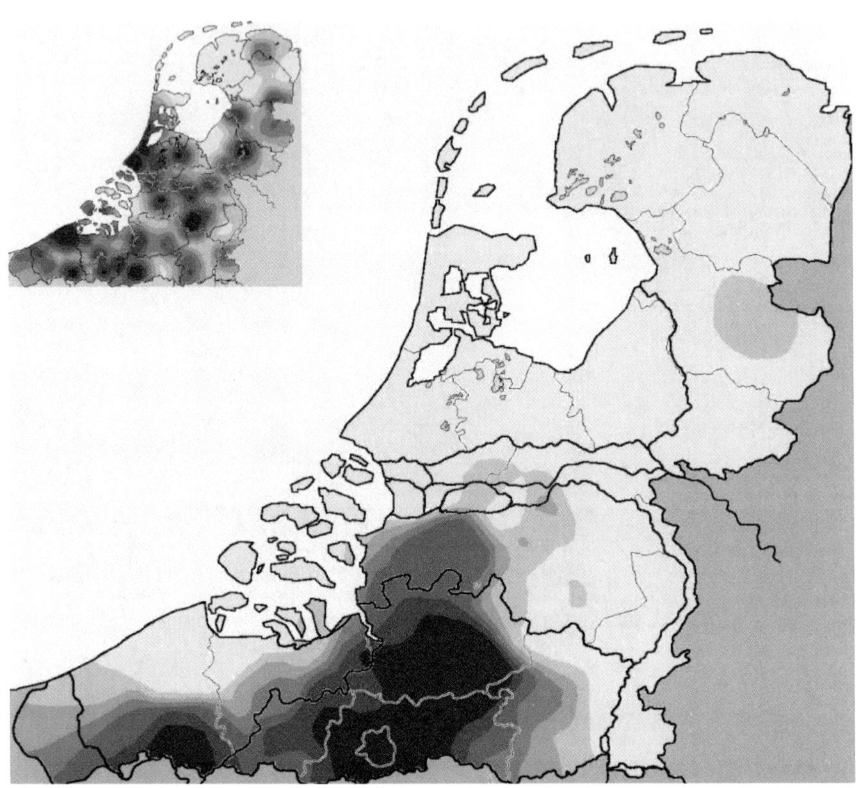

Map 3. *-chte-* versus *-chti-*, *-fti-*, *-fte-* in *vichtech* etc. versus other forms of 'fifty'.

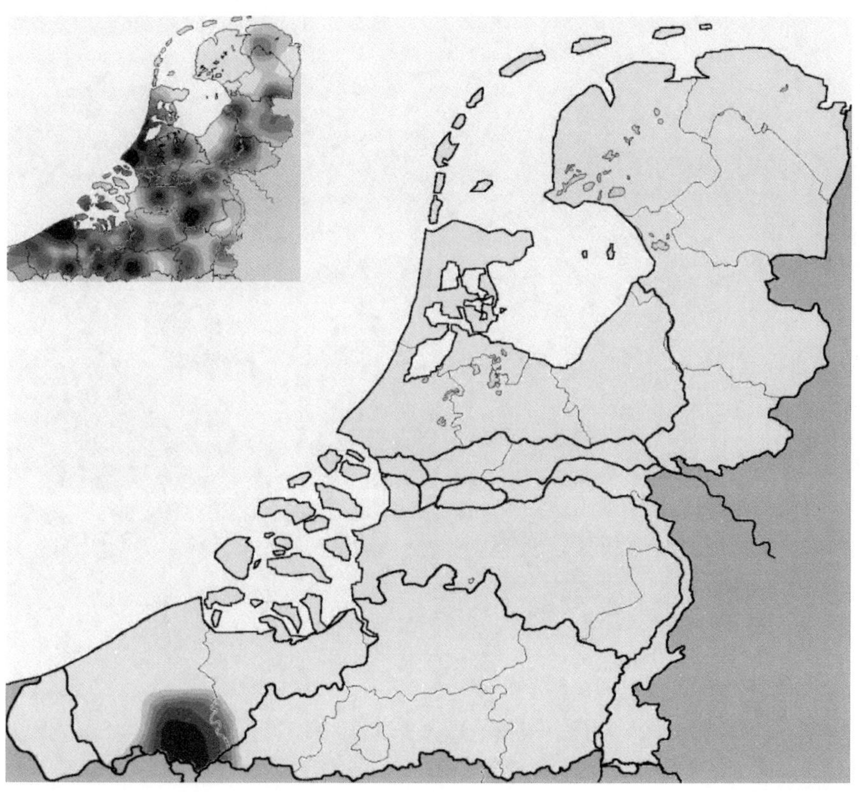

Map 4. Locator oppositions *sint* (light grey), *sent* (grey), *sont/sunt* (dark) *sant* (black), 'saint'. The transition area is white.

Map 5. *Of* (dark) versus *Af*: twice application of $\log_2$ function.

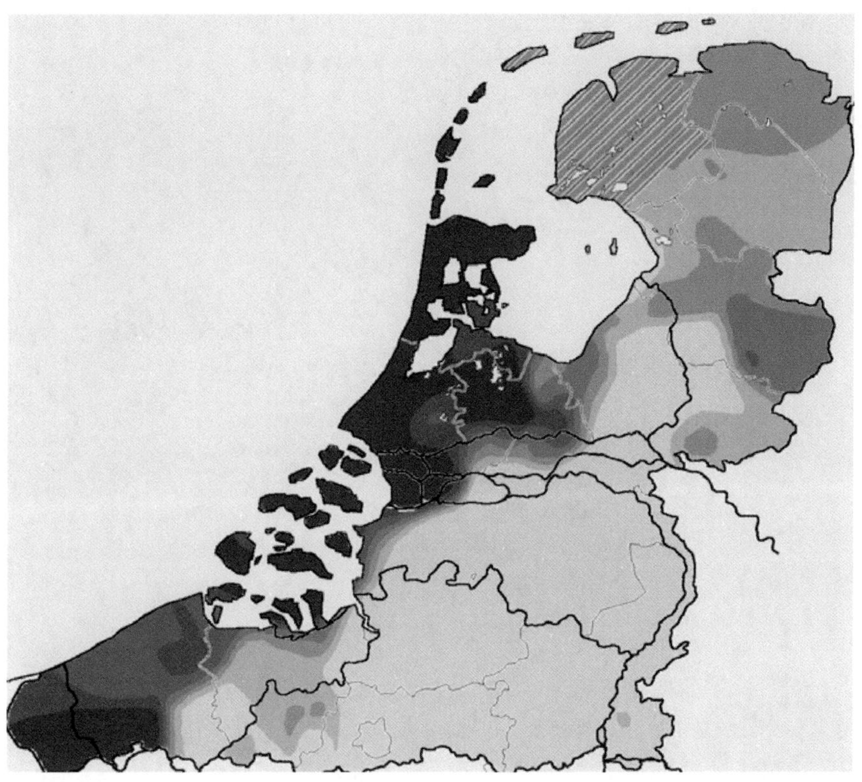

Map 6. *Of* (dark) versus *Af*: one settlement one witness.

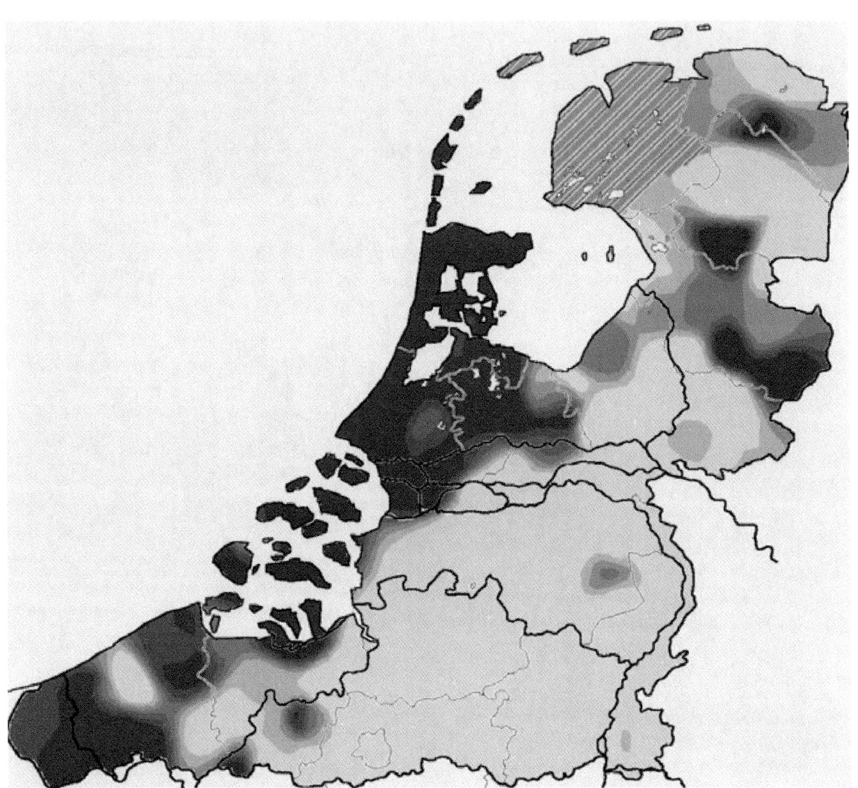

Map 7. Localization of the charters of Utrecht city as text with the charters of Utrecht city still in the database.

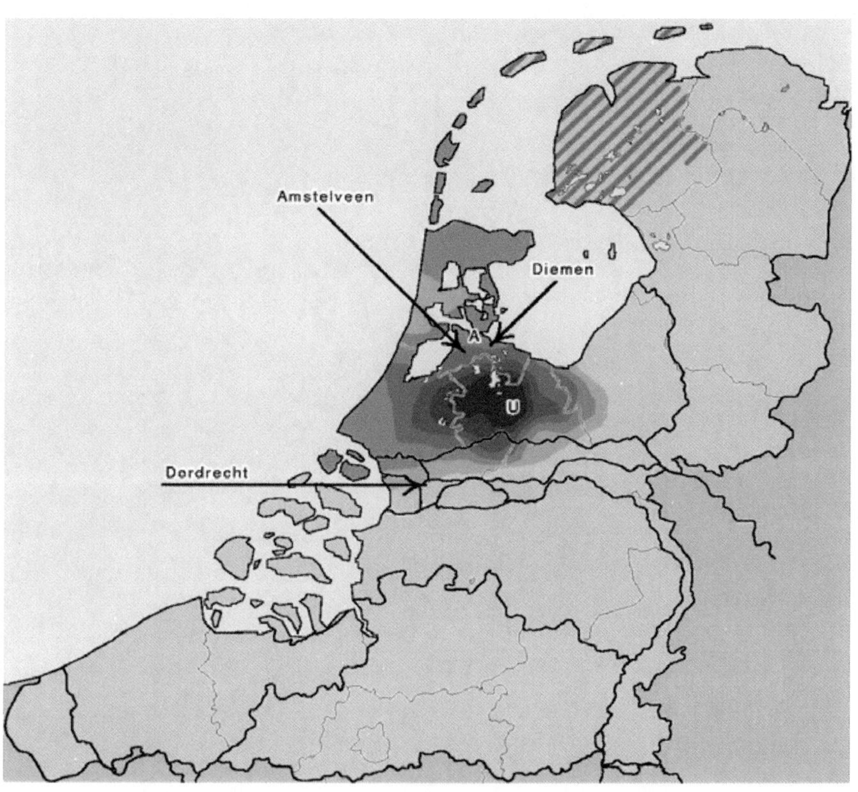

Map 8. Localization of the charters of Utrecht city as text without the charters of Utrecht city in the database.

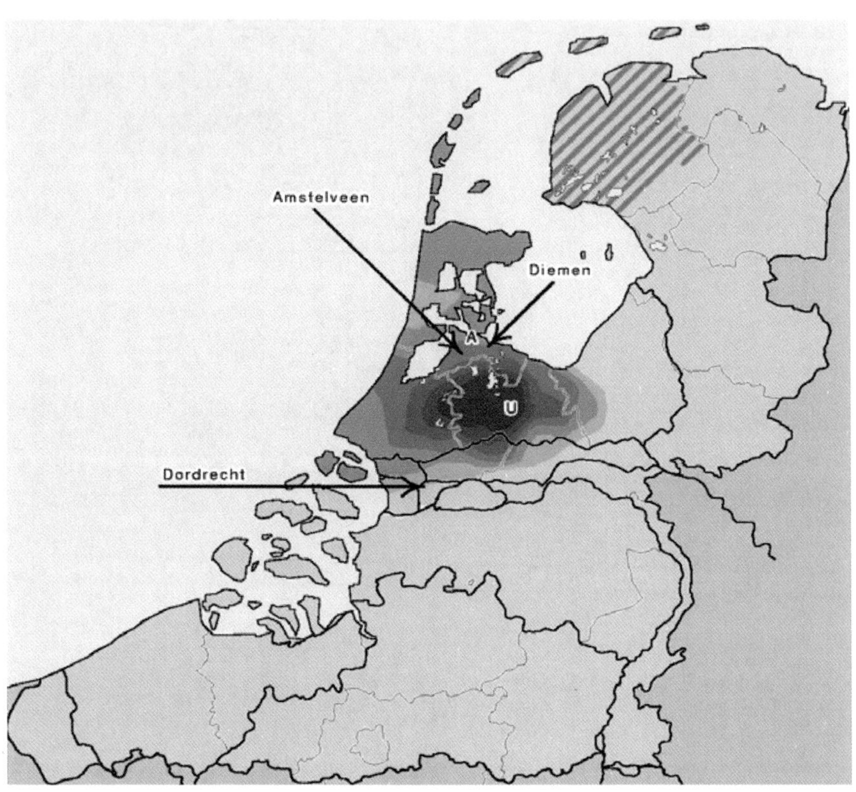

Map 9. Localization of the charters of Diemen as text with the charters of Diemen still in the database.

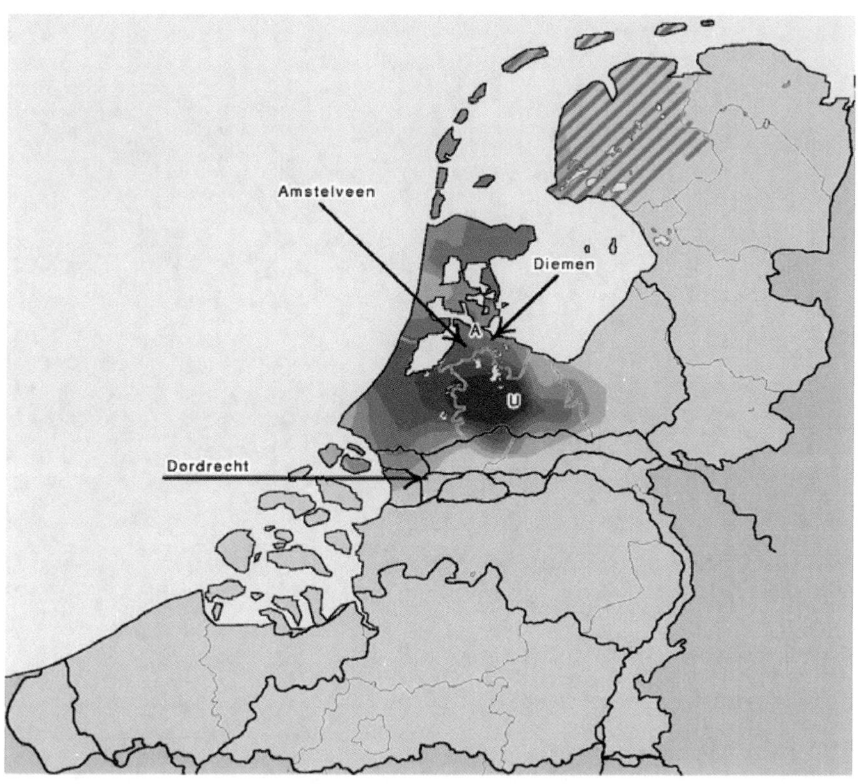

Map 10. Localization of the charters of Amsterdam as text with the charters of Amsterdam still in the database.

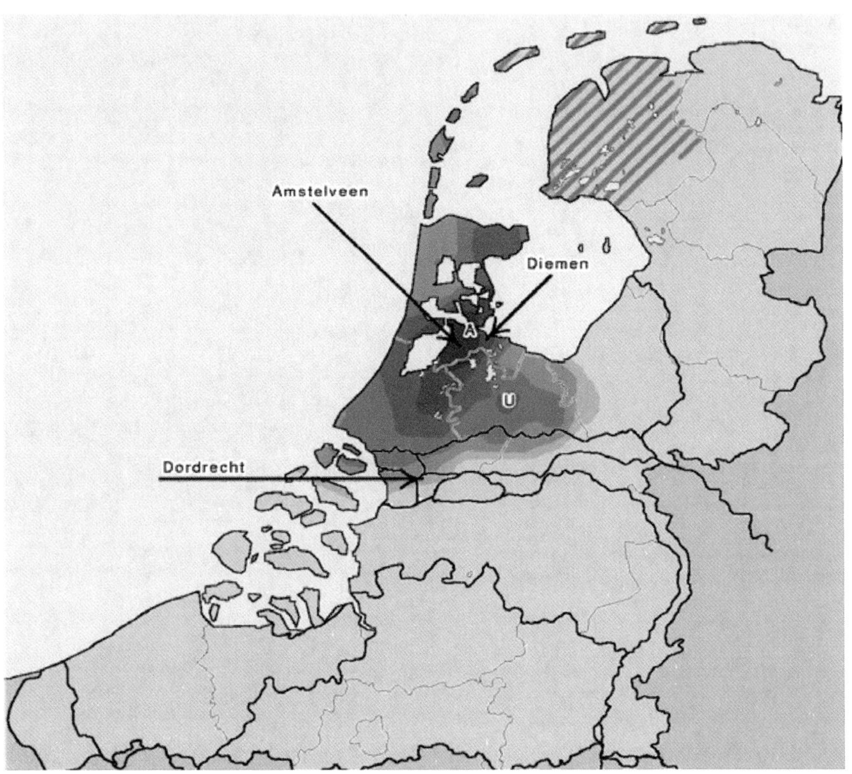

Map 11. Localization of the charters of Amsterdam as text without the charters of Amsterdam in the database.

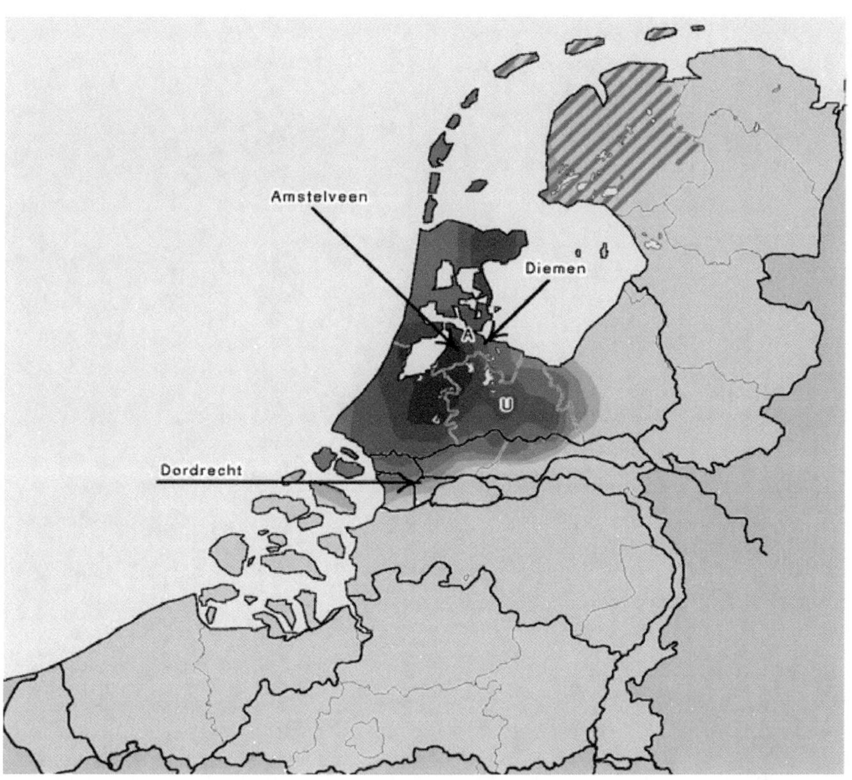

Map 12. Localization of the charters of Amstelveen as text with the charters of Amstelveen still in the database.

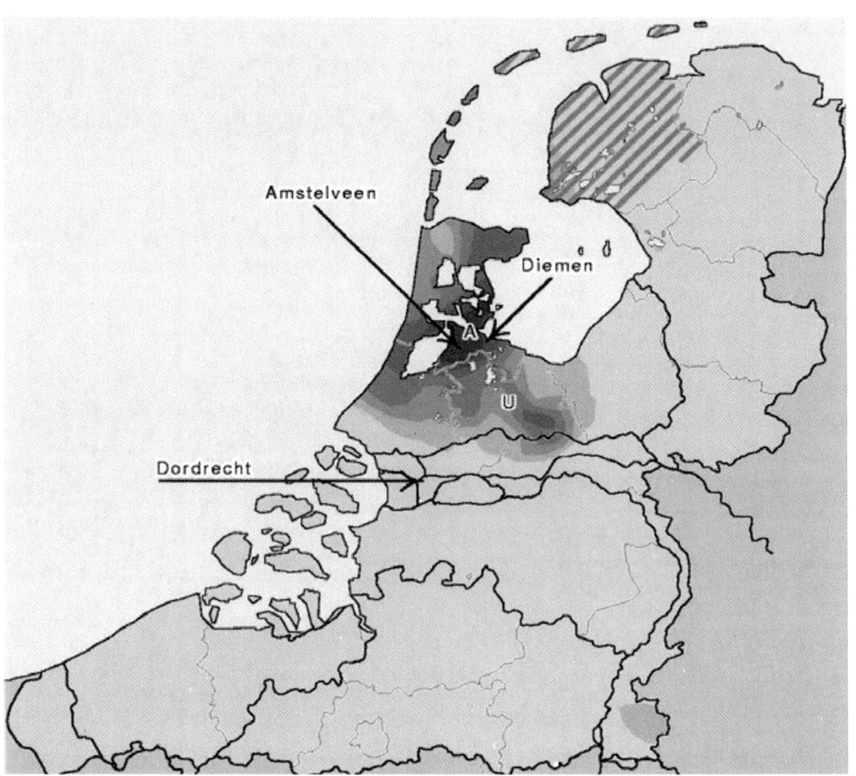

Map 13. Localization of the charters of Dordrecht as text with the charters of Dordrecht still in the database.

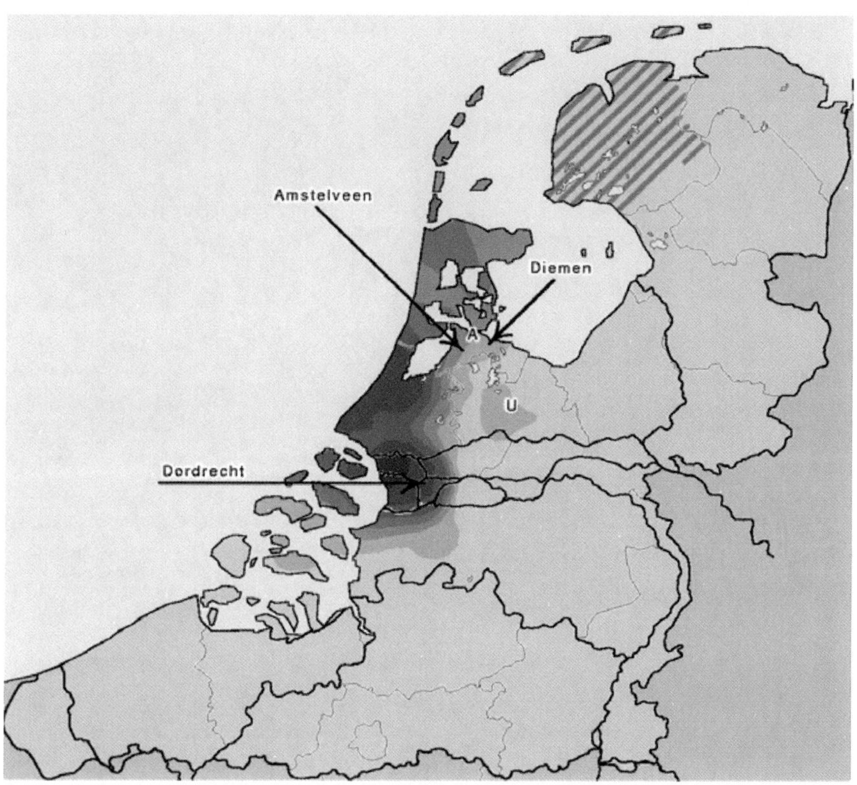

Map 14. Localization of the charters of Dordrecht as text without the charters of Dordrecht in the database.

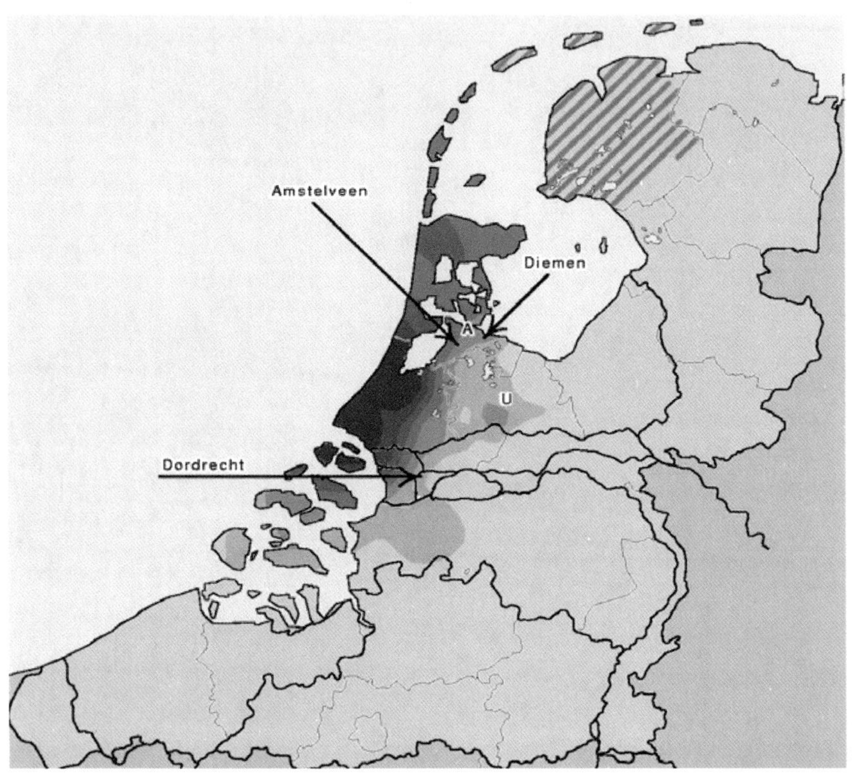

Map 15. Localization of the language of the clerks of Count Willem III.

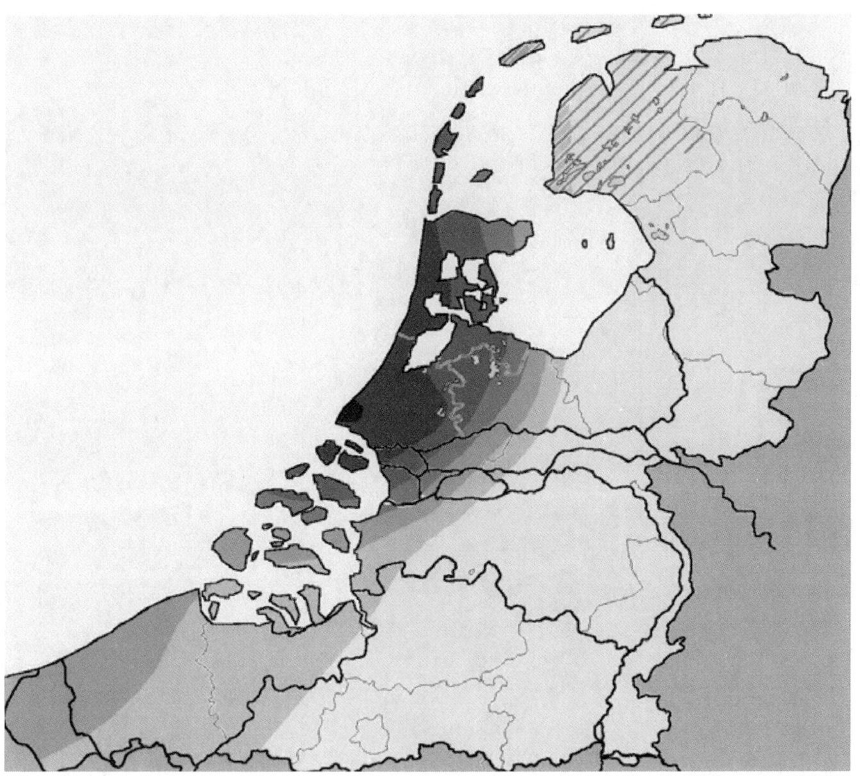

     Pieter van Reenen / Margit Rem / Evert Wattel

Map 16. Localization of the language of clerk Johannes.

HERMANN MOISL

Using Electronic Corpora
in Historical Dialectology Research:
The Problem of Document Length Variation

1. Introduction

The proliferation of computational technology has generated an explosive production of electronically encoded information of all kinds. In the face of this, traditional philological methods for search and interpretation of data have been overwhelmed by volume, and a variety of computational methods have been developed in an attempt to make the deluge tractable. These developments have clear implications for corpus-based linguistics in general, and for corpus-based study of historical dialectology in particular: as more and larger historical text corpora become available, effective analysis of them will increasingly be tractable only by adapting the interpretative methods developed by the statistical (Hair *et al.* 2005; Tabachnik/Fidell 2006), information retrieval (Belew 2000; Grossman/Frieder 2004), pattern recognition (Bishop 2006), and related communities. To use such analytical methods effectively, however, issues that arise with respect to the abstraction of data from corpora have to be understood. This study addresses an issue that has a fundamental bearing on the validity of analytical results based on such data: variation in document length. The discussion is in four main parts. The first part shows how a particular class of computational methods, exploratory multivariate analysis, can be used in historical dialectology research, the second explains why variation in document length can be a problem in such analysis, the third proposes document length normalization as a solution to that problem, and the fourth points out some difficulties associated with document length normalization.

2. Exploratory multivariate analysis
in historical dialectology

Historical dialectology is based on the study of collections of spoken or written language. A typical research question is: given a corpus comprising a collection of historical documents, can those documents be dialectally classified on the basis of their linguistic characteristics – phonetic, phonological, morphological, lexical, or syntactic? There are two main approaches to this type of question:

- Theoretically-driven: Classification criteria are selected by the researcher on the basis of an independently-specified theoretical linguistic framework supported by existing case studies conducted within that framework and by personal knowledge of the characteristics of the language in the historical period in question.
- Empirically-driven: Classification criteria are algorithmically abstracted from the corpus data itself without reference to any theoretical linguistic framework, existing analytical results, or personal knowledge of the subject domain.

The theoretically-driven approach is suitable where the corpus is embedded in a well understood dialectological context, while the empirically-driven one is suitable where little is known a priori about it. This contribution is concerned with analysis of historical corpora whose characteristics are not well known using an empirically-driven methodology called exploratory multivariate analysis.

2.1. The nature of exploratory multivariate analysis

In current scientific practice, a hypothesis about some natural phenomenon is proposed and its adequacy assessed using data obtained from observation of the domain of inquiry. But nature is dauntingly complex, and there is little practical or indeed theoretical hope of being able to observe even a small part of it exhaustively. Instead, the researcher selects particular aspects of the domain which seem salient to his or her research question. Each selected aspect is represented by a variable, and a series of observations is conducted in which, at each observation, the values of each variable are recorded. A body of data is thereby built up on the basis of which the hypothesis can be assessed. If only one aspect of the domain is observed – the height of individuals in a population, say – then the data consists of some number of values assigned to a single variable; that data is univariate. If two aspects are observed – say height and weight – then the data is bivariate, if three trivariate, and so on up to some arbitrary number *n*. Any data where *n* is greater than 1 is multivariate.

As the size of the data grows, that is, as the number of variables and/or the number of observations increases, it becomes ever more difficult to see any interesting regularities by direct inspection. Take, for example, data in which three persons p1, p2, and p3 are described in terms of two variables 'age' and 'weight'. If p1 is young, p2 middle-aged, and p3 old, and if p1's weight is low, p2's medium, and p3's high, it's easy enough to infer just by looking at the data that weight increases with age, at least for this sample. Adding a third variable 'height' makes it a little more difficult but not impossible to see such regularities. But what if there are a dozen variables, including such things as 'income', 'hair colour', and 'shoe size'? It is very difficult to see very much in the data, and, of course, there is no limit to the number of variables that might be used to describe people. How easy would it be to see any regularities in data with, say 100 variables, even for only three people? And, as the number of persons increases, so does the difficulty of interpretation. In short, as the number of variables and/or observations grows, so does the difficulty of conceptualizing the interrelationships of variables on the one hand, and the interrelationships of observations on the other.

Exploratory multivariate analysis is a general term for mathematically-based methods for discovering and understanding data that has too many variables for it to be comprehensible via direct inspection (Andrienko/Andrienko 2005). Exploratory methods have long been used in numerous science and engineering disciplines as a way of generating hypotheses about data whose characteristics are not well understood. Closer to home, the proliferation of electronic text in recent decades has seen the application of exploratory methods in processing of natural language text in areas like information retrieval (Belew 2000; Grossman/Frieder 2004) and data mining (Tan *et al.* 2006), as well as in linguistic analysis and in traditional philology more generally. The literature on linguistic and philological applications is too large and varied to cite here; representative dialectological examples are Heeringa/Nerbonne (2001), and Nerbonne/Heeringa (2001).

2.2. *Application of exploratory multivariate analysis*
to historical dialectology

Exploratory multivariate analysis methods are intended specifically to classify any given collection of objects described by more or less numerous variables. Because this is precisely the kind of research question with which historical dialectology is often concerned, their extension to corpus analysis is a natural step.

To exemplify this extension we consider the *Newcastle Electronic Corpus of Tyneside English* (NECTE), a corpus of dialect speech from Tyneside in North-East England (Allen *et al.* 2005). It includes phonetic transcriptions of 63 interviews together with social data about the speakers, and as such offers an opportunity to study the phonetic dialectology of Tyneside speech of the late 1960s. Moisl/ Jones (2005), Moisl *et al.* (2006), Moisl/Maguire (2008) have begun that study using exploratory analysis of the transcriptions with the aim of generating hypotheses about phonetic variation among speakers and speaker groups in the corpus. These studies were based on comparison of profiles associated with each of the Tyneside Linguistic Survey (TLS) speakers. A profile for any speaker S is the number of times S uses each of the phonetic segments in the NECTE transcription scheme in his or her interview. More specifically, the profile P associated with S is a vector having as many elements as there are segments such that each vector element P_j represents the *j*'th segment, where *j* is in the range 1..number of segments in the NECTE phonetic transcription scheme, and the value stored at P_j is an integer representing the number of times S uses the j'th segment. There are 156 segments, and so a speaker profile is a length-156 vector. There are 63 TLS speakers, and their profiles are represented in a matrix N, having 63 rows, one for each profile, and 156 columns, one for each segment; a fragment is shown in Figure 1:

	v1: ɪ	v2: i̯	...	v156: ʒ
Speaker 1	23	4	...	7
Speaker 2	3	56	...	4
...	...	...	...	...
Speaker 63	18	35	...	8

Figure 1. NECTE phonetic segment frequency data matrix N.

The aim is to classify the 63 speakers in accordance with the values in their speaker profiles.

N is an example of data that are simply too large and complex to be interpretable by direct inspection. It was therefore analyzed using hierarchical cluster analysis (Everitt *et al.* 2001), a widely used exploratory analytical method that represents relative similarity among items in high-dimensional data as a nested tree:

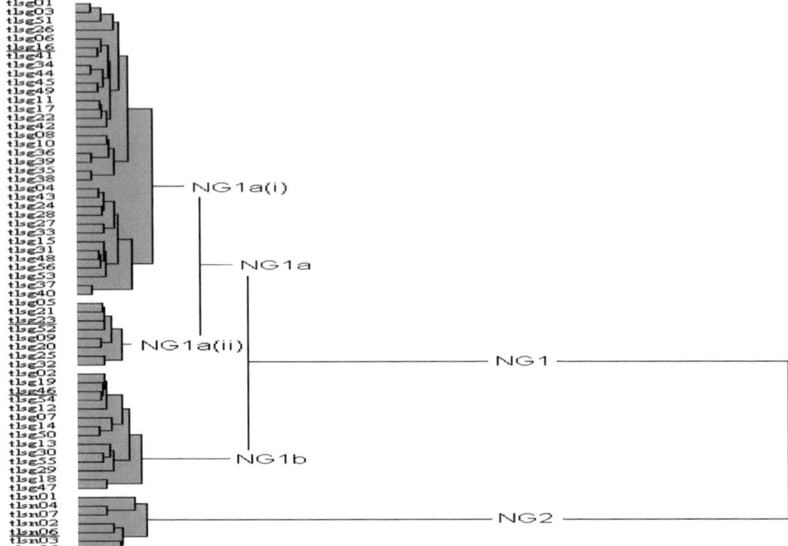

Figure 2. Cluster analysis of the NECTE data matrix N.

Cluster trees like this are familiar to linguists as representations of syntactic phrase structure, but differ from linguistic trees in that

- they are shown horizontally rather in the vertical orientation that is more usual for linguistic phrase structure trees in order to make them more readily representable on a page;
- the leaves are not lexical tokens but labels for the data items – here speaker labels;
- they represent not grammatical constituency but relativities of similarity between the vectors representing the data entities – here speakers. The lengths of the branches linking the subtrees represent degrees of similarity: the shorter the branch, the more similar the subtrees. Thus the subtrees labelled NG1 and NG2 above are very dissimilar, NG1a(i) and NG1a(ii) very similar, and so on.

The hierarchical analysis partitions the NECTE speakers on the basis of their phonetic usage (Moisl *et al.* 2006). The main distinction is between middle class, well educated speakers from Newcastle on the north side of the river Tyne, labelled NG2, and working class, less well educated speakers from Gateshead on the south side of the Tyne, labelled NG1. The Gateshead speakers are categorized into NG1b (exclusively male), and NG1a (mainly though not exclusively female); NG1a is subcategorized into NG1a(i) (working class females) and NG1a(ii) (males and females with relatively higher socio-economic status).

3. The problem of variation in document length

It is a simple fact of life that documents in any given collection can vary considerably in length. Where the data abstracted from such a corpus is based on frequency, such length variation is a problem for cluster analysis. This section shows why.

For concreteness of exposition the discussion is based on a small, artificially-constructed corpus C with known structural characteristics. It comprises 9 excerpts from historical English texts from OE to EModE. These are arranged chronologically in Figure 3:

Name	Date	Size
Sermo Lupi ad Anglos	996 - 1023 AD	13 kb
Beowulf	c.1000 AD	106 kb
Apollonius of Tyre	c.1000-1050	35 kb
The Owl and the Nightingale	c.1250-1300 AD	10 kb
Chaucer, *Troilus / Criseyde*	c.1370 AD	123 kb
Malory, *Morte d'Arthur*	c.1470 AD	132 kb
Everyman	c.1500 AD	37 kb
Spenser, *Faerie Queene*	1590 AD	34 kb
King James Bible	1611 AD	11kb

Figure 3. The contents of example corpus C.

3.1. Data creation

Prior to its standardization in the later eighteenth century, spelling in the British Isles varied considerably from time to time and place to place, reflecting on the one hand differences in phonetics, phonology and morphology at different stages of linguistic development, and on the other differences in spelling conventions. It should, therefore, be possible to categorize texts on the basis of their spelling, and to correlate the resulting categorizations with chronology. This, therefore, is the research question: can the documents in C be accurately categorized chronologically solely on the basis of their spelling?

How does one go about investigating spelling? The approach taken here is based on the concept of the tuple. A tuple is a sequence of symbols: AA is a pair, AAA a triple, AAAA a fourtuple, and so on. This concept of tuple offers an efficient way of comparing spellings among texts:

- Given a collection D containing m documents, compile a list of all letter tuples that occur in the texts. Assume that there are n such tuples;
- To each of the documents d_i in D (for $i = 1..m$) assign a vector of length n such that each vector element v_j (for $j = 1..n$) represents one of the n letter tuples;
- In each document d_i count the number of times each of the n letter tuples j occurs, and enter that frequency in the vector element v_j of the vector associated with d_i.

The result is a set of vectors each of which is an occurrence frequency profile of letter tuples for one of the documents in D. These document profile vectors can be stored as the rows of the data matrix.

A letter-pair frequency matrix was abstracted from C using the foregoing procedure. 554 letter pairs were found, and since there are 9 documents, the result is a 9 x 554 matrix henceforth referred to M. An example fragment is shown in Figure 4:

	v1: ic	v2: ch	v3: we	...	v554: qd
Sermo Lupi	67	1	86	...	0
Beowulf	400	15	737	...	0
...	...	...	...	...	...
King James Bible	18	18	21	...	0

Figure 4. Letter-pair frequency matrix M abstracted from C.

3.2. Hierarchical cluster analysis of M

From what is commonly known of the history of the English language and of spelling at various stages of its development, one expects cluster analysis of M to produce no surprises: the OE, ME, and EModE texts will form clusters. This expectation is not fulfilled, however, as is shown in Figure 5.

The texts do not cluster by chronological period, and the clustering in fact makes no obvious sense in terms of anything one knows about them and their historical context. When, however, one looks at the 'Size' column in Figure 3, the reason for the clustering immediately becomes clear. The texts have been clustered by their relative lengths: the short texts (*Owl, Sermo, King James*) comprise one cluster, the intermediate-length texts (*Apollonius, Faerie Queene, Everyman*) a second cluster, and the long texts (*Troilus, Morte d'Arthur*) a third, with *Beowulf* on its own commensurate with a length that falls between the intermediate-length and long texts.

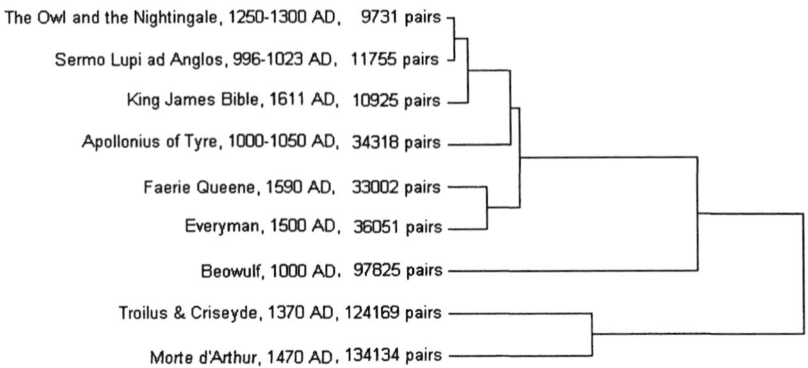

Figure 5. Cluster tree of the rows of data matrix M.

3.3. Explanation of document length based clustering

Clustering based on document length is best explained in terms of vector space geometry, for which see any textbook on linear algebra such as Fraleigh/Beauregard (1995). A vector space is a geometrical interpretation of a vector in which

- the dimensionality n of the vector defines an n-dimensional space which, for present purposes, is taken to be the familiar Euclidean one in which the axes are straight lines at right angles to one another;
- the sequence of numbers comprising the vector specifies coordinates in the space;
- the vector itself is a point at the specified coordinates in the space.

For example, the two components of a vector v = (30 70) in Figure 6 are coordinates of a point in a two-dimensional space, and those of v = (40 20 60) of a point in three-dimensional space:

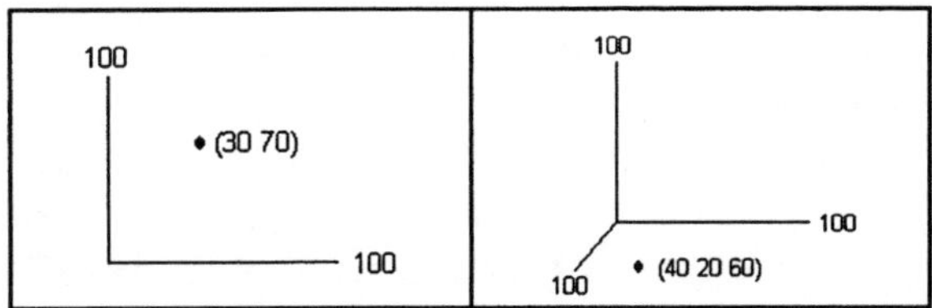

Figure 6. Vectors in two and three dimensional vector spaces.

A length-4 vector defines a point in 4-dimensional space, and so on to any dimensionality n. Mathematically there is no problem with spaces of dimension greater than 3. The only problem lies in the possibility of visualization and intuitive understanding: as the number of variables and thus dimensions grows beyond 3, graphical representation and intuitive comprehension of it become impossible. The two and three dimensional cases provide a very useful intuitive analogy for higher-dimensional ones, though.

More than one vector can exist in a vector space. Where $n = 2$, for example, a set of vectors in the two-dimensional space might look like Figure 7.

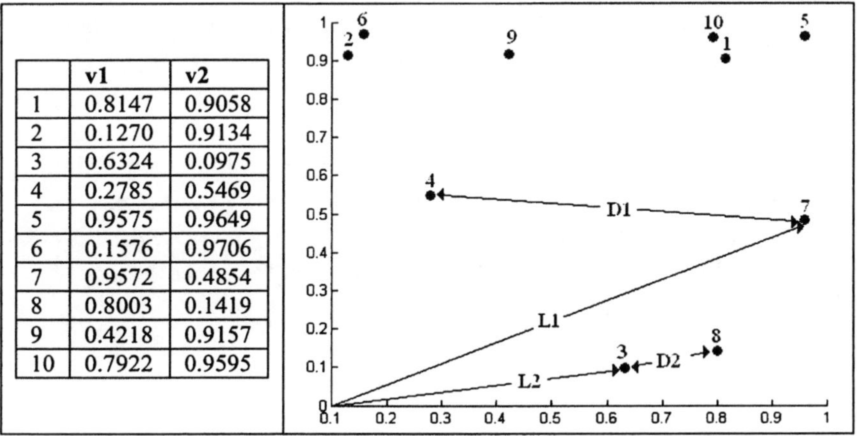
	v1	v2
1	0.8147	0.9058
2	0.1270	0.9134
3	0.6324	0.0975
4	0.2785	0.5469
5	0.9575	0.9649
6	0.1576	0.9706
7	0.9572	0.4854
8	0.8003	0.1419
9	0.4218	0.9157
10	0.7922	0.9595

Figure 7. Multiple vectors in two dimensional vector space.

Two concepts associated with vectors in a space are relevant here:

- The length of a vector is the length of a line drawn from the axis origin to the vector's coordinates in the space – for example L1 in Figure 7. Where two or more vectors exist in a space it is possible to compare their lengths: in Figure 7, L1 is greater than L2.
- Where two vectors exist in a space it is possible to measure the distance between them, and when there are more than two their relative distances can be compared; in Figure 7 D1, for example, is greater than D2.

Exploratory analytical methods use relativities of vector distance to identify clusters: vectors whose values are relatively similar have similar coordinates in space and are thus relatively close together in the space, whereas vectors whose values are relatively dissimilar are relatively far apart in space.

Figure 8 shows a two-dimensional data matrix, the corresponding vectors in two-dimensional space, and a hierarchical analysis showing the cluster structure.

Now observe what happens to the distribution of the row vectors in the space and the corresponding cluster tree when a proper subset of them is lengthened. A vector is lengthened by increasing the magnitude of the numbers that comprise it. The numerical values of all the vectors belonging to cluster B in Figure 8 were multiplied by 10; note that this is a random selection both of vectors and of multiplier, and the discussion to follow would have been the same with a different selection. The resulting matrix, together with the corresponding scatter plot and cluster tree, are shown in Figure 9.

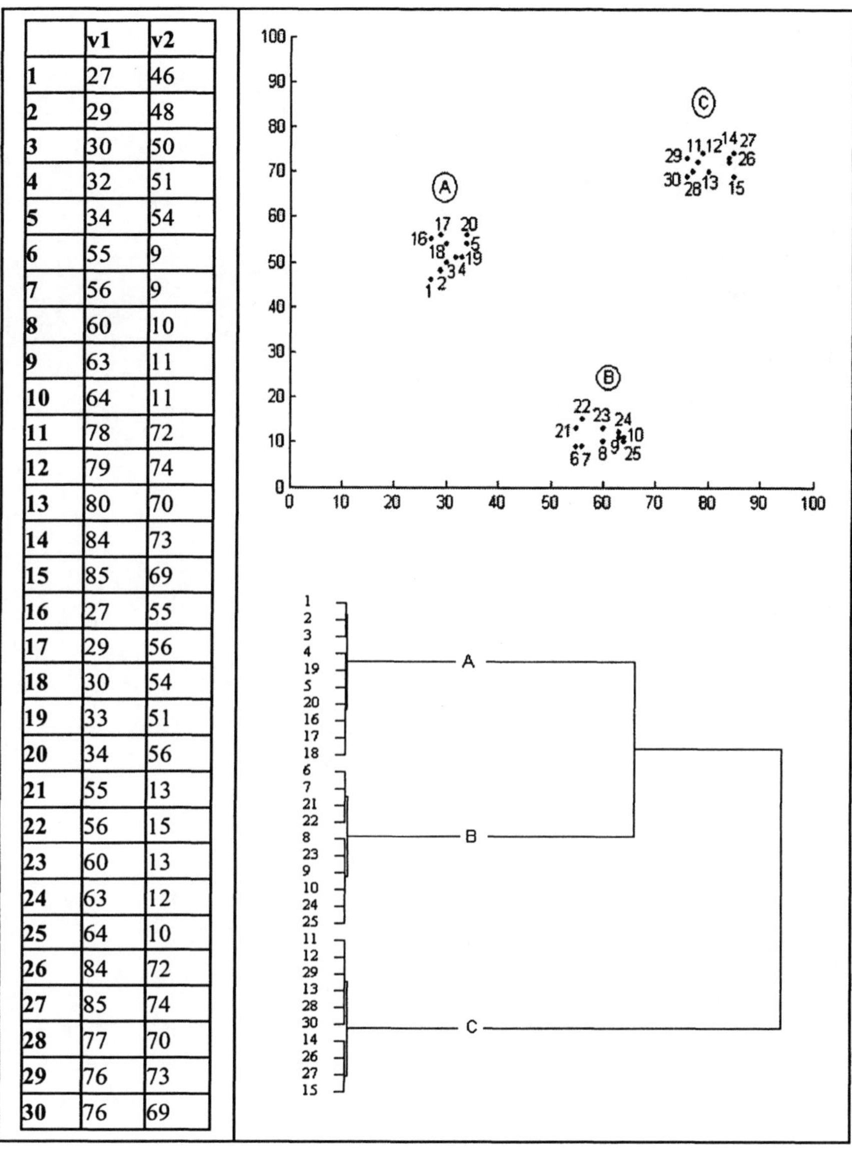

	v1	v2
1	27	46
2	29	48
3	30	50
4	32	51
5	34	54
6	55	9
7	56	9
8	60	10
9	63	11
10	64	11
11	78	72
12	79	74
13	80	70
14	84	73
15	85	69
16	27	55
17	29	56
18	30	54
19	33	51
20	34	56
21	55	13
22	56	15
23	60	13
24	63	12
25	64	10
26	84	72
27	85	74
28	77	70
29	76	73
30	76	69

Figure 8. Data matrix with scatter plot of row vectors in two-dimensional space and corresponding cluster tree showing distance relativities of row vectors in the space.

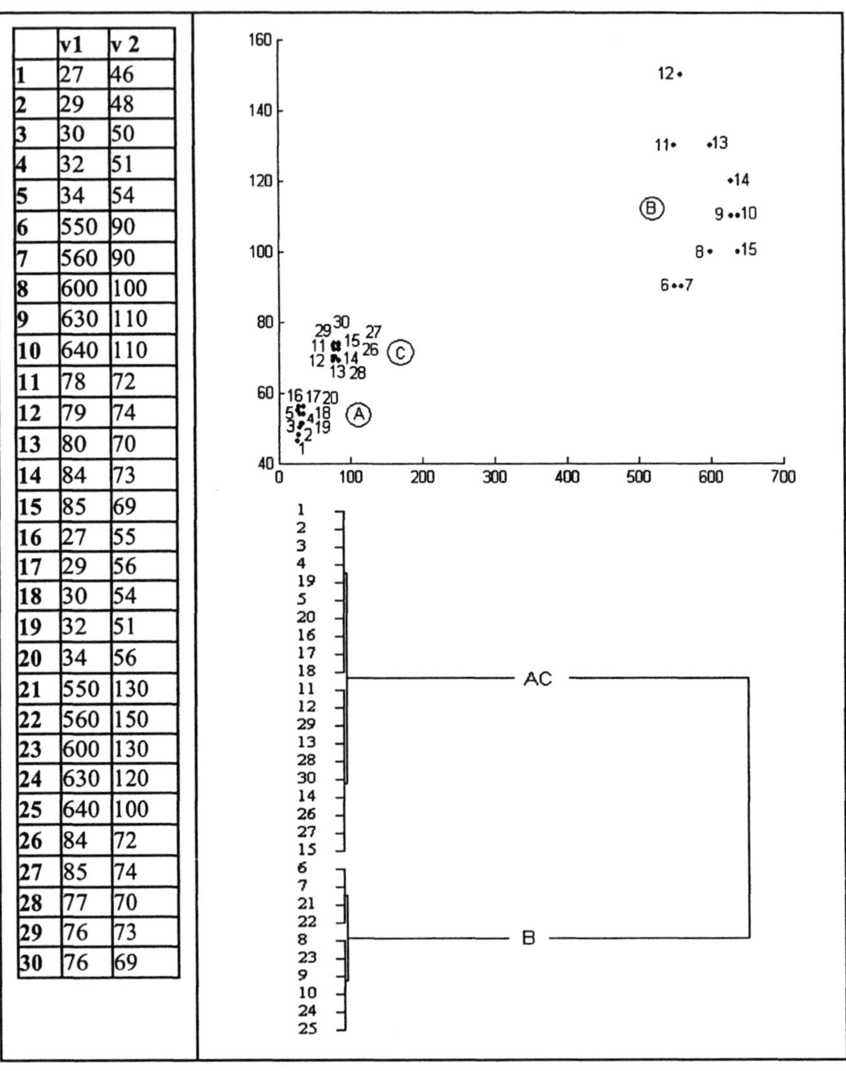

	v1	v2
1	27	46
2	29	48
3	30	50
4	32	51
5	34	54
6	550	90
7	560	90
8	600	100
9	630	110
10	640	110
11	78	72
12	79	74
13	80	70
14	84	73
15	85	69
16	27	55
17	29	56
18	30	54
19	32	51
20	34	56
21	550	130
22	560	150
23	600	130
24	630	120
25	640	100
26	84	72
27	85	74
28	77	70
29	76	73
30	76	69

Figure 9. Modified matrix from Fig. 8 with corresponding scatter plot and cluster tree.

Lengthening the row vectors of cluster B in Figure 8 has moved them far from A and C and brought A and C relatively much closer together. The consequence for clustering is shown in the corresponding tree, which now differs fundamentally from the one in Figure 8: A and C now form a composite cluster, and B is far from AC. In this case, therefore, it is clear that relative vector length is an important determinant of clustering, and, more specifically, that vectors of similar lengths cluster – long with long and short with short. The general case is not quite so simple, since the angles between and among vectors and not just their relative lengths also need to be taken into account (Fraleigh/Beauregard 1995), and it is more accurate to say that, in general, vectors of similar lengths *tend* to cluster.

How does all this apply to length-based clustering of varying-length document collections? When, as here, the data abstracted from a collection is a frequency matrix based on counting all occurrences of a set of features in each text, the sum of magnitudes of the frequencies in the vector representing a long document will be greater than the sum of magnitudes of frequencies in the vector representing a short one – or, in other words, vectors representing long documents are longer than vectors representing short documents in a way that is proportional to the difference in document lengths. This is shown in Figure 10, where row vector lengths in M are plotted against the lengths of the corresponding documents in C, and where vector length grows near-linearly with document length.

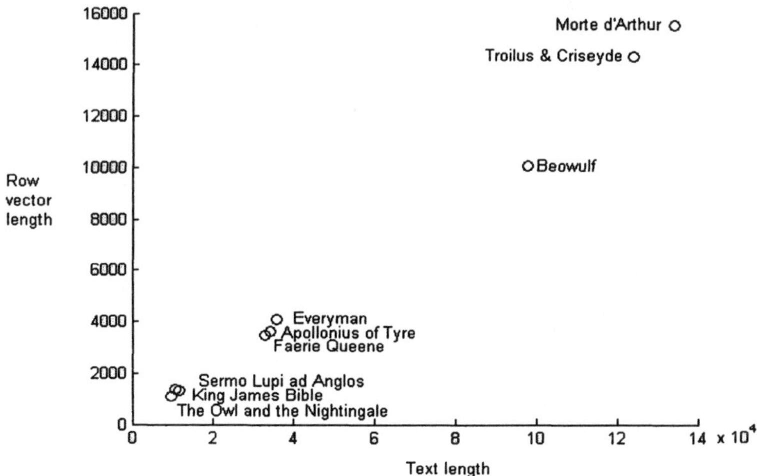

Figure 10. Plot of row vector lengths in M against the lengths of the corresponding documents in C.

Comparison of Figure 10 with the cluster tree in Figure 5, moreover, shows an isomorphism between the vector length relations in Figure 10 and the document clustering in Figure 5: the documents have been clustered by relative vector length.

4. Solutions

There is an obvious solution to the problem of variation in document length: truncate all the documents to the length of the shortest, thereby making them all equal in length. There are, however, two problems with this approach. On the one hand, where the variation is large and the shortest documents are very short, it entails throwing away a good deal of potentially useful information. And, on the other, there is no obvious basis for choosing what material to retain from the longer texts and what to discard. For these reasons, alternatives to truncation have been developed.

The literature contains a variety of ways of mitigating or eliminating the effect of variation in document length on data matrix row vector clustering (Buckley 1993; Singhal/Buckley/Mitra 1996; Singhal *et al.* 1996). We will consider the one that is probably the intuitively most accessible: normalization by mean document length. This normalization adjusts the lengths of each row vector of an m x n frequency matrix, here M, in relation to the mean length of documents in the collection:

$$M'_i = M_i \times \frac{\mu}{length(i)}$$

where:

- M'_i is the normalized i'th row vector of the matrix M, for i = 1..the number of rows m in M.
- M_i is the unnormalized i'th row vector of the matrix M
- μ is the mean number of letter pairs across the m documents
- *length(i)* is the number of letter pairs in any given document i

The value in each document vector M_i is multiplied by the ratio of the mean number of letter pairs across all the documents in the collection to the number of pairs in document i. The effect is to decrease the values in the vectors that represent long documents, increase them in vectors that represent short ones, and, for documents that are near or at the mean, to change the corresponding vectors little or not at all. Conceptually, therefore, this normalization constitutes a conjecture about what the row vectors in a data matrix would have been like if the corresponding documents had all been the same length.

Cluster analysis of the normalized matrix M' is shown in Figure 11:

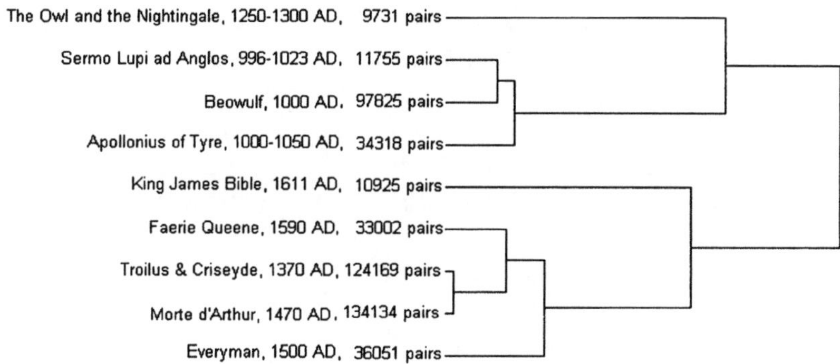

Figure 11. Cluster tree of the rows of length-normalized matrix M'.

The row vectors are now clustered by the chronological periods of the texts they represent, and make sense in terms of what is known of those texts in relation to the history of English. There are two main clusters. The upper one subclusters into a group of OE texts and the single EME text irrespective of length variation. The lower one contains the LME and the EModE texts. Here, the most recent of the Early Modern texts, *King James*, is on its own; the *Faerie Queene*, though chronologically near to *King James*, is known deliberately to have archaized its spelling, and is thus classified with the ME texts. Document length normalization has, therefore, solved the problem of clustering by document length in this instance. The NECTE data matrix discussed in Section 1 above was, moreover, normalized prior to cluster analysis, and the tree shown in Figure 2 is based on the normalized matrix.

5. Discussion

Document length normalization is not as straightforward as the foregoing discussion suggests, for two main reasons.

Firstly, the normalization procedure used in Section 3 solved the problem of variation in document length in the sense that, for the small example corpus C, it supported a cluster analysis that gave the expected answer, and, for NECTE, supported an analysis that is socio-linguistically plausible. But how does its performance compare to the other available normalization methods, both with respect to these and to more general applications? Selection of an appropriate method must be based on an evaluation of its relative effectiveness; the plan is to undertake such an evaluation as part of future research on document length normalization.

Secondly, frequency matrices based on collections of varying-length documents can have characteristics that compromise the effectiveness of existing normalization procedures. One of these is nonlinearity in the growth of variable frequency with increasing text length, and another is unreliable population probability estimation for variables in very short documents. An adequate account of the former would excessively prolong the discussion and is therefore not attempted here, but see Moisl (2007) for an indication of what is involved. A brief account of the latter follows.

Given a population E of n events, the frequency interpretation of probability (Milton/Arnold 2003: 1-17) says that the probability $p(e_i)$ of $e_i \ \varepsilon$ E (for i in 1..n) is the ratio (*frequency* (e_i) / n), that is, the proportion of the number of times e_i occurs relative to the total number of occurrences of events in E. For example, if a document contains 100,000 letters and the letter g occurs 320 times, then the probability $p(g) = 320/100000$. A sample of E can be used to estimate

$p(e_i)$, as is done with, for example, human populations in social surveys. The Law of Large Numbers (Grinstead/Snell 1997: 305-320) says that, as sample size increases, so does the likelihood that the sample estimate of an event's population probability is accurate; a small sample might give an accurate estimate but is less likely to do so than a larger one, and for this reason larger samples are preferred.

With specific reference to document corpora, it was pointed out earlier that, where the data abstracted from a multi-document corpus is a frequency matrix based on counting all occurrences of a set of features in each document, the sum of magnitudes of the frequencies in a vector representing a relatively longer document is greater than the sum for the vector representing a relatively shorter one. The longer the document, therefore, the more accurate its estimation of the population probabilities of the selected textual features can be expected to be. To exemplify this, a randomly selected document – Dickens' *Dombey & Son* – was partitioned into a corpus D of 100 increasing-length segments: the first segment contains the first 1000 words of the novel, the second segment the first 2000 words, and so on, adding the next 1000 words to segment i to create segment $i + 1$. A matrix Q of letter-pair frequencies was abstracted from D as in Section 2.1 above. For convenience of exposition, the matrix rows were arranged in ascending order of row vector length so that the one representing the shortest segment was at Q_1 and the longest at Q_{100}, and the columns so that the highest-frequency variable was represented by the leftmost column and the lowest frequency variable in the rightmost one. The probabilities for each of the letter-pair columns of Q were then calculated to find out the relationship between segment length and accuracy of population probability estimation for each pair across the entire 100-segment collection. The probability distributions for the three most frequent pairs *he*, *th*, and *in* are shown in Figure 12; the distributions for the remaining columns are similar.

The horizontal axis represents the 100 segments and the vertical axis the probability estimates for *he*, *th*, and *in*. In each distribution, the probabilities fluctuate for the shorter segments on the left and then settle down to a fairly constant value representing the increasingly-accurate estimate of the population probability as one moves to the longer segments on the right, which is what one expects from the Law of Large Numbers. The fluctuations on the left are caused by frequency values that are too large or too small relative to the length of the segment to estimate the population probability accurately. In other words, frequency values for variables in short texts can be and in the present instance are unreliable estimators of population probabilities.

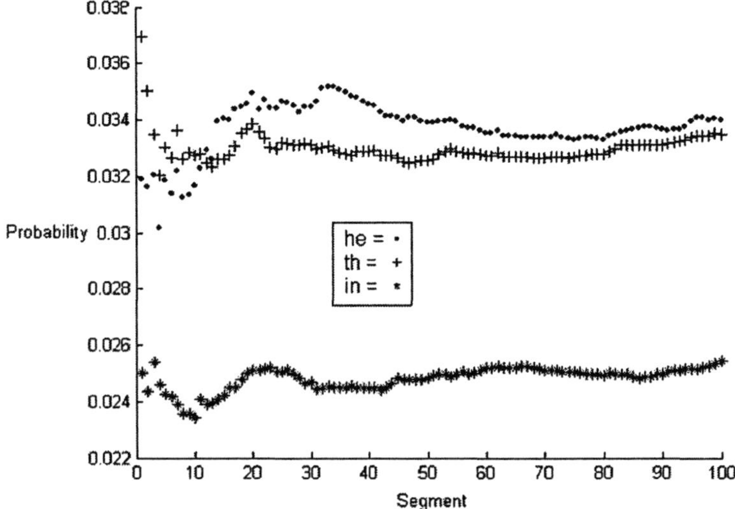

Figure 12. Probability estimates of the letter pairs he, th, and in, where the horizontal axis represents segments of increasing length and the vertical axis probability.

This unreliability can render document length normalization unreliable as well. To show how, Q was normalized using the same procedure as in Section 3, and the effect on the values in the *he* column is shown in Figure 13. Figure 13 shows a normalized frequency distribution curve isomorphic with the probability curve in Figure 12: for the shorter segments, the normalized values fluctuate between about 5100 and 5900 before settling down to a value around 5600. This degree of variation can be expected to affect assignment of the shorter segments to clusters in cluster analysis. The suspicion, moreover, is that Q is not unique in this respect, and that the effect just described will occur for matrices derived from other document collections – that, in short, this is a general problem in document length normalization. How widespread it is, and how important its effect can be on exploratory analysis, is a matter for further research. And, if it is both widespread and important, it is therefore also important to do something about it.

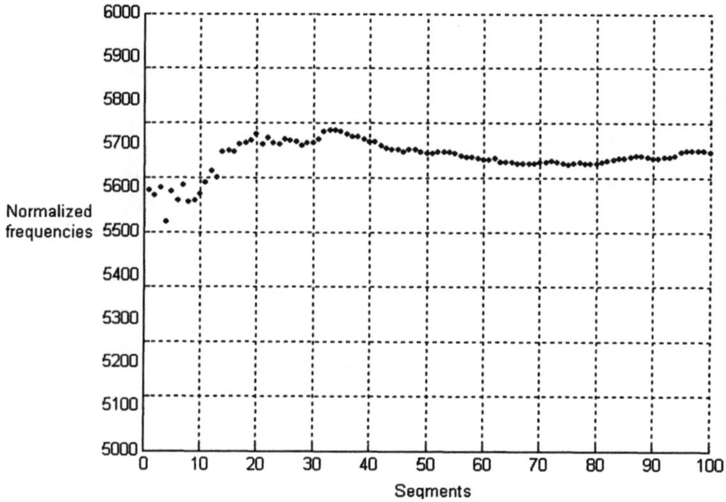

Figure 13. Normalized values for the letter pair he, where the x-axis represents texts of increasing length and the y-axis the normalized values.

6. Conclusion

To use exploratory multivariate methods effectively in the analysis of document collections, issues that arise with respect to the abstraction of data from such collections have to be understood. The foregoing discussion explained how one of these issues, variation in document length, can be a problem in historical dialectology research, proposed normalization of document length relative to the mean length of documents in a collection as a solution, and pointed out some difficulties associated with that solution. The conclusion is that failure to normalize for variation in document length can generate fundamentally erroneous cluster analytical results, but that normalization itself has some unresolved problems.

References

Allen, Will / Beal, Joan / Corrigan, Karen / Maguire, Warren / Moisl, Hermann 2006. A Linguistic 'Time Capsule': The Newcastle Electronic Corpus of Tyneside English. In Allen, Will / Beal, Joan / Corrigan, Karen / Maguire, Warren / Moisl, Hermann (eds) *Creating and Digitizing Language Corpora, Volume 2: Diachronic Databases*. Basingstoke: Palgrave Macmillan, 16-48.

Andrienko, Natalia / Andrienko, Gennady 2005. *Exploratory Analysis of Spatial and Temporal Data: A Systematic Approach*. Heidelberg: Springer.

Belew, Richard 2000. *Finding out about: A Cognitive Perspective in Search Engine Technology and the WWW*. Cambridge: Cambridge University Press.

Bishop, Christopher 2006. *Pattern Recognition and Machine Learning*. New York: Springer.

Buckley, Chris 1993. The Importance of Proper Weighting Methods. *ARPA Workshop on Human Language Technology*. Princeton, NJ: Morgan-Kaufmann, 349-352.

Everitt, Brian / Landau, Sabine / Leese, Morven [4]2001. *Cluster Analysis*. London: Arnold.

Fraleigh, John / Beauregard, Raymond [2]1995. *Linear Algebra*. Menlo Park, CA: Addison-Wesley.

Grinstead, Charles / Snell, J. Laurie [2]1997. *Introduction to Probability*. American Mathematical Society.

Grossman, David / Frieder, Ophir [2]2004. *Information Retrieval*. Dordrecht: Springer.

Hair, Joseph / Black, William / Babin, Barry / Anderson, Rolph / Tatham, Ronald [6]2005. *Multivariate Data Analysis*. New Jersey: Prentice-Hall.

Heeringa, Wilbert / Nerbonne, John 2001. Dialect Areas and Dialect Continua. *Language Variation and Change* 13, 375-400.

Milton, J. Susan / Arnold, Jesse [4]2003. *Introduction to Probability and Statistics*. Boston: McGraw-Hill.

Moisl, Hermann 2007. Data Nonlinearity in Exploratory Multivariate Analysis of Language Corpora. In Nerbonne, John / Ellison, Mark / Kondrak, Greg (eds) *Computing and Historical Phonology. Proceedings of the 9th Meeting of the ACL Special Interest Group in Computational Morphology and Phonology*. Association for Computational Linguistics, 93-100.

Moisl, Hermann / Jones, Val 2005. Cluster Analysis of the Newcastle Electronic Corpus of Tyneside English: A Comparison of Methods. *Literary and Linguistic Computing* 20, 125-46.

Moisl, Hermann / Maguire, Warren 2008. Identifying the Main Determinants of Phonetic Variation in the Newcastle Electronic Corpus of Tyneside English. *Journal of Quantitative Linguistics* 15, 46-69.

Moisl, Hermann / Maguire, Warren / Allen, Will 2006. Phonetic Variation in Tyneside: Exploratory Multivariate Analysis of the Newcastle Electronic Corpus of Tyneside English. In Hinskens, Franz (ed.) *Language Variation. European Perspectives*. Amsterdam: Benjamins, 127-141.

Nerbonne John / Heeringa, Wilbert 2001. Computational Comparison and Classification of Dialects. *Dialectologia et Geolinguistica* 9, 69-83.

Singhal, Amit / Buckley, Chris / Mitra, Mandar 1996. Pivoted Document Length Normalization. *Proceedings of the 19th ACM Conference on Research and Development in Information Retrieval (SIGIR-96)*, 21-29.

Singhal, Amit / Salton, Gerard / Mitra, Mandar / Buckley, Chris 1996. Document Length Normalization. *Information Processing and Management* 32, 619-633.

Tabachnik, Barbara / Fidell, Linda [5]2006. *Using Multivariate Statistics*. Boston: Allyn/Bacon.

Tan, Pang-Ning / Steinbach, Michael / Kumar, Vipin 2006. *Introduction to Data Mining*. Boston: Pearson Addison Wesley.

Roger Lass / Margaret Laing

Databases, Dictionaries and Dialectology. Dental Instability in Early Middle English: A Case Study[1]

1. Preliminaries

1.1. An Old English alternation

Consider a situation in which a particular etymological category is expected to be represented by the *littera* 'x', but also appears (variably) as the *littera* 'y'.[2] If both 'x' and 'y' appear in a given text language or group of text languages, how do we discriminate between two possible interpretations of the variation 'x'~'y'?

1

1   These observations arise from detailed analytical work on EME manuscript texts being undertaken at the Institute for Historical Dialectology, Linguistics and English Language, School of Philosophy, Psychology and Language Sciences, University of Edinburgh, towards the compilation of *A Linguistic Atlas of Early Middle English* (*LAEME*). This research project was supported from 2000–2006 by AHRC for which gratitude is here expressed. We are also grateful to the University of Cape Town for support.

2   In this study we use the terminology of the medieval doctrine of *littera*. For the discussion parts of the paper we adopt our usual conventions (established by Michael Benskin (1997: 1 n. 1 and   2001: 194 n. 4). *Littera* is the abstract notion of the letter, and when referred to independently of manuscript citation, *litterae* are enclosed in single inverted commas. *Figura* is the shape of a letter in a particular script or a particular realisation within that script; manuscript *figurae* are here enclosed in angle brackets or are italicised when combined as whole words or longer. *Potestates* are sound values and are represented by IPA symbols in phonetic brackets. Glosses and names of lexical categories are in small capitals. For illustrative manuscript forms cited from any of the *LAEME* corpora, we use the relevant 'internal format' for which see below.

(a)   There has been a variable sound change in which the *potestas* traditionally associated with 'x' has become that associated with 'y' or vice versa.
(b)   The variation is a case of litteral substitution without phonetic change.[3]

One simple interchange that has been commonly noted, is the appearance of 't' where historically one would expect 'þ' 'ð' or 'th'. This phenomenon appears early in the history of English. The occasional use of 't' for 'þ' or 'ð' in the 3rd person singular present indicative in Old English is observed by Campbell (1959: §735 (b)):

> The 3rd sg. has in some texts -*it*, -*et* beside -*iþ*, -*eþ*. While in *Ep.*, *Cp.* this might be regarded as graphic [...] the appearance of the form in later texts suggests a genuine phonetic variant.

Campbell (1959: §57 (7)) further notes:

> *t* rarely represents a spirant: instances are *earbet*- (Ep. 619, Cp. 1320), *hāēt*- (Cp. 570), *flītat* (Cp. 680), *Sūtangli* (Ct. 9), *Cuutfert* (Ct. 11), for *earfoþ*-, *hǣþ*-*flītaþ*, *Sūþ*-, *Cūþferþ*.

In other words, Campbell is suggesting that in these forms *t* represents [θ]. He gives no justification for why he identifies any particular form as a 'phonetic' or 'graphic' phenomenon, but his observations do raise an important issue. The use of 't' for 'þ' or 'ð' in Old English is found not just in weak syllables like the verbal inflections, but also in the strong syllables of lexical items. What is also apparent is that by the

---

3   Interpretation (b) invokes what we call a Litteral Substitution Set (LSS) (Laing 1999, Laing/Lass 2003) where a scribe has a number of orthographic choices for a particular segment. For a rich example, scribe D of Trinity College Cambridge 323 has the following variants for the reflex of OE -*ht*: {'ct', 'st', 't', 'ch', 'cht', 'dt', 'tht', 'tt', 'ʒt', 'd', 'tf'}. There is no reason to suppose that this set represents more than two sound values, one with a preceding fricative and one without (although a third in [θ] is also possible). The problem of differentiating between interpretations (a) and (b) above arises in the complex interchange of dental consonant graphs in early Middle English and this paper attempts to make the case for interpretation (a) being desirable in this instance.

time we get to early Middle English the 't'~'þ'/'ð' alternation takes its place within a set of possibly related patterns of variation. These involve *litterae* that typically have (on historical grounds) phonetically similar but not identical reference:

(a)   the use of 't' for expected 'þ', 'ð' or 'th';
(b)   the use of 'd' for expected 'þ', 'ð' or 'th';[4]
(c)   the use of 'þ', 'ð' or 'th' for 'd';
(d)   the use of 'þ', 'ð' or 'th' for 't'.

What is the status of this variation?

1.2. A Linguistic Atlas of Early Middle English corpus of tagged texts

We first noticed the existence of this series of variations while working with the corpus of tagged texts (CTT) created in the making of *A Linguistic Atlas of Early Middle English* (*LAEME*). For *LAEME* (and for *A Linguistic Atlas of Older Scots – LAOS*), we have developed a corpus-based approach to historical dialectology. Instead of using a questionnaire, we transcribe entire texts (or extensive samples of very long texts) in a format that can be lexico-grammatically 'tagged'. From each tagged text is derived a text dictionary, which is the equivalent of a linguistic profile in *LALME*, but whose content is not limited to questionnaire items. A text dictionary is a taxonomised inventory of the entire surviving output of a text witness (or of the entire sample transcribed), and the resulting assemblage is a proper subset of a given scribe's total usage. Sets of tags (equivalent to (non-preselected) *LALME* questionnaire items) and their associated scribal forms may be sorted, analysed and compared electronically (using software written for the purpose by Keith Williamson). This means that for the entire *LAEME* CTT we have access to all possible lexical and grammatical contexts for any linguistic phenomenon. So in practice, the *LAEME* CTT becomes both the source of observations,

---

4   Evidence for this appears later than that for (a); i.e. it seems to be a Middle English phenomenon not an Old English one.

such as the dental variations listed above, and also the facilitating tool for their investigation.

2. Etymologies as heuristics

2.1. The corpora[5]

As well as the CTT, there is now an added, purely historical utility: a Corpus of Etymologies (CE). This is currently under construction and aims to give the history of every spelling recorded in the *LAEME* CTT. *LAEME* etymologies are not like those of standard lexico-graphy, such as are provided in OED. By contrast, a *LAEME* etymology unpacks and makes explicit the *narrative* that brings a particular attested form into existence. Each etymology is a step-by-step history of the form it labels. Within the narrative histories of the CE, accounting for all the variant spellings recorded in the CTT has made it necessary to construct a further corpus – of changes (CC), which names, describes and comments on all the phonological and morphological changes occurring in the etymologies.

Spellings, and the underlying phonic substance inferable from them, may be compared within single lexical items, and also across sets of etymologically equivalent segments. The facility to compare the appearances of linguistic phenomena across the full range of EME lexis, and across a large number of texts, throws up some surprising sets of variants such as those listed in Section 1.1 above. The discovery of hitherto largely unnoticed sets of variants has made it necessary to construct 'new' changes that are often not listed as such in the handbooks.

---

5   The *LAEME* CTT has been compiled by Margaret Laing between ca. 1990
       and the present. The added utilities of the Corpus of Etymologies (CE) and the
       Corpus of Changes (CC) are the work of Roger Lass since he joined *LAEME*
       in 2002.

2.2. *Etymologising rare variants of* CHILD

The map of a *LAEME* etymology is:

\$tag[6]
morphological category
etymology proper in the form:
‖ *root ((change 1)) > new derived form ((change 2)) > new derived form etc.
Commentary if needed

The first stage in our observation of the phenomena under discussion here arose when the etymological narrative for the word CHILD was being undertaken. This involved a complete search of the *LAEME* 'tag dictionary' to identify all forms for CHILD and its derivatives.[7] Construction of the root etymology appeared to be straightforward. The final result was:

(a)   Etymology

\$child/n
SNt[8]
‖ *kilþ* - ((EDH)) > *kild* ((VP)) > [ʧild]. OE *cild*
Cf. Go *kilþei* WOMB, *inkilþō* PREGNANT WOMAN. This root does not appear to be attested outside of EGmc except in this word.

The initials in double parentheses are links to the *LAEME* Corpus of Changes.

(b)   Links to Corpus of Changes

The map of a CC entry is:

---

6   A prototypical tag consists of a lexical element ('lexel') and a grammatical element ('grammel'). \$ introduces the lexel, / introduces the grammel. Some tags may consist of a grammel only, but none of a lexel only. In this paper the grammel-only tags will be the verbal endings. The lexels are usually modern English equivalents or OE etyma and are mostly transparent. But for discussion of the ongoing key to the lexels see Section 5.1 below.

7   The *LAEME* 'tag dictionary' is a complete inventory of all forms in the *LAEME* corpus listed alphanumerically by their 'tags'. See further below.

8   SNt = Strong Neuter.

((abbreviated name of the change)); %flags indicating the status and variability of the change; full name of the change [time of the change]
Commentary.

The changes invoked in the etymology of CHILD are:

((EDH))% n, ?v:[9] Early Dental Hardening [WGmc]
After Voiced Fricative Hardening ((VFH)) turned the reflexes of IE *bh, *dh, *gh to their homorganic stops, *þ > [d] (presumably via [ð]) after *l, *n: Go *in-kilþ-ō* PREGNANT WOMAN, cf. OE *cild* CHILD, Go *falþan, finþan,* cf. OE *fealdan, findan* FOLD, FIND. This change is given as exceptionless in the handbooks, but may not have been in the ancestor of OE, judging from the occasional ME spellings of CHILD with final <y, d, TH>.[10] (For an alternative interpretation of these spellings see s.v. ((LDS)).[11]

((VP))% r:[12] Velar Palatalisation [OE]
In front vowel environments *k >[tʃ], *g > [j] except after nasals and in gemination where it becomes [dʒ:].

3. Further developments

3.1. More on CHILD

This explanation appeared to account for most of the *LAEME* forms for CHILD. But, aside from <CILD>, <CHILD>, spellings that require no further etymologising, some forms were recorded that prompted the invocation of further changes. For instance, <CHILT> appears to

---

9   The flags after the change title mean respectively 'named in *LAEME* for the first time (or in recent times outside of the standard handbooks)', and 'possibly variable'.

10   In this and following examples from the CE, citations from the *LAEME* CTT are in angle brackets and are in 'internal format', i.e. capital letters for plain text manuscript letters (manuscript capitals or *litterae notabiliores* are preceded by *); lower case for expansions of abbreviations and for 'special' letters as follows: ae = aesc, d = edh, g = insular 'g', w = wynn, y = thorn, z = yogh.

11   I.e. Late Dental Spirantisation. We will return to this sound change in Section 3.6 below.

12   r = 'regionally restricted'

have undergone a change, which we call Final Devoicing 2 ((FD2)).[13]
So some Middle English forms for CHILD may have longer and more
complex stories than their Old English etyma.[14] Examination of all the
forms of CHILD and its derivatives in *LAEME* CTT took us back to the
early history: four further forms stood out as having the 'wrong' final
consonant.

$child/n CHILd[15]
$childhood/n<pr CHILd+HOd
$childing/vn CHILTH+ING CHILd+INGE

Cf also:

$childing/vn CHILDy+INGE

If they are not 'merely orthographic', the first four spellings in -d- and
-TH- could be due either to sporadic failure of ((EDH)) (see above) or,
at least as likely, a later spirantisation. In order to come to a judgement about their status it is essential to look at the entire writing
system(s) of the text language(s) in which they occur. A directed
search for the textual origins of these forms in the CTT gave us the
following results:

arundel248t.dic[16]

---

13   ((FD1)) Final Devoicing 1 is an OE change which affects only the final
      voiced velar, e.g. *burg ~ burh*.
14   In the case of ((FD2)), this is a very frequently observed phenomenon, but
      does not form part of the set of changes we are mainly dealing with here
      except insofar that it may provide input to one of them, but see Section 5.1
      below.
15   Here the format is that of the *LAEME* 'tag dictionary'. For details see n. 6
      above.
16   The .dic labels are the filenames of the text dictionaries derived from the
      relevant tagged texts in the *LAEME* CTT. The tagged texts themselves have
      identical filenames but with a .tag suffix instead of a .dic suffix. For a full list
      of the *LAEME* CTT filenames and their associated manuscript designations
      see Appendix 1. Those listed in this section correspond to: London, BL
      Arundel 248, fols. 154r-155r: 4 lyrics; Cambridge, Gonville and Caius
      234/120, pp. 1-185: extracts from *Ancrene Riwle* – sample tagged pp. 1-59;
      London, British Library, Cotton Caligula A ix, fol. 246v: *Orison to Our Lady*;
      Oxford, Jesus College 29, part II, English on fols. 144r-195r; 198r-200v –

childing/vn<pr CHILTH+ING 1

caiusart.dic
child/n CHILd 1
$childhood/n<pr CHILd+HOd 1

cotorisont.dic
childing/vn<pr{rh} CHILd+INGE 1

jes29t.dic
childing/vn<pr{rh} CHILDy+INGE 1

3.2. arundel248t.dic

The spelling CHILTHING in arundel248t.dic needs to be assessed in
the light of the scribe's other spellings for CHILD and in the light of his
use of TH elsewhere. The relevant entries in arundel248t.dic give the
following sequence for CHILD and its derivatives:

$child/n CHILD 1
$child/n<pr CHILD 1
$child/n<pr{rh} CHILDE 1
$child/nG CHILDES 1
$child/nOd CHILD 2
$child/nOi CHILD 1
$childing/vn<pr CHILTHING 1
$childing/vn<pr{rh} CHILTINGE 1 CHILTInGE 1

Beside seven 'normal' spellings in -D- we find two in -T- as well as
our one -TH- form. The Arundel scribe uses TH in the following
further contexts:

---

sample tagged fols. 156r-168v, 169r-174v, 179v-180v, 182r-185v, 187r-188v.
Note that the example of the word CHILDING in Jesus 29 is from that
manuscript's version of *Orison to Our Lady* and corresponds to the same
word in Cotton A.ix: the shared texts in these manuscripts go back to a
common exemplar. The numbers following the citations in internal format
indicate text frequency: in the present example, one occurrence of each form.

1. Word initially (very occasionally beside much more common thorn-spellings) in e.g. THIN THINE; THROWE (< OE *þrāg* TIME);[17]
2. Medially in e.g. BLITHE BLITHE; BOTHEN BOTH; OTHER and OTHRE OTHER;
3. Syllable finally in e.g. DETH DEATH; FELTHE FILTH; SOTH, SUTH SOOTH and in 3rd sg. present indicative endings: +TH (contracted forms only beside uncontracted +ET only).

He also uses TH in contexts where we would not expect historical [θ], viz:

4. Commonly in words with *ht* in Old English, e.g. ARITH(E) ARIGHT; BRITH(E) BRIGHT; LITH(E) LIGHT; MITH(E) MIGHT;
5. Occasionally word finally where we would expect historical [t], e.g. *FETH beside FET FEET; LETH beside LET for LET past tense.

On the basis of this information, how do we determine what the status of the TH in CHILTHING is? The evidence on face value presents us with the following possibilities for the Arundel scribe's use of TH in his recorded output:

(a) TH can represent varyingly both [θ~ð] and [t] (as well as possibly [xt]).
(b) TH represents [t] only, alongside more common T-spellings.
(c) TH represents [θ~ð] only, and we are observing a varying set of sound-changes for segments that would normally be spelled with D or T (or fricative +T).

It can be seen from the above that manuscript spellings can never be analysed in isolation. They are parts of systems of scribal praxis where each usage may influence our interpretation of each other usage. Here, because the Arundel scribe has left us with only limited output, and because his sound to symbol mapping is in other ways

---

17 Word initially, the Arundel scribe also occasionally uses H-spellings for historical [θ].

idiosyncratic,[18] this is perhaps as far as we can go in our assessment of
CHILD in this particular text language. However, if we hypothesise
that interpretation (c) is at least a possibility, we would have to seek
further support for the sound changes implied by these spellings. In
the case of CHILTHING there are two possible trajectories for a
sound change:

(a)   devoicing (cf. CHILTING) followed by spirantisation;
(b)   direct spirantisation of [d] to [ð].

Are there similar kinds of variants in any other text languages
represented in the *LAEME* CTT?

3.3. jes29t.dic

The spelling CHILDyINGE seems to be a compromise between a stop
and a fricative spelling, unless it implies an affricate which would be a
reasonable step on the way to spirantisation. Again, this form needs to
be assessed beside the Jesus scribe's spellings for other dentals that
might be involved in change processes. The text dictionary derived
from the tagged sample for the Jesus scribe in the *LAEME* CTT shows
the following possible support for spirantisation of original [d]:

```
$forweorYan/vSpp-aj FURWRyE 2
$forweorYan/vSpp{rh} FOR-WURyE 2
$weorYan/vSpp{rh} IWORyE 1
```

These are past participles of the reflex of OE *weorþan*, which would
be expected to show [d] from Verner's Law. The thorn-spellings
would seem to indicate a fricative, which in turn suggests spirantisation of the original. However, in this verb, a likely alternative
interpretation of the thorn-spellings would be analogy to the present
system. Reducing the number of alternants in strong verbs is
extremely common throughout Middle English. Thorn-spellings in the

---

18   See further Laing (2008).

past participle and past plural of *weorþan* are very frequent across the whole *LAEME* corpus.

However, the Jesus scribe also shows a number of spellings that seem to suggest spirantisation not of [d] but of [t]. These can occur initially, medially or finally. Words in which these spellings occur are cited in bold below alongside any 'normally spelled' variants with which they co-occur:

$begitan/vsjps13{rh} **BI-GETHE** 1
$efete/npl **EUETHEN** 1
$outsi:Y/npl<pr{rh} **HOUy-SYyE** 1
$sot/aj SOT 1 **SOTH** 1
$sot/n *SOT 1
$teach/vi TECHE 3
$teach/vi-m TECHE 1
$teach/vi{rh} TECHE 1
$teach/vps11 **THECHE** 3 TECHE 2
$teach/vps12 TECHEST 1
$teach/vpt13 TAUHTE 1
$teach/vpt13{rh} TAHTE 1
$teach/vsjps12 TECH 1
$tear/npl<pr TERES 1 **THERES** 1
$tear/nplOd *TERES 1
$tooth/npl TEy 1
$tooth/npl<pr{rh} **THEy** 1

There are also sporadic spellings that may indicate the opposite change to spirantisation, i.e. occlusivisation of fricatives either voiced or voiceless. See the emboldened variants below, again cited alongside co-occurring 'normal' spellings:

$breath/nOd{rh} BREy 1
$breath/n{rh} **BRED** 1 BREy 1
$lothly/aj **LODLICH** 4 **LODLICHE** 1
$lothly/ajOd **LODLICH** 1
$si:Y/n-av SYyE 1
$si:Y/n-av{rh} **SID** 1 SIyE 1 SYyE 1
$si:Y/n<pr SYyE 1
$si:Y/n<pr{rh} SIyE 1
$si:Y/npl<pr-k{rh} -SYyE 1
$with{a}/pr WIy 27 WYy 1 **wIT** 1
$with{f}/pr WIy 3
$with{t}/pr *WYy 1

$with{w}/pr WIy 18 WYy 3 *WYy 1

If we have apparent evidence for two sound changes going in opposite directions we have to consider two possibilities:

(a)   that the two historical categories have merged and that either spelling will serve to represent the output;
(b)   we may have an instance of two changes competing for the same environment (cf. Wang 1969).

3.4. *cotorisont.dic*

The Cotton scribe of *An Orison to Our Lady* is the same as copied *The Owl and the Nightingale* in the same manuscript. He is a well known literatim copyist whose language reflects whatever variability he found in his exemplars. There is no further relevant evidence in the short text of *An Orison to Our Lady*, but in his other texts, which are all in types of language belonging not far from each other in the South West Midlands, we have examples of three of the four possible changes evidenced in jes29t.dic. The Cotton scribe has both +ED and +ET spellings for the 3rd sg pres indicative endings beside more common +Ey spellings. These occlusivations are also evidenced sporadically in lexical words. He also shows +wORyE spellings for the reflexes of the past participle of OE *weorþan*.

But it is when we come to caiusart.dic that we see the full possible extent of these alternations in large enough numbers to make it difficult to deny them phonetic status or to suppose them due merely to 'scribal error' or to the workings of analogy.

3.5. *caiusart.dic*[19]

Below we present all the examples of unexpected spellings (emboldened) of dental reflexes, alongside any alternants, in the text dictionary derived from caiusart.tag. For the purposes of this paper, we omit ordinal numbers and Scandinavian loan words, because of uncertainties of etymological developments. Adding such material would certainly increase possible examples. Grammel-only tags in the material below are as follows: $/v-imp22 = imperative plural; $/vpp = weak past participle; $/vps13 = present indicative 3rd sg.; vps21, 22 and 23 = present indicative first, second and third plural.

$-hood/xs-n<pr +HAD 3 **+HOd 1** -HADE 1
$/v-imp22 **+ET 6 +D 5 +ED 5** +Ed 5 +IEd 1 +d 1
$/vpp +ED 80 +D 11 +ET 4 **+Ed 3** +EDE 3 +DE 1 +ID 1 **+d 1 +de 1**
$/vps13 **+ED 142** +d 48 **+D 31 +ET 27** +Ed 21 **+T 4 +ID 2 +IED 2 +IT 1** +de 1
$/vps21 **+ED 6 +D 3 +ET 3** +Ed 3 +ETH 1 **+IED 1**
$/vps22-apn **+ED 4 +ET 2** +Ed 1 **+IED 1**
$/vps23 **+ED 18 +ET 8** +Ed 4 **+D 3 +IED 3** +IEGH 1 +IEd 1 +ETH 1 +TH 1 +d 1
$be/vps21 **BEOD 2 BEOT 1** BEOd 1 BOTH 1
$be/vps23 **BEOD 20** BEOd 9 **BEOT 2 +BED 1 BED 1**
$child/n CHILD 4 **CHILd 1**
$child/npl CHILDREN 4
$childhood/n<pr CHILDHAD 2 CHILD-HADE 1 **CHILdHOd 1**
$cweYan/vSpt13 CwEd 2 **CwED 1**
$cweYan/vps13 Qd 2 **QD 1**
$dead/aj DEAD 2 DEADE 2 DED 1 **DEd 1**

---

19   The Gonville and Caius text of *Ancrene Riwle* was written by a scribe using an idiosyncratic form of script with cursive features, influenced by contemporary document hands. He was apparently working at high speed. Neil Ker (in Wilson 1954: xii-xiii) says that the scribe was "trained abroad", an opinion taken up by Dobson (1976: 295); and also Millett (2005: xvi). This explanation is supposed to account for the scribe's 'corrupt orthography'. Such an opinion is however no longer tenable. Ker's judgement was based on the putative 'Continental' formation of the scribe's <r>, (and less often <s> and <f>) with an extra 'tail' being added to the stem to take it below the baseline. *Figurae* formed like this do, however, appear in other English book hands of the early thirteenth century (Malcolm Parkes, p.c. 2002). They are also found in document hands of the late twelfth and early thirteenth century; for some examples (beside others that may have been made with a single backward curving stroke) see Johnson/Jenkinson (1915: vol. 2, pls. VIIc and d, VIII, IXa and X).

$earth/n EORdE 5 EORyE 3 **EORDE 1** ORyE 1
$end/n ENDE 4 **ENdE 1**
$forth-/xp-n **FORD- 2** FORd- 1
$forth/av **FORD 9** FORd 5 **wORD 1** wORd 1
$forweorYan/vSpp-pl **FORwURyEN 1**
$gold/n **GOLd 1**
$good/aj/n GOD 27 GODE 7 **GOd 2**
$lae:YYu/nOd **LEADyE 1**
$lord/n LAUERD 19 **LAUERd 2** LEAUERD 2 LOUERD(+) 2
$lothless/ajOd **+LADLES 1**
$ly:Yerli:ce/av LUyERLICHE 1
$ly:Yre/aj<pr **LUDER 1**
$mae:Ylessli:ce/av **MEDLESLICHE 1**
$mouth/n MUd 2 **MUD 1** MUTH 1
$murder/n<pr **MURDRE 1** MURyRE 1
$murder/vpt12K2 **MURDREDEST 1**
$other/aj OyER 11 OdRE 2 **ODER 1** OyERE 1
$scendful/ajpl<pr SCHENDFULE 2 SHENT-FULE 1
$scendfulleikr/nOd SCHENDFULLEC 1
$scendfulli:ce/av **SCHENdFULLICHE 1**
$sooth/aj SOd 3 **SOD 2**
$stalwartly/av **STEALEwARDLICHE 1**
$swi:De/av SwIyE 4 SwIdE 3
$swi:De/av-cpv **SwIDERE 1**
$unlothness/n **VNLADNESSE 1**
$weorYan/vi **IwURDEN 1** IwURyEN 1 wURyEN 1
$whether/cj **HwEDER 1**
$with-/xp-v **wID- 2**
$withal/av MID-ALLE 3 **wID-ALLE 1**
$within/av INwId 4 **INwID 2** IN-wId 1 **wID-INNEN 1**
$without/pr **wID-UTEN 8** UTEwID 2 UTEwId 2 **wIDUTEN 2** wIdUTEN 1
$with/pr **wID 51** wId 9 **VID 2** wIND 1 wIT 1
$world/n wORLD 9 **wORLd 1**
$worth/aj **wURD 2** wURd 1 wURyE 1
$wrath/n **wREDyE 2 WARTyE 1**
$yet/av GET 6 *GET 1 GETEN 1 **GETH 1** IGEcTEN 1 yET 1

The data listed above reveal extensive interchange among the dental obstruent graphs, which may well indicate phonetic change. One explanation is that historical [d] and [ð] have merged and historical [t] and [θ] have merged, and the traditional *litterae* are interchangeably adopted for the outputs. We cannot tell in this case whether the outputs are stops or fricatives. But the 'competing changes' explanation would support a face-value reading for:

(a)   spirantisation of [d] in e.g. DEAD, GOLD, GOOD, LORD and in the reflex of the past participle of OE *weorþan* as well as in the weak past participle endings;

(b)   spirantisation of [t] is confined to one example of YET spelled GETH;

(c)   very extensive occlusivisation of the voiced dental fricative in e.g. EARTH, LOTHLESS, MOUTH, MURDER, UNLOTHNESS, WHETHER, WITH as well as the (presumably previously voiced) present indicative verbal endings in +(E)D;

(d)   extensive occlusivisation of the voiceless fricative in the present tense verbal endings in +(E)T and in the wIT-spelling of WITH.

The assumption in (c) above is that voiced [ð] has hardened to [d] and in (d) above that voiceless [θ] has hardened to [t]. But what are we to make of apparent (rather unlikely) voicing in final position e.g. in the +(E)D spellings in the present tense verbal endings and spellings like MUD for MOUTH and wID for WITH? The 'received wisdom' response might be to suggest scribal carelessness in failing to cross the 'underlying' or 'intended' <ð>.[20] But the sheer numbers of these spellings (20 in BEOD for ARE, 51 in wID for WITH etc) makes this explanation scarcely credible. This same phenomenon is observable in

---

20   We are grateful to Michael Benskin for reminding us that Anglo-Latin or Anglo-French orthographic traditions should also be considered as possible inputs for or influences on early Middle English spelling systems. *The Ancrene Riwle* contains Latin quotations interspersed in the English text. The Caius scribe's renditions of these Latin passages show no idiosyncratic use of dental graphs. There is no French surviving in his hand for comparison. However, early Old French does use 'd' for [ð~θ]. By the time of the Norman Conquest, the dental fricative had been deleted in intervocalic position and in post-vocalic final position in all French dialects other than those of the West (Britton 1992: 283; Pope 1934: §§346-347). [ð~θ] survives in Old West French, and thence in Anglo-French, into the thirteenth century (see spellings in 'd' and 't' in AND s.v. *bonté, charité, deinté, dru, fei, nativité*; and there are likely to be many more examples, given the extent to which AND is based on normalised texts). Sporadic spellings of dentals in 'dh' and 'th' are also found in Anglo-French texts (we owe this observation to Philip Bennett). It would be of great interest to examine the dental graph systems in the works of thirteenth-century scribes for whom output in both Anglo-French and Middle English survives, e.g. those of Oxford, Bodleian Library, Digby 86 and London, British Library, Cotton Caligula A.ix, part II.

numerous other text languages in the *LAEME* CTT. A voicing in syllable-final position might seem unusual, but in the face of such widespread evidence must be seriously considered. We might then postulate an extension of the environment of (c) above so that [θ] > [d] presumably via [ð]. We now lay out below the entries in the CC that relate to our four postulated changes.

3.6. The changes[21]

(a)   ((LDS)) %n, v: Late D Spirantisation [ME]
[d] > [ð, θ]. This manifests as unexpected <d, y, TH> spellings for historical [d]. Examples: <dON> for DO, <yRUNC> for DRINK, <wORyE> for past participle from OE *weorþan*, <GOd> for GOOD, <+TH> for weak past participle. The forms <CHILd, CHILTH+> may be the result either of this change or failure of ((EDH));[22] it is impossible to tell. Note that there are survivals of a later Middle English version of this change: *mother, father, weather, gather, together.*

(b)   ((LTS)) %n, v: Late T Spirantisation [ME]
[t] > [θ]. Examples <yATH> for THAT <THECH> for TEACH, <YEFyE> for GIFT.

(c)   ((LDH)) %n, v: Later Dental Hardening [ME]
[ð] > [d] and [θ] > [ð] > [d]. This manifests in writings of <D> for expected <d, y, TH>. A particularly rich source is caiusart.tag, which has among others, variable <+ED> for 3rd sg pres indicative, <DED> for DEATH, <FORD> for FORTH, <MUD> for MOUTH.

(d)   ((TH))%n, v: Theta Hardening [OE, ME]
[θ] > [t]. This occurs as early as the 8thc. OE glosses (Corpus, Epinal), and sporadically later. In ME it is commonest in verb endings that would normally end in <y, d> e.g. imperative pl, pres indicative 3 sg and pl as <+ET, +IT>. It does however occur very frequently also in other forms, e.g. chertseyt.tag <+TEOF> for -THIEF, bestiaryt.tag <wIT> for WITH, <BOYT> for BOTH.

---

21   For a 'map' of a Corpus of Changes entry and a key to the conventions used here see Section 2.2 (b) and n. 9 above.

22   Early Dental Hardening, see Section 2.2 (b) above.

3.7. Significance

Of the 167 different text languages so far sampled in the *LAEME* CTT, 23 show evidence of all four changes, 30 show evidence of three out of the four, 40 show evidence of two out of four, 50 show evidence of one of the four. Only 24 texts show no evidence of our changes. Of these 24 texts, only two are longer than 500 words, and for some very short texts there may simply have been no suitable contexts for the changes to surface.[23] Given the widespread evidence for spellings across the CTT, covering a broad geographical range, we consider that the phenomena they represent should be added to the inventory of genuine English sound changes.[24]

The process we have followed shows how there has to be a balanced approach to the assessment of idiosyncratic manuscript spellings. As we pointed out in Section 2.4 above, looking at individual scribal systems is vital for detailed interpretation of sound to symbol mappings, but it can lead to a certain myopia. In the text dictionary for bod34t.tag (the sample in the *LAEME* CTT taken from Oxford, Bodleian Library, Bodley 34 – the 'B' element of the famous AB language) we find evidence for three of our changes. Theta Hardening occurs occasionally in e.g. +ET endings for 3rd sg pres indicative, and in WIT-UTEN for WITHOUT. Late dental hardening

---

23   For a listing of the tagged texts grouped according to the evidence they display of the changes, see Appendix 2.

24   Spirantisation and 'despirantisation' in the dental series have been sporadically recognised in the standard handbooks. For a recent treatment see Wełna (2004). Wełna also cites such handbook references as there are (2004: 252). For EME citations Wełna's data is not wholly accurate: in Table 4 *burdene* cited from *Gen. & Ex.* 1467 should read *birdene*, while *burdene* cited from *Lamb. Hom.* 5 should in fact read *burðene*. The latter does not therefore belong in the table and it should also be removed from Table 7. In Table 7 Wełna has *Owl and Night.* listed as a South-Western text (confusingly with the label *Sur.*, a south-eastern county). The dialect of the 'original' is disputed; both surviving manuscripts, however, belong in the South-West Midlands. Wełna cites two examples of *d*-spellings for the word 'earth' from *Owl and Night.* (he does not say which manuscript); these spellings (in both manuscripts) are in fact for the word *eard* DWELLING and do not belong in the table. Similarly the citations of EARTH from *Lambeth Hom.* and *Layamon A* and those in Table 8 for *Trin. Coll. Hom.* and *Genesis & Ex* should be removed as they all also belong to *eard.*

occurs more frequently in e.g. +ED endings for 3rd sg pres indicative, and in CLADES for CLOTHES, EORDLICH for EARTHLY, LADLI for LOTHLY and ODER for OTHER. Late D Spirantisation occurs in e.g. GOd for GOOD, HIRd for OE *hīred* HOUSEHOLD, LEAd+Ed plural pres indicative of LEAD, and LAUerd for LORD. We have recorded no examples in this text sample of Late T Spirantisation.

In the phonology section of her edition of *Þe Liflade ant te Passiun of Seinte Iuliene*, d'Ardenne (1961: 197, §36) makes a detailed assessment of spelling peculiarities in the Bodley text and her judgement is that:

> [...] the letters *ð* and *d* are frequently confused by misplacing or omission of the bar: phonetic change from *ð* and *d* is thus usually doubtful. It certainly has occurred before *l* (so already in OE.) in *ladlich* loathly [...] in which *d* is usual in AB.

This statement shows that assessment of individual text languages in isolation can lead to a tendency to 'explain away' observed spelling phenomena. It is true that the two *litterae* 'ð' and 'd' differ in their formation only in the presence or absence of a bar on the ascender, and the possibility of scribal error in the use of these *figurae* must always be considered. But in the ca. 13,000-word sample from Bodley 34 in the *LAEME* CTT we find 19 examples of 'ð' for 'd' and 27 examples of 'd' for 'ð': this looks like something more significant than 'confusion'. When we set this evidence beside the observations of similar phenomena across the whole extent of EME usage, especially in the light of spellings in 'þ' as well as 'ð' (e.g. ALyER+ for the prefix ALDER- in five tagged texts and ELyERNE-MAN in creditonbt.tag for ALDERMAN), it seems to us that the scribe of Bodley 34 is showing normal and unconfused scribal behaviour, merely registering minor and as yet undiffused sound changes.[25]

---

25   In our ca. 15,000-word sample from Cambridge, Corpus Christi College 402, *Ancrene Wisse* (the A element of AB language) we find sporadic evidence of all four of our changes. Late T Spirantisation is represented by the single occurrence of IFEdERET for the past participle of the verb FETTER. There are far fewer examples of the other three changes than appear in bod34t.tag.

4. Some difficult evidence

4.1. Problematic spellings

Beside the recorded spellings in D/T for historical [ð, θ] and the y/d/TH-spellings for historical [d, t], there are sporadic other forms which may be evidentially interesting. Given the necessity for looking at spelling phenomena both in the context of individual scribal systems and across the whole CTT, we first present the equivocal spellings as they appear in the individual text dictionaries. To save space, this time we cite only the forms in question, not any co-occurring forms. The relevant segments are in bold.

4.1.1. Listing by tagged text

add25031t.dic
$witness/nOd **WITHTENESSE** 1

adde6at.dic
$sooth/av **SODT** 1

adde6bt.dic[26]
$/vps13 **ETz** 3 +**EzT** 1 +**ITz** 2 +**Tz** 1 +**YTz** 1 +**z** 2 +**zT** 2
$/vps23 +**ITz** 2 +**ETz** 1
$hence/av **HEzE** 1
$without/pr **WITz**-OUTE 1 **WITz**-OUTIN 1
$with/pr **WITz** 1

bodley26t.dic
$truth/n **TROUHT** 1

caiusart.dic
$lae:YYu/nOd **LEADyE** 1

---

26   In the verbal endings and other citations in this text and in some others, the lower case z stands for a *figura* that is identical with the scribe's yogh used in [j] and in [x] contexts. Here, where it seems to stand for [θ~ð], it is possible that the *figura* goes back not to yogh but to the syllabic abbreviation (from Latin and French usage) for *-et* which was transferred in early Middle English via verbal endings to stand also for *-eþ/-eð/-eth*, i.e. for [eθ], and thence also for [θ] alone, not just in verbal endings, whence also for [ð] in medial position.

     Roger Lass / Margaret Laing

$wrath/n wREDyE 2 WARTyE 1

clericot.dic
$dead/aj{rh} DEDH 1

corp145selt.dic
$white/aj WIzT 2

cotcleoBvit.dic
$without/pr WITy-HUTIN 1

cotvespcmat.dic
$selcu:Y/av SELCUHT 1

dulwicht.dic
$mouth/n MUHT 2
$what/pn WAHT 1

edincmat.dic
$la:Yian/vps23 LEHTES 1
$wit/npl WIHTIS 1

edincmbt.dic
$without/pr *WIHT-OUTEN 1
$with{w}/pr WIHT 3

egpm2t.dic
$ni:Yful/ajplOd NIHTFULLE 1
$with{a}/pr wIHT 1

emmanuel27t.dic
$mouth/n<pr MUTy

genexodt.dic
$loth/aj{rh} LOdT 1
$scri:Dan/vSpt13{rh}SCROdT 1

jes29t.dic
$childing/vn<pr{rh} CHILDyINGE 1

lamhomA1t.dic
$strengthen/vps13 STRENGdDEd 1
$wrath/n wREDdA 1 wREDdE 1

lampmt.dic
$sot/n *SOHT 1

laud108at.dic
$forth/av FORHT 2
$sooth/aj{rh} SOTy 1
$soothness/n<pr SOTyENESSE 1
$with{w}/pr WIHT 1

laud471dwct.dic
$/vps13 +EyT 1

laud471kst.dic
$/vps13K2 +EDH 1
$be/vps23 BIEDH 1
$mouth/n MUDH 1

layamonAat.dic
$li:Yan/vpt13 LIDdE 1
$li:Yan/vpt23 LIDdEN 2
$writ/n WRIH 1

layamonAbt.dic
$aeYele/ajOd aeDdELE 1
$forth/av FORH 5 FEORH 1 FOR 1 FORHD 1
$send/v-imp22 SENDdE 1
$with-/xp-v WIH- 1
$within/pr WIH-INNEN 1
$withthat/cj WIH-yON-yE 1
$with/pr WIH 7 WIHT 1

nerowgt.dic
$wrath/n<pr yREDdE 1

ramseyat.dic
$cy:Yan/vps11 KYDHEN 2

ramseycott.dic
$cy:Yan/vps11 KIDHEN 1

tencmFft.dic
$oath/nOd ADH 1

titusart.dic
$wrath/n wRADdE 4

tr323dt.dic
$/vps13K2 +IDy 1

trincleoDt.dic
$death/nG DETyIS 1

vitelld3t.dic
$/vps13[V] +yT 1

vvat.dic
$cy:Yan/vps13-ct KYDH 1

wellsat.dic
$forth/av FURHT 1

winchestert.dic
$cu:Yrae:den/n gE-CUyDREdENE 1

worcthcreedt.dic
$eft/av EFTd 1

worcthfragst.dic
$geddian/vpt13K2 gEOdD^EDE 1

It is very difficult to know how to comment on this array of unhistoric
spellings. If we take as our starting point the historic origins [t], [d],
[θ] and [ð], we can arrange the various spellings under those headings.

4.1.2. Listing by historical segment

Historic [t]
H $writ WRIH
HT $sot/n *SOHT $what/pn WAHT $wit/npl WIHTIS
THT $witness/nOd WITHTENESSE
Td $eft/av EFTd
zT $white/aj WIzT

Historic [d]
DH $dead/aj{rh} DEDH
Dd $send/v-imp22 SENDdE
Dy $childing/vn<pr{rh} CHILDyINGE

Historic [dd]
dD $geddian/vpt13K2 gEOdD^EDE

Historic [θ]
0       $forth/av FOR

DH   present indicative endings and $cy:Yan/vps13-ct **KYDH** $mouth/n **MUDH**
      $oath/nOd **ADH**
DT $sooth/av **SODT**
Dy   pres indicative endings
H $forth/av **FORH FEORH** $with/pr **WIH(-)**
HD $forth/av **FORHD**
HT $forth/av **FORHT FURHT** $mouth/n **MUHT** $ni:Yful/aj **NIHT-** $selcu:Y/av
      SELCUHT $truth/n **TROUHT** $with/pr **WIHT** w**IHT**
Ty $mouth/n<pr **MUTy** $sooth/aj{rh} **SOTy(-)** $with/pr **WITy-**
Tz   pres indicative endings and $with/pr **WITz(-)**
dT $loth/aj{rh} **LOdT** $scri:Dan/vSpt13{rh}**SCROdT**
yD $cu:Yrae:den/n gE-**CUyDREdENE**
yT   pres indicative ending
zT   pres indicative endings

Historic [θθ]
Dd $wrath/n y**REDdE** w**RADdE** w**REDdA** w**REDdE**
Dy $lae:YYu/nOd **LEADyE** $wrath/n w**REDyE**
Ty $wrath/n **WARTyE**

Historic [ð]
DH $cy:Yan/vps11 **KIDHEN KYDHEN**
Dd $aeYele/ajOd ae**DdELE** $li:Yan/vpt13 **LIDdE** $li:Yan/vpt23 **LIDdEN**
HT $la:Yian/vps23 **LEHTES**
Ty $death/nG **DETyIS**
dD $strengthen/vps13 **STRENGdDEd**
z $hence/av **HEzE**

4.2. Significance

4.2.1. Phonographic profiling:
Litteral and Potestatic Substitution Sets

It is unlikely that this large number of problematic spellings have the
same sound to symbol mappings across all the text languages in which
they occur. Before one can make claims about whether orthography
represents sound change in progress (and if so what change) or
whether it represents 'merely' litteral substitution, it is necessary for
any one text language to produce what we call a 'phonographic
profile' (Lass/Laing 2005: 289; Laing 2008: 22-28). This can be done
for the entire text language, or for a subset of chosen etymological
categories/graphs under consideration. A phonographic profile

presents in list, tabular or graphic form the mappings between orthographic and phonological segments in a text language. It thus invokes both Litteral Substitution Sets and the phonic equivalents of LSSs, Potestatic Subsitution Sets (PSSs) (Laing/Lass 2003).

We exemplify with a phonographic profile in graph form of the spellings for our historic [t], [d], [θ] and [ð] appearing in a single text language – that of dulwicht.tag. Once the historic segments have been linked to the *figurae* that realise them, any other historic segments realised by those same *figurae* are then added to the profile, giving us the full set for these sounds and *figura* mappings:[27]

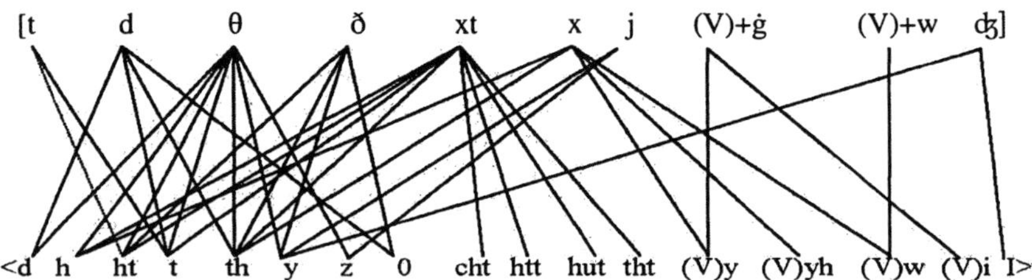

Figure 1. Phonographic profile of dental consonant mappings in dulwicht.tag (London, Dulwich College MS XXII, fols. 81v-85v: *La Estorie del Euangelie* Lincs).

To progress further in our assessment of the problematic spellings, these mappings of etymological categories to orthographic segments would then have to be analysed. Any possible conclusions about sound-symbol equivalences could be drawn only in the light also of other text languages' profiles. Some cases will always remain equivocal.

4.2.2. *Further caveat*

In Figure 1 above the line joining [t] with 'ht' is dotted as a caveat. The single form in the text language that it represents is WAHT for

---

27   Note that in this text language the NE Midland scribe uses the *figura* <y> in both [i~j] contexts and [θ~ð] contexts as well as once for [ʤ] (in YOYE for JOY). This complex usage combined with spellings showing diphthongisation in words with OE V+[x], triggers the addition to the profile of certain of these vocalic and palatal categories.

WHAT, which at face value might suggest HT for [t]. Consider, however, the following extract from dulwicht.dic:

```
$what/RTI>pr *WAT 1
$what/pn WAHT 1
$when/cj >W>EN 6 *WEHN 3 *WEN 2 WEHN 2 VEHN 1
$whenthat/cj *WEN-YAT 1 WAN-YAT 1
$wherefore/av-k WAR-FORE 1
$whereof/av-k >W>ARE-OF 1
$wherethrough/av-k *WARE-YORU 1
$whether/cj *WEHER 1 *WEHR 1
$which/pn<pr WIHLC 1
$while/cj WIHL 1
$whom/pn<pr WAHM 1 WAM 1
$whoso/pn >W>OH-SWO 1
$why/av *WI 1
```

For the reflexes of OE initial *hw-* there are spellings in W+vowel and also spellings in W+vowel+H. WAHT is one of these. In the light of the other evidence for OE initial *hw-* in this text language it seems less likely that HT is here a spelling for [t] than that WAH is a spelling indicating the presence of frication in the syllable not tied to a specific segment. In other words something like a Firthian prosody (Firth 1942). This assessment of the Dulwich scribe's use of H as a prosodic marker is perhaps supported by the following spellings in his text language: FOULH, FUHL, FOUHL beside FOUL for FOWL. It is also possible that in some words H is on its way to being lost which would account for the spelling OHLD beside OLD and HOLD for OLD.

The scope of this paper does not allow us to make phonographic profiles of the dental obstruents in all the relevant text languages. We will not attempt here therefore to account further for any of the problematic spellings listed in Section 4.1 above, except to say that some, such as Dd and possibly DH may perhaps imply affrication as a way station on the path to spirantisation.

5. Conclusions and connections

5.1. Heuristics and external sources

In this paper we have shown how observation of detailed data in the
LAEME CTT has driven the creation of new historical utilities – the
LAEME CE and CC. The corpora themselves thus have complementary heuristic functions, enabling both the serendipitous capture of hitherto unnoticed phenomena and also their more detailed investigation.

The wider contextualisation of such investigations of early
Middle English is made possible by the ability to access external
sources such as the OED Online and the electronic MED. For
instance, one might be examining a specific early Middle English text
witness and be interested in a form or set of forms appearing in it for a
particular item: e.g. spellings for the word DEAD in Laȝamon A, Hand
B. Accessing the text dictionary for the sample of Laȝamon A, Hand
B in the *LAEME* CTT would enable a comparison of all the recorded
spellings for that word in that scribal text language, viz:

```
$dead/aj DEAD 4 DEaeD 3 DaeD 2 DEeD 1
$dead/ajOd{rh} DEAD 1
$dead/ajn DEaeDE 1
$dead/ajnpl<pr DaeDEN 1
$dead/ajpl DEaeDDE 1
$dead/ajpl{rh} DEAD 1 DEAd 1
$dead/aj{rh} DEAd 1 DED 1
```

The tagged text itself could be searched by means of the tag $dead/aj
to find all the textual contexts for the spellings, to determine whether
there is any patterning in the use of different variants. Alternatively, a
general interest in early Middle English spellings for DEAD would
trigger entry to the main tag dictionary of the entire *LAEME* CTT
where all the recorded spellings for $dead/aj are listed as follows:

```
$dead/aj *DEAD *DED *DEDE +DED DE DE>H>IT DEAD DEADE DEAT DEAd
     DED DEDE DEID DET DETD DEYD~ DEaeD DEd DEeD DIED DYAD
     DaeD Daed
$dead/aj-cpv DEAD+RE DEAD+URE DEADD+RE
$dead/aj-k +DED
```

$dead/aj<pr DEAD DEADE DED DEDE DYADE
$dead/ajG DEAD+E DED+E
$dead/ajOd *DED +DED+ DEAD DEAD+ DEADE DED DEDE
$dead/ajOd-k -DED
$dead/ajOd{rh} DEAD DED
$dead/ajn DED DEDE DEaeDE DYAD
$dead/ajn-av DEDE
$dead/ajn<pr DED DEDE
$dead/ajn<pr{rh} DEDE
$dead/ajnG DEAD+^ES DED+ES DaeD+AN
$dead/ajnOd DEDE [D]EADE
$dead/ajnOi DEDE
$dead/ajnpl DEAD+E DED+E
$dead/ajnpl<pr DEAD+E DYAD+E DaeD+EN
$dead/ajnplOd *DED+E DEAD+E DEAD+EN DED DED+E DED+EN DEED+E
        DYAD+E
$dead/ajnplOd{rh} DEAD+E DED+E DIED+E
$dead/ajpl *DED+E DEAD DEAD+E DED DED+E DEaeDD+E DYAD+E
$dead/ajpl-k +DED+E
$dead/ajpl<pr DED DYAD+E
$dead/ajpl<pr{rh} DED+E
$dead/ajplG DEAD+RE
$dead/ajplOd *DED DED+E
$dead/ajplOd{rh} DED+E
$dead/ajpl{rh} DEAD DEAD+E DEAd DED DED+E
$dead/aj{rh} DE DEAD DEAd DED DEDE DEDH DEED DETD DYAD DaeD

From here, special interest in, say, spellings in DEAd would direct the
enquirer, via a special search program, to the text dictionaries derived
from those text witnesses that employ the spellings DEAd – in this
case only the two scribes (A and B) of Laȝamon A. An enquirer with
interest in the use of the word in early Middle English could consult
the entry for $dead/aj in the Key to the Lexels where there is brief
semantic information and cross references to MED and OED:

> $dead/aj (1) = "having ceased to live, deprived of life; bereft of sensation,
> benumbed; insensible to, indifferent to; futile, useless; deadly, mortal"; *be
> dead* = "to have died"; as noun "a dead person, one who has died" (< OE
> *dēad*). <u>MED s.v. *dēd* adj.</u> and <u>MED s.v. *dēd* adj. as n.</u> <u>OED s.v. *dead* a. (n.[1],
> adv.).</u> Cf. $deadly/aj, $deadly/av, $death/n, $die/vpp. <u>CE $dead/aj.</u>

Anyone requiring detailed citation of variants of the word in later
Middle English can then link to MED. Anyone wishing to access

earlier cognates and an OED-type etymology of the word DEAD can direct their steps to OED. The Lexel Key also cross references to the relevant entry in the *LAEME* CE, which gives the narrative-type etymology of the word, accounting for all its spelling variants in the *LAEME* CTT, including DEAd, with a cross-reference to the relevant change ((LDS)) in the CC. See below:

> $dead/aj
> ‖ *ðauð ((VFH)) > *daud ((AUF)) > daeud ((DHH)) > [dæad] *dēad* ((EAM))
> > [dae:d] ((LAER)) > [dɛ:d]
> The difference in final consonant between this word and $death is due to an original accented suffix (IE form *dhau-t-ó-s, probably a perfect participle, which would make the adjective deverbal). The Gmc reflex of *t, i.e. *þ, is, because of the following accent, voiced by Verner's Law and follows the normal pathway for *ð. There are quite a number of cases in which $dead appears to end with a fricative, and $death with a stop; we attribute these instances to well motivated sound changes (e.g. ((LDS)), ((LDH))), but with a pair of related words like this there is always the possibility of analogical 'contamination' or litteral substitution. The appearances however match the outputs of the sound changes, so we build them into the narrative. See also $death.

<u>phonology</u>
/aj DEAD(E) DED(E) DEED(E) DEID DEYD~ DEaeD(E) DEeD DIED(E) DaeD
All these medial vowel combinations are possible spellings for [ɛ:], though EI, EY are more normally used for diphthongs and IE for close [e:]. Sound changes of these kinds however appear to be ruled out. See further s.v. $death/n.
?((LDS)) > DEDH
DH possibly to indicate fricative
((FCD)) > DE
((KD)) > DYAD(E)
((FD2)) > DEAT DET DEHIT
((LDS)) > DEAd DEd Daed
DETD
Difficult. T would seem to indicate ((FD2)) and D is expected. Perhaps TD is a complex litteral substitution
DEaeDDE
DD may be dittography rather than gemination.

<u>Links to changes that have not been discussed above</u>

((AUF))%n: au-fronting [OE]

Gmc *au > [æ:u]. The output is subject to ((DHH)) in OE, giving [æ:a], i.e. *ēa*.

((DHH))%n: Diphthong height harmony [OE]
First named in Lass/Anderson (1975). This is a well-formedness constraint on the most characteristic kind of OE diphthong: the second elements come to agree in height with the first, so that e.g. [æu] > [æa], [eu] > [eo]. DHH affects both the original Germanic diphthongs and those formed by OE changes like breaking.

((EAM))%n: ea-merger [lOE]
ă > *ǽ*. The change of short *ea* leads to merger with *œ*, and then further merger with *a*, so that the histories of the three categories, in those varieties and forms where they are initially distinct, collapse. For the history of *ǣ* see ((LAER)).

((FCD))%v: Final Coronal Deletion [ME]
t, d delete when second members of clusters before another C or #. This is scattered throughout the texts, never constant. Deletion is promoted by the presence of an initial consonant in the following word or absolute finality in the phrase, less so by a following vowel. This is still common in ModE casual speech: coronal stops delete in final position, especially if the preceding consonant is homorganic (prototype in *LAEME*: frequent <CHIL> for $child/n both in absolute finality and as first element of a compound). For a relevant discussion of modern instances and the complex variability patterns associated with them, see Chambers/Trudgill (1998: §9.9.2). The conditioning environments and variable status of this process appear to have changed little if at all from eME times.

((FD2)) %v, r{?SW}: Final Devoicing 2 [ME]
Voiced stops *b, d, g* > *p, t, k* in final position. This is relatively uncommon and geographically scattered, though some scribes, e.g. that of tr323at.tag, show it extensively.

((KD))%n, v, r{Kt}: Kentish Diphthongisation [ME]
Long mid vowels (both 'open' and 'close') diphthongise by raising the first element, so that for expected <O, E> the results are <UO>, <YA>. These are not entirely parallel (diphthongisation of back vowels appears in our sample to occur only after *b*, *g*, while that of front vowels occurs in initial position and after *h* and dentals. But they are the same general and cross-linguistically very common type, and occur in the same text, ayenbitet.tag. Typical examples are $good/aj <GUOD>, $bone/npl <BUONES>, $be:odan/vpt12 <BYAD>, $dead <DYAD>, $deaf <DYAF>.

((LAER))%n: Long æ-raising [lOE/eME]
After monophthongisation of *ēa* [æːa] ((EAM)), [æː] > [ɛː]. This change is posited in the standard handbooks, but there is really very little evidence one way or the other; since we are uncertain about the quality of OE) *ǽ*, it could well have been [ɛː] virtually from the beginning.

Now that *LAEME* and its associated corpora are web-mounted and active,[29] they too can serve as 'external sources' in the same way as MED and OED do now. For a diagram showing all these potential connections see Section 5.2 below.

5.2. The Paths of the $dead/

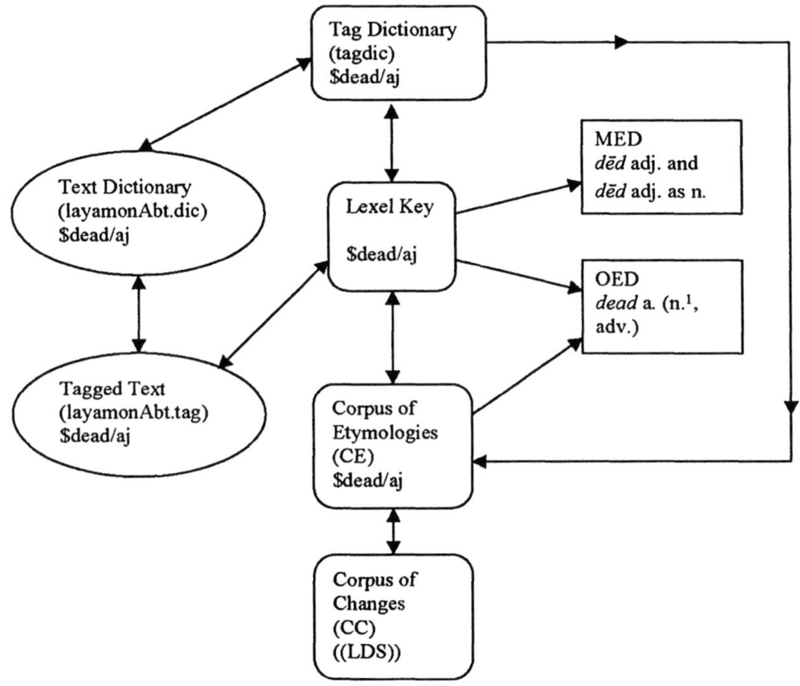

---

29   See <www.lel.ed.ac.uk/ihd/laeme1/laeme1.html>.

References

Primary sources

See Appendix 1.

Secondary sources

AND = *Anglo-Norman Dictionary* online edition at <www.anglo-norman.net/>

Benskin, Michael 1997. Texts from a Township in Late Medieval Ireland. *Collegium Medievale* 10: 91-173.

Benskin, Michael 2001. The Language of the English Texts. In Hunt, Tony (ed.), *Three* receptaria *from Medieval England*. Oxford: The Society for the Study of Medieval Languages and Literature. Chapter 4, 193-230.

Britton, Derek 1992. Of *contreth* Matters. *Neophilologus* 76, 283-289.

Campbell, Alistair 1959. *Old English Grammar*. Oxford: Clarendon.

Cartlidge, Neil 1997. Orthographical Variation in the Middle English Lyrics of BL Cotton Caligula A. 9. *Neuphilologische Mitteilungen* 98, 253-259.

Chambers, Jack K. / Trudgill, Peter [2]1998. *Dialectology*. Cambridge: Cambridge University Press.

d'Ardenne, S.T.R.O. (ed.) 1961. *Þe Liflade ant te Passiun of Seinte Iuliene*. EETS OS 248. London: Oxford University Press.

Dobson, E.J. (ed.) 1972. *The English Text of the Ancrene Riwle edited from B.M. Cotton MS. Cleopatra C VI*. EETS OS 267. London: Oxford University Press.

Dobson, Eric J. 1976. *Origins of* Ancrene Wisse. Oxford: Clarendon.

Firth, John R. 1948. Sounds and Prosodies. *Transactions of the Philological Society* 1948, 127-152 (1949).

Holthausen, Ferdinand (ed.) 1888. *Vices and Virtues*, part 1. EETS OS 89. London: Oxford University Press.

Hupe, Heinrich 1893. *Cursor Mundi, edited by Richard Morris, part VII Essay on the Manuscripts and Dialect by H. Hupe.* EETS OS 101. London: Oxford University Press.

Johnson, Charles / Jenkinson, Hilary 1915. *English Court Hand A.D. 1066 to 1500.* 2 vols. Repr. 1967. New York: Frederick Ungar.

LAEME = Laing, Margaret / Lass, Roger 2008. *A Linguistic Atlas of Early Middle English.* Online at <www.lel.ed.ac.uk/ihd/laeme1/laeme1.html>.

Laing, Margaret 1999. Confusion *wrs* Confounded: Litteral Substitution Sets in Early Middle English Writing Systems. *Neuphilologische Mitteilungen* 100, 251-270.

Laing, Margaret 2004. Multidimensionality: Time, Space and Stratigraphy in Historical Dialectology. In Dossena, Marina / Lass, Roger (eds) *Methods and Data in English Historical Dialectology.* Bern: Peter Lang, 49-96.

Laing, Margaret 2008. The Middle English Scribe: *Sprach er wie er schrieb?* In Dossena, Marina / Dury, Richard / Gotti, Maurizio (eds), *English Historical Linguistics 2006. Volume III: Geohistorical Variation in English.* Amsterdam: Benjamins, 1-44.

Laing, Margaret / Lass, Roger 2003. Tales of the 1001 Nists. The Phonological Implications of Litteral Substitution Sets in 13th-Century South-West-Midland Texts. *English Language and Linguistics* 7.2, 1-22.

Laing, Margaret / McIntosh, Angus 1995a. The Language of *Ancrene Riwle*, the Katherine Group Texts and *Þe Wohunge of ure Lauerd* in BL Cotton Titus D xviii. *Neuphilologische Mitteilungen* 96, 235-263.

Laing, Margaret / McIntosh, Angus 1995b. Cambridge, Trinity College MS 335: Its Texts and their Transmission. In Beadle, Richard / Piper, A.J. (eds) *New Science out of Old Books: Studies in Manuscripts and Early Printed Books in Honour of A.I. Doyle.* Aldershot: Scolar Press, 14-52.

LALME = McIntosh, Angus / Samuels, Michael L. / Benskin, Michael (eds) with the assistance of Margaret Laing and Keith Williamson. 1986. *A Linguistic Atlas of Late Mediæval English,* 4 vols. Aberdeen: Aberdeen University Press.

LAOS = Williamson, Keith 2008. *A Linguistic Atlas of Older Scots.* Online at <www.lel.ed.ac.uk/ihd/laos1/laos1.html>.

Lass, Roger 1997. *Historical Linguistics and Language Change.* Cambridge: Cambridge University Press.

Lass, Roger / Anderson, John M. 1975. *Old English Phonology.* Cambridge: Cambridge University Press.

Lass, Roger / Laing, Margaret 2005. Are Front Rounded Vowels Retained in West Midland Middle English? In Ritt, Nikolaus / Schendl, Herbert (eds) *Rethinking Middle English: linguistic and literary approaches.* Frankfurt a.M.: Peter Lang, 280-290.

MED = Kurath, Hans *et al.* 1952–2001. *Middle English Dictionary.* Ann Arbor: University of Michigan Press. Online at <ets.umdl.umich.edu/m/med/>

Millett, Bella (ed.) 2005. *Ancrene Wisse: A Corrected Edition of the Text in Cambridge, Corpus Christi College, MS 403, with variants from other manuscripts.* EETS OS 325. Oxford: Oxford University Press.

OED = Murray, J.A.H. *et al.* 1884–1928. *The Oxford English Dictionary.* Supplement 1933. [2]1989. Oxford: Clarendon Press. Online at <www.oed.com/>.

Pope, Mildred K. 1934. *From Latin to Modern French with Especial Consideration of Anglo-Norman.* Manchester: Manchester University Press.

Wang, William S.-Y. 1969. Competing Changes as a Cause of Residue. *Language* 45, 9-25.

Wełna, Jerzy 2004. Spirantisation and Despirantisation. In Kay, Christian / Hough, Carole / Wotherspoon, Irené (eds) 2004. *New Perspectives in English Historical Linguistics. Vol. II: Lexis and Transmission.* Amsterdam: Benjamins, 251-265.

Wilson, R.M. (ed.) 1954 [for 1948, repr. 1957]. *The English Text of the Ancrene Riwle, with an introduction by N.R. Ker.* EETS OS 229. London: Oxford University Press.

Wright, Cyril E. 1960. *English Vernacular Hands from the Twelfth to the Fifteenth Centuries.* Oxford: Clarendon.

Appendix 1

Key to the filenames in the *LAEME* Corpus of Tagged Texts

The *LAEME* CTT filename is in the form filenamet.tag. This is
followed by the manuscript repository reference, including folio
references and the title or description of text(s) in the relevant text
language. For full information on the tagged texts, including date,
localisation (if any), and the tagged sample see *LAEME*, Auxiliary
Data Sets, Index of Sources.

aberdeent.tag = Aberdeen University Library 154, fol. 368v: couplet and 3 quatrains
add25031t.tag = London, British Library, Add 23501, fol. 5v: *Ten Commandments*
add27909t.tag = London, British Library, Add 27909, fol. 2r: *Penitence for Wasted Life*
adde6at.tag = Oxford, Bodleian Library Add E.6, roll, hand A: *Sayings of St Bernard*
adde6bt.tag = Oxford, Bodleian Library, Add E.6, hand B: *XV Signs before Doomsday*
adde6ct.tag = Oxford, Bodleian Library, Add E.6, roll, hand C: *Pater Noster*
arundel248t.tag = London, British Library Arundel 248, fols. 154r-155r: four lyrics
arundel292vvt.tag = London, British Library, Arundel 292, fol. 3r-v: *Creed, Pater Noster, Ave Maria* etc
ashmole1280t.tag = Oxford, Bodleian Library, Ashmole 1280, fols. 48r, 192v: prayers
ashmole360t.tag = Oxford, Bodleian Library, Ashmole 360, fol. 145v, hand B: lyric
ayenbitet.tag = London, British Library, Arundel 57, fols. 2r-4r; 13r-96v: *Ayenbite of Inwyt, Pater Noster* etc.
bardneyt.tag = Oxford, Bodleian Library, Rawlinson C 510, fol. 3r: Fragment of *Stella Maris*
benetholmet.tag = London, British Library, Cotton Galba E ii, fols. 30r-v: clauses in English
bestiaryt.tag = London, British Library, Arundel 292, fols. 4r-10v: *The Bestiary*
beverleyt.tag = London, British Library, Cotton Charter iv 18: Athelstan's Charter
blicklingt.tag = Private: Blickling Hall, Norfolk 6864, fol. 35r: *Creed*
bod34t.tag = Oxford, Bodleian Library, Bodley 34, fols. 1r-80v: *St Katherine, St Margaret, St Juliana, Hali Meiðhad, Sawles Warde*
bodley26t.tag = Oxford Bodleian Library, Bodley 26, fols. 107r-108r: macaronic sermon
bodley57t.tag = Oxford, Bodleian Library, Bodley 57, fol 102v: lyric
buryFft.tag = Cambridge University Library Ff.II.33: Bury documents
caiusart.tag = Cambridge, Gonville and Caius 234/120, pp. 1-185: *Ancrene Riwle*

candet1t.tag = Durham, Dean & Chapter Library A.III.12, fol. 49r: *Candet Nudatum Pectus*

candet2t.tag = Oxford, Bodleian Library, Digby 45, fol. 25r: *Candet Nudatum Pectus*

candet3t.tag = Oxford, Bodleian Library, Digby 55, fol. 49r: *Candet Nudatum Pectus*, etc

candet4t.tag = Oxford, Bodleian Library, Rawlinson C 317, fol. 89v: *Candet Nudatum Pectus*

candet5t.tag = Cambridge, St John's College A.15, fols. 72r, 120v: *Candet Nudatum Pectus*, etc

candet6t.tag = Oxford, Bodleian Library, Bodley 42, fol. 250r: *Candet Nudatum Pectus*, etc

candet7t.tag = London, British Library, Additional 11579, fols 35v–36v; 72v–73r: *Candet Nudatum Pectus*, etc.

candet8t.tag = Cambridge, Sidney Sussex College 97 (Δ.5.12), fol. 111r: *Candet Nudatum Pectus*

candet9linzat.tag = Linz, Staatsbibliothek Sankt Florian XI.57, fol. 9v hand A: *Candet Nudatum Pectus*

cccc8t.tag = Cambridge, Corpus Christi College 8, p. 457: lyric with musical notation

ccco59t.tag = Oxford, Corpus Christi College 59, fols. 66r–v, 113v, 116v: verses

chertseyt.tag = London, British Library, Cotton Vitellius A xiii, Chertsey Cartulary, fols. 50r–51v, 53v: six documents

cleoarat.tag = London, British Library, Cotton Cleopatra C.vi, hand A, fols. 4r–198v: *Ancrene Riwle*

cleoarbt.tag = London, British Library, Cotton Cleopatra C.vi, hand B's corrections

clericot.tag = London, British Library, Add. 23986 verso of roll: *Interludium de Clerico et Puella*

corp145selt.tag = Cambridge, Corpus Christi College 145, hand A, fols. 1r–210v: *South English Legendary*

corpart.tag = Cambridge, Corpus Christi College 402, fols. 1r–117: *Ancrene Wisse*

cotabusest.tag = London, British Library, Cotton Caligula A ix, part 2, fol. 248v: *The Ten Abuses*

cotcleoBvit.tag = London, British Library, Cotton Cleopatra B vi, fol. 204v: *Pater Noster* and *Creed* etc.

cotdoomsdayt.tag = London, British Library, Cotton Caligula A ix, part 2, fol. 246v–247r: *Doomsday*

cotdwct.tag = London, British Library, Cotton Caligula A ix, part 2, fol. 246r–v: *Death's Wither Clench*

cotfaustat.tag = London, British Library, Cotton Faustina A.v fols. 10r–v, hand A: fragments of English in a Latin sermon

cotfaustbt.tag = London, British Library, Cotton Faustina A.v, fols. 105v–106r, hand B: verses on Lazarus in a Latin sermon

cotlastdayt.tag = London, British Library, Cotton Caligula A ix, part 2, fol. 247r–248v: *The Latemest Day*

cotorisont.tag = London, British Library, Cotton Caligula A ix, part 2, fol. 246v: *Orison to Our Lady* cotowlat.tag = London, British Library, Cotton Caligula A ix, part 2, *The Owl and the Nightingale*, language 1

cotowlbt.tag = London, British Library, Cotton Caligula A ix, part 2, *The Owl and the Nightingale*, language 2

cotsermont.tag = London, British Library, Cotton Caligula A ix, part 2, fols. 248v-249r: *Lutel Soth Sermun*

cotvespcmat.tag = London, British Library, Cotton Vespasian A.iii, hand A: fols. 2r-91v; 93va line 9-95vb line 19; 99ra-112vb; 119rb-139va line 36 *Cursor Mundi* and fols. 139va line 37-163ra: *Exposition of the Creed*, and *Lord's Prayer*, Prayers for the Hours of the Passion and to the Trinity, *Book of Penance*

cotwillt.tag = London, British Library, Cotton Caligula A ix, part 2, fol. 246v: *Will and Wit*

coventryt.tag = Stratford-upon-Avon, Shakespeare Birthplace Library, DR 10/1408, pp. 23-24: Coventry Writ

creditonat.tag = London, British Library, Cotton Roll ii.11, language A: 3 Crediton documents

creditonbt.tag = London, British Library, Cotton Roll ii.11, language B: Credition document

cuckoot.tag = London, British Library, Harley 978, fol. 11v: *Svmer is icumen in*

culhht.tag = Cambridge University Library Hh.6.11, fol. 70v: *Pater Noster* and *Ave Maria*

digby2a1t.tag = Oxford, Bodleian Library, Digby 2, fol. 6r, hand A language 1: verse

digby2a2t.tag = Oxford, Bodleian Library, Digby 2, fol. 6v, hand A language 2: verse

digby2bt.tag = Oxford, Bodleian Library, Digby 2, fol. 15r, hand B: verse

digby2ct.tag = Oxford, Bodleian Library, Digby 2, fol. 111r, hand C: verse

digby86bodysoult.tag = Oxford, Bodleian Library, Digby 86, fols. 195v-197v: *Debate between Body and Soul*

digby86hendingt.tag = Oxford, Bodleian Library, Digby 86, fols. 140v-143r: *Proverbs of Hending*

digby86mapt.tag = Oxford, Bodleian Library, Digby 86, all the texts that are suitable for mapping

digby86painst.tag = Oxford, Bodleian Library, Digby 86, fols. 132r-134v: *XI Pains of Hell* and *Sweet Ihesu*

digby86siritht.tag = Oxford, Bodleian Library, Digby 86, fols. 165r-168r: *Dame Sirith*

digpmt.tag = Oxford, Bodley Digby 4, fols. 97r-110v: *Poema Morale*

dulwicht.tag = London, Dulwich College MS XXII, fols. 81v-85v: *La Estorie del Euangelie*

edincmat.tag = Edinburgh, Royal College of Physicians, MS of *Cursor Mundi*, hand A, fols. 1r-15v

edincmbt.tag = Edinburgh, Royal College of Physicians, MS of *Cursor Mundi*, hand B, fols. 16r-36v: Extracts from the *Northern Homily Collection*

edincmct.tag = Edinburgh, Royal College of Physicians, MS of *Cursor Mundi*, hand C, fols. 37r-50v

egblessedt.tag = London, British Library, Egerton 613, hand C, fol. 2r-v: *Blessed beo*

eglitelt.tag = London, British Library, Egerton 613, hand D, fol. 2v: *Litel uoit eni man* egpm1t.tag = London, British Library, Egerton 613, hand G, fols. 64r-70v (e): *Poema Morale*

egpm2t.tag = London, British Library, Egerton 613, hand F, fols. 7r-12v (E): *Poema Morale*

egsomert.tag = London, British Library, Egerton 613, hand A, fol. 1v: *Somer is comen*

egstellat.tag = London, British Library, Egerton 613, hand B, fol. 2r: *Stella Maris*

emmanuel27t.tag = Cambridge, Emmanuel College 27, fols. 111v, 162r-163r: Lyrics

eul107t.tag = Edinburgh University Library MS 107, fol. 89r: six verse lines

fmcpmt.tag = Cambridge, Fitzwilliam Museum, McClean 123, fol. 114v: Old English letters; fols. 115r-120r: *Poema Morale*

gandccreedt.tag = Cambridge, Gonville and Caius College 52/29, fol. 43r: *Creed, Pater Noster, Ave Maria, In manus tuas*

genexodt.tag = Cambridge, Corpus Christi College 444, fols. 1r-81r: *Genesis and Exodus*

gospatrict.tag = Carlisle, Cumbria RO, D/Lons/L Medieval Deeds C1: Gospatric's Writ

hale135t.tag = London, Lincoln's Inn Hale 135, fol. 137v: *Nou sprinkes the sprai*

hat26tct.tag = Oxford, Bodleian Library, Hatton 26, fol. 211r: *Ten Commandments* and *Seven Gifts of the Holy Ghost*

havelokt.tag = Oxford, Bodleian Library, Laud Misc 108, fols. 204r-219va, hand C: *Havelok*

herefordverset.tag = Hereford Cathedral Library O.III.11, fol. 122v: verse on the passion

huntproct.tag = Kew, The National Archives, C66/73 (Patent Roll 43 Henry III), membr. 15 item 40, Chancery enrollment of proclamation in English by Henry III, dated from London, 18 October 1258

iacobt.tag = Oxford, Bodleian Library, Bodley 652, fols. 1r-10v: *Iacob and Iosep*

jes29t.tag = Oxford, Jesus College 29, part II, English on fols. 144r-195r; 198r-200v

johnstandt.tag = Cambridge, St John's College 111 (E8), fol. 106v: *Stand wel moder*

lam499t.tag = London, Lambeth Palace Library 499, fols. 64v-69r, 125v: lyrics

lamhomA1t.tag = London, Lambeth Palace Library 487, fols 1r-21v, 30v-51v, hand A language 1: Lambeth Homilies I-V, IX-XIII

lamhomA2t.tag = London, Lambeth Palace Library 487, fols. 21v-30v, 51v-65r, hand A, language 2: Lambeth Homilies VI- VIII, XIV-XVII

lampmt.tag = London, Lambeth Palace Library 487, fols. 59v-65r, hand A: *Poema Morale*

lamursnt.tag = London, Lambeth Palace 487, fols. 65v-67r, hand B: *On ureisun of ure louerde*

laud108at.tag = Oxford, Bodleian Library Laud Misc 108, part 1, fols. 1r-200v, hand A: *Life of Christ, Infancy of Christ, South English Legendary*

laud108bt.tag = Oxford, Bodleian Library, Laud Misc 108, hand B, fols. 200v-203v: *Debate between Body and Soul*

laud471dwct.tag = Oxford, Bodleian Library, Laud Misc 471, hand A, fol. 65r: *Death's Wither-Clench*

laud471kst.tag = Oxford, Bodleian Library, Laud Misc 471, hand B, fols. 128v-133v: *Kentish Sermons*

layamonAat.tag = London, British Library, Cotton Caligula A.ix, part 1, hand A, fols.
     3r–17rb (foot); 17va line 5–18vb line 6; 27ra lines 1–6 (BLIdE); 88ra–89rb line 3:
     Laȝamon A
layamonAbt.tag = London, British Library, Cotton Caligula A.ix, part 1, hand B, fols.
     17va lines 1–4; 18vb line 7–26vb (foot); 27ra line 6 (yAT)–87vb (foot); 89rb line
     4–194v (end): Laȝamon A
layamonBOt.tag = London, British Library, Cotton Otho C.XIII, fols 1r–146v:
     Laȝamon B
linzbt.tag = Linz, Staatsbibliothek Sankt Florian XI.57, fol. 9v, hand B: fragment of
     verse
linzct.tag = Linz, Staatsbibliothek Sankt Florian XI.57, fol. 9v, hand C: quatrain
maidsdwct.tag = Maidstone Museum A.13, main hand of English, fol. 93v: *Death's
     Wither-Clench*
maidspat.tag = Maidstone Museum A.13, main hand of English, fol. 93r: *Proverbs of
     Alfred*
maidststt.tag = Maidstone Museum A.13, main hand of English, fol. 243v: *Three
     Sorrowful Tidings*
merton248t.tag = Oxford, Merton College 248, fols. 166r–167r: lyrics and sermon
neroart.tag = London, British Library, Cotton Nero A.xiv, fols. 1r–120v, hand:
     Ancrene Riwle
nerowgt.tag = London, British Library, Cotton Nero A.xiv, fols. 120v–131v, hand B:
     Wooing Group texts
newcoll88t.tag = Oxford, New College 88, fols. 31r, 179r–v, 488v: lyrics and *Ten
     Commandments*
ormt.tag = Oxford, Bodleian Library, Junius 1, fols. 3r–: *The Ormulum*
oxproct.tag = Oxfordshire Record Office (Temple Road, Cowley), OCA/H.29.1: a
     proclamation in English of Henry III (single sheet copy), dated from London, 18
     October 1258.
petchront.tag = Oxford, Bodleian Library, Laud Misc 636, fols. 88v–91v:
     Peterborough Chronicle, final continuation
pofh145t.tag = Cambridge, St John's College F.8 (145): 17 fragments of *Proverbs of
     Hending*
prisprayt.tag = London, Corporation of London Records Office, Guildhall, *Liber de
     antiquis Legibus*, fols. 160v–161v: *Prisoner's Prayer*
ramseyat.tag = Kew, The National Archives, E 164/28, hand A, fols. 52v–53r, 59v–
     60r, 165v–166v: Register of Ramsey Abbey
ramseybt.tag = Kew, The National Archives, E 164/28, hand B, fol. 229v: Register of
     Ramsey Abbey
ramseycott.tag = London, British Library, Cotton Otho B xiv, fol. 263r–v: Fragment
     of a Ramsey Register
rawlg18t.tag = Oxford, Bodleian Library, Rawlinson G.18, fols. 105v–106r: *Worldes
     blis*
rawlg22t.tag = Oxford, Bodleian Library, G 22, fol. 1v: [M]Irie it is
royal12e1at.tag = London, British Library, Royal 12.E.i, fols. 193r–194v, Hand A:
     Stond wel moder

royal12e1bt.tag = London, British Library, Royal 12.E.i, fol. 194v, hand B: versions of *My Leman on the Rood*, and *Thenk man*

royal2f8t.tag = London, British Library, Royal 2.F.viii, fol. 1v

royalkgat.tag = London, British Library, Royal 17.A.xxvii, hand A, fols. 1r-8v, 11r-45v: *Sawles Warde* (part), *St Katherine*, *St Margaret* (part)

royalkgbt.tag = London, British Library, Royal 17.A.xxvii, hand B, fols. 9r-10v, 58v-70v: ends of *Sawles Warde* and of *St Juliana*, *Oreisun of Seinte Marie*

royalkgct.tag = London, British Library, Royal 17.A.xxvii, hand C, fols. 45v para 2-58r: End of *St Margaret*, first bit of *St Juliana*

salisbury82t.tag = Salisbury Cathedral Library 82, f. 271v: *Paternoster*

scotwart.tag = London, British Library, Cotton Julius A v, fols. 180r-181v: *Prophecy of the Scottish Wars*

sherbornet.tag = London, British Library, Add 46487, Sherborne Cartulary, fols. 24v-25r: boundary clause

swinfieldt.tag = Herefordshire Record Office AL 19/2, *Registrum Recardi de Swinfield*, fol. 152r: Bromfield Writ

tanner169t.tag = Oxford, Bodleian Library, Tanner 169*, p. 175: *Stabat iuxta crucem Christi*

tcd432t.tag = Dublin, Trinity College 432, fol. 22r: version of *My Leman on the Rood*

tencmFft.tag = Cambridge University Library Ff.VI.15, fol. 21r: *Ten Commandments*

thorneykt.tag = Cambridge University Library, Add 3021, *Red Book of Thorney* 2, fol. 372: Kingsdelf document

thorneymt.tag = Cambridge University Library, Add 3020, *Red Book of Thorney* 1, fol. 18r: Will of Mantat

titusart.tag = London, British Library, Cotton Titus D xviii, fols. 14r-105r: *Ancrene Riwle*

titushmt.tag = London, British Library, Cotton Titus D xviii, fols. 112v-127r: *Hali Meiðhad*

tituslang2t.tag = London, British Library Cotton Titus D xviii, language T2: *Ancrene Riwle*

titusskt.tag = London, British Library, Cotton Titus D xviii, fols. 133v-147v: *Saint Katherine*

titusswt.tag = London, British Library Cotton Titus D xviii, fols. 105v-112v: *Sawles Warde*

tituswoht.tag = London, British Library, Cotton Titus D.xviii, fols. 127r-133r: *Wohunge of ure lauerd*

tr323at.tag = Cambridge, Trinity College B.14.39 (323), hand A: fols. 19r, 25rb, 25v, 27rb, 28r-29v, 32r-33v, 36r-46r, 47r-v, 83v-84r

tr323bt.tag = Cambridge, Trinity College B.14.39 (323), hand B: fols. 20r-25r, 26r-27ra, 27v, 34r, 35r-v

tr323ct.tag = Cambridge, Trinity College B.14.39 (323), hand C: fols. 30r-31v, 81v

tr323dt.tag = Cambridge, Trinity College B.14.39 (323), hand D: fols. 81v-82r, 85r-87v

trhom34ct.tag = Cambridge, Trinity College B.14.52, hand C, pp. 153-154: Trinity Homilies XXXIV

trhomAt.tag = Cambridge, Trinity College B.14.52, Trinity Homilies, hand A: all the
    texts in this hand apart from *Poema Morale* are tagged in this sample
trhomBt.tag = Cambridge, Trinity College B.14.52, Trinity Homilies, hand B: all the
    texts in this hand are tagged in this sample
trin43Bt.tag = Cambridge, Trinity College 43 (B.1.45), hand B, fol. 73v: lyric on the
    approach of death
trincleoDt.tag = The work of 'Scribe D' viz:
    Cambridge, Trinity College 43 (B.1.45), fols. 24r-v, 41v-42r: verses and sermon
    and London, British Library, Cotton Cleopatra C vi, hand D continuous texts:
    fols. 22v-23r, 57v, 199r and London, British Library, Cotton Cleopatra C vi, hand
    D additions and corrections.
trinpmt.tag = Cambridge, Trinity College B.14.52, hand A, fols. 2r-9v: *Poema Morale*
vitelld3t.tag = London, British Library, Cotton Vitellius D iii, fols. 6r-8v: *Floris and
    Blancheflur*
vvat.tag = London, British Library, Stowe 34, hand A, pp. 1-74 line 17; 74 line 22-75
    line 3: *Vices and Virtues*
vvbt.tag = London, British Library, Stowe 34, hand B, pp. 74 lines 17-22; 75 line 3-
    95: *Vices and Virtues*
vvcorrt.tag = London, British Library, Stowe 34: *Vices and Virtues*, the main
    correcting scribe
vvtit.tag = London, British Library, Stowe 34: *Vices and Virtues*, the scribe of the
    titles
wellsat.tag = Wells Cathedral Library, *Liber Albus* I, language 1, fol. 14r
wellsbt.tag = Wells Cathedral Library, *Liber Albus* I, language 2, fols. 17v-18r
westminstert.tag = London, Westminster Abbey Library MS 34/3, fol. 36v: verse on
    impossibilities
winchestert.tag = London, British Library, Add 15340, fols. 116v-117r: *Vision of
    Edwin*
wintneyt.tag = London, British Library, Cotton Claudius D iii: *Benedictine Rule*
worcdoct.tag = Worcester, Herefordshire and Worcestershire Record Office, BA
    3814, fol. 38v
worcsermont.tag = Worcester Cathedral, Chapter Library Q 29, fols. 130v-131r
worcthcreedt.tag = Oxford, Bodleian Library, Junius 121, fol. vi: *Nicene Creed*
worcthfragst.tag = Worcester Cathedral, Chapter Library F 174, fols. 63r-66v:
    Worcester Fragments
worcthgrglt.tag = Worcester Cathedral, Chapter Library F 174, fols. 1r-63r: Ælfric's
    Grammar and Glossary

Appendix 2

List of filenames in the *LAEME* Corpus of Tagged Text according to which show evidence of presence of the spelling alternations implying the possibility of the dental changes discussed in the paper. Those with evidence of all four types are listed first, then those with evidence of three, two, one, and finally those with no evidence of the alternations are listed last. Note that ordinal numbers and Scandinavian loanwords are not included in the assessment.

Tagged texts with spelling alternations implying the possibility of all four changes (23 texts):

ayenbitet.tag	havelokt.tag	merton248t.tag
bestiaryt.tag	jes29t.tag	neroart.tag
buryFft.tag	lam499t.tag	royalkgat.tag
caiusart.tag	lamhomA1t.tag	tr323at.tag
cleoarat.tag	lampmt.tag	tr323dt.tag
cotvespcmat.tag	laud471kst.tag	vvat.tag
digby86mapt.tag	layamonAat.tag	vvbt.tag
genexodt.tag	layamonAbt.tag	

Tagged texts with spelling alternations implying the possibility of three of the four changes (30 texts):

adde6at.tag	edincmat.tag	scotwart.tag
arundel248t.tag	edincmbt.tag	tituslang2t.tag
bod34t.tag	egpm2t.tag	titusskt.tag
candet8t.tag	lamhomA2t.tag	titusswt.tag
cccc8t.tag	laud108bt.tag	trhomBt.tag
clericot.tag	layamonBOt.tag	trincleoDt.tag
corp145selt.tag	newcoll88t.tag	wellsat.tag
corpart.tag	petchront.tag	wintneyt.tag
cotowlat.tag	ramseyat.tag	worcthfragst.tag
dulwicht.tag	ramseycott.tag	worcthgrglt.tag

Tagged texts with spelling alternations implying the possibility of two of the four changes (40 texts):

adde6bt.tag
adde6ct.tag
benetholmet.tag
beverleyt.tag
bodley57t.tag
candet5t.tag
candet7t.tag
chertseyt.tag
cotlastdayt.tag
cotowlbt.tag
cotsermont.tag
digby2a2t.tag
digby86bodysoult.tag
edincmct.tag
egpm1t.tag
gandccreedt.tag
gospatrict.tag
johnstandt.tag
laud108at.tag
maidsdwct.tag
maidspat.tag
maidststt.tag
nerowgt.tag
ormt.tag
pofh145t.tag
prisprayt.tag
rawlg18t.tag
royal12e1at.tag
royal2f8t.tag
royalkgbt.tag
royalkgct.tag
titusart.tag
titushmt.tag
tr323bt.tag
tr323ct.tag
trhom34ct.tag
trhomAt.tag
trin43Bt.tag
vitelld3t.tag
wellsbt.tag

Tagged texts with spelling alternations implying the possibility of one of the four changes (50 texts):

aberdeent.tag
add25031t.tag
arundel292vvt.tag
blicklingt.tag
bodley26t.tag
candet1t.tag
candet4t.tag
ccco59t.tag
cleoarbt.tag
cotcleoBvit.tag
cotdoomsdayt.tag
cotfaustat.tag
cotfaustbt.tag
cotorisont.tag
coventryt.tag
creditonat.tag
creditonbt.tag
culhht.tag
digby2a1t.tag
digby2bt.tag
digby2ct.tag
digby86hendingt.tag
digby86siritht.tag
digpmt.tag
eglitelt.tag
egsomert.tag
egstellat.tag
emmanuel27t.tag
fmcpmt.tag
hat26tct.tag
iacobt.tag
lamursnt.tag
laud471dwct.tag
linzct.tag
ramseybt.tag
rawlg22t.tag
royal12e1bt.tag
sherbornet.tag
swinfieldt.tag
tanner169t.tag
tcd432t.tag
tencmFft.tag
thorneymt.tag
tituswoht.tag
trinpmt.tag
vvcorrt.tag
vvtit.tag
winchestert.tag
worcdoct.tag
worchthcreedt.tag

Tagged texts showing none of the spelling alternations (24 texts):

add27909t.tag	cotabusest.tag	herefordverset.tag
ashmole1280t.tag	cotdwct.tag	huntproct.tag
ashmole360t.tag	cotwillt.tag	linzbt.tag
bardneyt.tag	cuckoot.tag	oxproct.tag
candet2t.tag	digby86painst.tag	salisbury82t.tag
candet3t.tag	egblessedt.tag	thorneykt.tag
candet6t.tag	eul107t.tag	westminstert.tag
candet9linzat.tag	hale135t.tag	worcsermont.tag

MARÍA JOSÉ CARRILLO-LINARES / EDURNE GARRIDO-ANES

Middle English Word Geography:
External Sources for Investigating the Field

1. Introduction

The purpose of this contribution is to examine to what extent the research in ME word geography – an area much neglected within ME dialectal studies[1] – can benefit from the available external sources, and to assess how technological developments may help in the investigation of the field. The publication of *A Linguistic Atlas of Late Medieval English (LALME)* in the mid eighties, the completion of the *Middle English Dictionary* (*MED*), and the recent publication of both *A Linguistic Atlas of Early Middle English (LAEME)* and *A Linguistic Atlas of Older Scots (LAOS)*, have certainly improved the scenario for researchers. Additionally, the availability of these resources in electronic format makes things somewhat easier.[2] Furthermore, the

---

1   Studies in the field are very few and widely scattered in time. Nevertheless, the need for undertaking lexical dialectal research has been put forward by several scholars. For further details see Carrillo-Linares/Garrido-Anes (2007 and 2008) and Carrillo-Linares (2005-2006).

2   *MED* has been online for a while now as part of the Middle English Compendium, and just recently free access has been provided as well. A project for carrying out an online version of *LALME* has been funded by the UK Arts and Humanities Research Council Resource Enhancement Scheme (1 Sept 2007 – 31 Aug 2010). *e-LALME* is being compiled by Michael Benskin, of the University of Oslo, Derek Britton, Margaret Laing and Keith Williamson at the Institute for Historical Dialectology at the University of Edinburgh. It will contain corrections to the printed edition (1986). There will also be re-analysis of some texts and the addition of new LPs, including Hiberno-English and 'State' material. It is to be published as a freely accessible, dynamic, interactive web-site. *LAEME* has been compiled by Margaret Laing in collaboration with Roger Lass. The publication of *LAEME* (2008) is also a freely accessible, dynamic, interactive web-site. It is based on

publication of several corpora and collections of electronic versions of ME texts are likewise tools that could be of utility for this field. Nevertheless, in spite of the current technological advances, and the contributions of external sources and software, one of the most obvious difficulties in the investigation of dialectal lexis lies in the fact that many of the tasks that need to be undertaken are, un-avoidably, extremely time-consuming, since in almost all the cases they involve the consultation of manuscript sources.

Most external sources have some limitations for our purpose because none of them has been conceived with word geography in mind. We regard them as excellent auxiliary tools, though, and the limitations for our purposes do not have to be considered a criticism of them, since they have their own aim and objectives, which they fulfil perfectly. The external sources we have considered here can be divided into three main groups:

1.   Historical corpora and electronic collections of ME texts;
2.   Linguistic atlases for medieval material: specifically, *LALME, LAEME* and *LAOS*; and
3.   Dictionaries, especially the *Middle English Dictionary (MED)*, the *Oxford English Dictionary (OED)*, the *Dictionary of the Older Scottish Tongue (DOST)* and the *English Dialect Dictionary (EDD)*.

2. Historical Corpora and Electronic Texts

Historical corpora and electronic collections of ME texts may, in principle, seem to be excellent resources for research in ME word geo-graphy since working manually with texts is hugely time-consuming.

---

an extensive corpus of lexico-grammatically tagged texts, transcribed from manuscript and it deals with English written between 1150 and 1325 (see also Lass/Laing, this volume). *LAOS* (2008) is a 'sister' project of the latter, and it has been published also as a web-site. It has been compiled by Keith Williamson and it includes Older Scots material from 1380-1500.

The sources considered for this paper have been: The Corpus of Early Middle English Tagged Texts and Maps in *LAEME*, The Edinburgh Corpus of Older Scots in *LAOS*, *The Helsinki Corpus (HC)*,[3] *The Corpus of Early English Medical Writing (MEMT)*,[4] *The Innsbruck Computer Archive of Middle English Texts (ICAMET)*,[5] *The Corpus of Middle English Prose and Verse (CMEPV)*,[6] *The Oxford Text Archive (OTA)*,[7] *The Electronic Text Centre's Collection (ETCC)*[8] and *Literature On-Line (LION)*.[9] There are unquestionably several general advantages in the use of these sources. The main benefit from corpora comes from the quick identification of certain lexical items and the easier access to occurrences that electronic texts provide. Likewise, performing electronic searches minimises the probability of human readers missing some of the occurrences. Moreover, if the electronic texts have been specifically designed for linguistic research, the value of this resource increases even more, for they provide more accuracy.

However, whenever we seek the assistance of corpora, we encounter some general limitations in our attempt to use them. These constraints can be due to intrinsic features of corpora, such as their

---

3   The diachronic part of the Helsinki Corpus is published in the *ICAME Collection of English Language Corpora* (1999) in a compilation made by Knut Hofland, Anne Lindebjerg and Jorg Thunestvedt. It consists of a selection of texts covering the OE, ME, and EModE periods, in all 242 text files.

4   This corpus has been produced by the research team of the Department of English at the University of Helsinki under the supervision of Irma Taavitsainen and Päivi Pahta with the assistance of Martti Mäkinen. *MEMT* contains about half a million words of running text of edited medical treatises and early printed books from c. 1375 to c. 1500 and an appendix of texts written c. 1330. It is available on CD-ROM.

5   A subset of this corpus is devoted to prose texts with "129 unabridged Middle English prose pieces from 1150 to 1500, stored to the full on a CD-ROM" (Markus 2002). It is also now available in the *ICAME Collection of English Language Corpora*.

6   Published as part of the Middle English Compendium, this online corpus consists of a collection of 146 items.

7   26 editions of ME texts have been retrieved in electronic format.

8   The University of Virginia has made available 65 titles in ME: see <etext.lib. virginia.edu/collections/languages/english/mideng.browse.html>.

9   This resource is a fully searchable library of more than 350,000 works of English and American poetry, drama and prose. It includes 3,917 entries for OE and ME literature and electronic editions of several texts are provided.

structure and the selection of their sources. In that respect, the existing electronic texts are uneven in the benefits they can provide for our research. Likewise, the limitations may be due to external factors that have more to do with the methodology employed for the study of ME word geography than with the value of corpora themselves. As we explain further on, their contribution is then only complementary to our approach.

2.1. Structure of the corpus

The structure of the corpus determines how far it can be used for our purposes. Most of the existing historical corpora and collections of electronic texts are compilations of transcripts normally taken from scholarly editions. This is the case of *HC, MEMT, ICAMET, CMEVP, OTA, ETCC* and *LION*. Of all the corpora searched for this paper only *LAEME* and *LAOS* include texts transcribed and presented specifically with linguistic analysis in mind. This distinction is important because the research value of these resources in the lexical field is not entirely the same. Some of the problems raised by the use of this kind of texts in historical research are not exclusive to the study of dialectal lexicon.[10] The main obstacle we have to face is that texts taken from scholarly editions are sometimes renderings of more than one manuscript of the same work. This is exemplified by the electronic texts of *The Pricke of Conscience* in *OTA* and *CMEPV,* which are based on the only edition of the complete text that has been published so far (see Morris 1863). Morris edited the text found in London, British Library, Cotton Galba E.9 but he supplied ll. 1538-1729 and 6923-9210 from London, British Library, Harley 4196. Although the language of both texts is similar and they both have been localised in

---

10   Some of these problems in historical research have been discussed by Anneli Meurman-Solin (2001). Likewise, in the introduction to *LAEME,* Laing/Lass (2008: ch. 3.3.1), though not specifically dealing with electronic corpora, consider extensively the inconveniences of using non-manuscript sources for this purpose. In addition, Lass (2004: 22) provides further and more detailed argumentation for avoiding the use of edited texts.

the north of England,[11] the two manuscripts are two different sources and they should be treated as such. There is also an electronic version in the *HC* which is, nonetheless, not affected by this problem, since in this corpus only extracts corresponding to ll. 2892-3293 and 9214-9624 have been included, and all of them correspond to the text in the edition found in London, British Library, Cotton Galba E.9.

An additional problem, not completely disconnected from the previous issue, is that the electronic texts based on scholarly editions are included in the corpus without the additional material accompanying the texts. This causes additional troubles to the users, especially because the textual apparatus found in the printed versions of the editions is not included. Most of the times, the editors' conjectures, emendations, additions, etc. are clearly explained in the apparatus. By leaving out this information, the reader is made unable to reconstruct the copy-text at all, and this can lead to erroneous conclusions not only about lexis but also about other linguistic matters. Even if there should always be a preference for using manuscript material for any linguistic historical research, the printed editions normally provide information, either in an introduction or in notes, about the editorial procedures and conventions which are essential for our grasping and understanding of the text found in the manuscript copy. In the electronic versions of these editions the user cannot discriminate among the occurrences found there because the tools to do it are missing. It is obvious that the interpretations made by the editors cannot be taken into account in order to carry out a linguistic analysis, even if the conjectures seem to be perfectly acceptable, or if the editor emended a very probable scribal error. Let us take, as an example, one of the emendations made by Eccles (1969) in his edition of the medieval play *Mankind.* In l. 863 (p. 183), he emends the word 'sawle' which, according to the apparatus, appears as 'sowe' in the manuscript. The electronic version in *LION* gives only the emended item. Not only are we not getting all the information, but also, if we were going to perform a lexical search, this occurrence would not be a valid one.

---

11   Both London, British Library, Cotton Galba E.9 and London, British Library, Harley 4196 are broadly localised as NME. (*LALME* 1: 106, 113).

If the texts compiled for the corpus have been transcribed with a specific linguistic purpose in mind, some of these problems are not so noticeable, since they are diplomatically edited from one single manuscript. Sometimes, there are even two or more texts retrieved from different manuscripts of the same work. This is the case, for instance, of the different early copies of *Ancrene Riwle* found in *LAEME*.[12] This kind of corpus is also more convenient and suitable for electronic searches of lexical items. The spelling variation encountered in the corpus of ME texts makes both manual and electronic searches tricky, since the spelling possibilities for lexical items can sometimes be numerous and not always predictable. *LAEME* and *LAOS* are examples of corpora designed with a specific linguistic purpose. The texts included in them have been linguistically tagged, and thus one can perform the searches through a lexical element ('lexel') and/or a grammatical element ('grammel'). This 'lexel' is either the present-day counterpart for the medieval lexical item or, if the word is lacking or ambiguous, a form of its etymon. The searches carried out in these corpora are likely to be far more accurate because searching via tag identifiers should prevent the possibility of missing any occurrences, no matter how odd the spelling might be, or what grammatical form might occur in the text. Thus, for example, if we were looking for the ME lexical item DELVEN, we could perform a search of the form and/or the tag 'delve' and the result of the search would be something like: \$delve/vi_DELF \$/vi_0.[13] Thus, corpora

---

12   Extracts from all the early extant copies of this work have been tagged and are
      part of this corpus. See Laing/Lass (2008: ch. 3.1). The later copies of the
      work found in Cambridge, Magdalene College, Pepys 2498 (datable a. 1400),
      London, British Library, Royal 8.C.1 (datable a. 1500) and Oxford, Bodleian
      Library, Eng. poet. a.1 (datable c. 1390) are not included, since they are
      beyond the time-span covered by *LAEME*.

13   Example taken from the *LAEME* corpus from the Edinburgh, Royal College
      of Physician Manuscript for the *Northern Homily Collection*. Other examples
      for the variation in spelling and grammatical forms found in the same texts
      are:
      \$Yolian/vps23K2_THOL+ES \$/vps23K2_+ES. An explanation of the labels
      in the tags is offered in Laing/Lass (2008: ch. 4). In this example '\$' marks
      the beginning of a tag, 'Yolian' is the lexel, 'vps' stands for verb present, '2 =
      plural, 3 = third person, K2 = Old English Class 2.
      \$Yolian/viK2_THOL \$/viK2_0

with elements of lexico-grammatical tagging do, in fact, facilitate somewhat the study of the lexicon.[14]

An alternative method to fully tagged texts is offered by Manfred Markus' suggestions for *ICAMET*. Markus (2002) proposes to provide interlinear normalised lines of a given text. This normalisation would only be, according to him, a preliminary step to a later tagging of all the texts in the corpus. Having a parallel normalised version of ME texts would help to solve the problem of spelling variation. These two types of corpora, where the texts have been encoded for linguistic research, or at least provided with a normalised 'gloss', can be far more useful than those in which the texts are uncoded.

Another aspect that needs consideration is the selection of our sources in corpora. When allowing for all the available corpora as a whole, it could seem, in principle, that the sources used provide certain benefits since electronic corpora contain texts of diverse nature, of different length, multi-genre texts, texts of multiple origins, etc. Thus, there are specialised corpora devoted to literary texts (*LION* and *ETCC*), or focusing on one register of writing, for example including scientific material (*MEMT*) or more general ones including all sorts of texts (*HC, CMEPV, OTA*). Likewise, the sources can also be exclusively prose texts (*ICAMET*) or they may contain only early sources in ME (*LAEME*). Certainly, using all of them in the investigation of the lexical field ensures that the data used in the research would not be monolithic.

Nevertheless, there are also some problems relating to the use of these sources as presented in electronic corpora. One of them is that many texts in the existing corpora are not complete. This has un-questionably more negative implications for lexical research than for syntactic, phonetic or morphological research, since words do not occur in a given pattern throughout a work. Words occurring only in parts of a work that have not been included in the corpus would thus be missing from our study. The bigger the corpus the better, but still

---

$Yolian/vpt13K2_THOL+ED $/vpt13[L]K2_+ED
$Yolian/vpt13K2_THOL+ID $/vpt13[L]K2_+ID

14   Williamson (2000) discusses the value of this kind of corpora for phonetic and syntactic analysis of texts, but he does not mention the analysis of the lexicon.

there is no guarantee that because we have only an extract, we will not miss important occurrences, which we might pick up simply from browsing the glossary of an edition of the complete text.

Another problem arises because the geographical location para-meter is not always adequately represented in the texts of the corpus. The organisation of texts in corpora is generally done according to chronological parameters while spatial factors are not considered. This is the case of all corpora revised here, except for *LAEME* and *LAOS* which follow both. Even if we take all the existing corpora including ME as a whole for our purposes, certain dialect areas are better represented than others and this provokes a lack of balance in the sources. It is obvious that having an equivalent number of texts for the different dialect areas would not represent reality either, since some areas are much better documented than others. This problem is inherent in the investigation of the field, since we are dependent on the fortuitous survival of certain texts. Nevertheless, even for carrying out a purely quantitative analysis of the data extracted from corpora, it would be necessary to have more or less proportionally geo-graphically-organised data. The spatial localisation of the texts in corpora is a matter of fundamental importance for the research of the dialectal lexicon,[15] but the structure of most of the ones analysed here does not allow for an adequate result.

2.2. Research methodology

The second type of limitation mentioned above has to do more with our own methodology than with the intrinsic value of corpora themselves. The methodology we have devised for the study of ME dialectal lexicon has benefited from electronic texts only tangentially, given that using certain corpora is advantageous only as a complemen-tary tool. The main hindrance is that our approach is not greatly facilitated by corpus-based analysis.[16] This is so, partially, because of the nature of dialectal lexicon itself. Many of the words considered

---

15   On this issue see also van Reenen/Rem/Wattel (this volume).
16   General works on Corpus Linguistics are available in Aarts/Meijs (1990),
      Kennedy (1998), Biber/Conrad/Reppen (1998) or Meyer (2002).

dialectal (i.e. to have local associations) have a low frequency of occurrence. They appear only sporadically in ME texts, since many of them have a restricted semantic usage. Only a few local lexical discriminants, such as the adjective SERE or the adverb AY, or some function words, as for example TIL (as an equivalent to TO, infinitive marker or preposition) have a high frequency of occurrence within the corpus of localised ME texts.[17] When the words have a low frequency of occurrence, the chances of finding them in the texts included in corpora are restricted, and the problem increases if the texts included are not complete, as we have mentioned before. The consequence is, then, that the texts included in corpora may not be at all representative of the totality.

Furthermore, since we set out from the assumption that a given word occurring in a particular copy of a work could be maintained as such, omitted, or substituted by either a lexical equivalent or a paraphrase in other copies of the same work, we would need to have all the existing copies of a work in the corpus in order to examine the scribes' preferences for such a lexical notion. Our methodology seeks to examine only those sources where the lexical item we are concerned with might occur. Thus, the sources for our study must be selected carefully only among those in which there are reasons to believe that there is a potential occurrence of a given item, or if the item does not occur, we would seek for the possibility of finding a clear omission, or the occurrence of a lexical equivalent or paraphrase for that particular item. For this reason, the sources cannot be selected at random because we could get very poor and doubtful results. Moreover, if what we are looking for is the avoidance of a particular lexical item in a particular copy, the electronic texts are of little use. Electronic searches of dialectal lexical items can be done with more or less effort as we remarked before, but looking for lexical equivalents

---

17   For example, in Morris' edition of the *Prick of Conscience* based on the texts found in London, British Library, Cotton Galba E.9 and London, British Library Harley 4196, the item SERE has 133 occurrences and the item AY 304, while most of the other dialectal terms in the same copy have a much lower frequency, some of them occurring just once. With regard to the infinitive TIL there is a difference in the frequency which seems to be related to text-type, there being a contrast between the usage of local documentary texts and literary texts in northern English. See Williamson (2002: 270-271).

is far more complicated since the possibilities multiply as the scribes had different options, and our quest may not cover them all.

Lastly, as our main objective is the establishment of the geographical distribution of the lexical items, the quantification of the data would be relevant only in relation to spatial distribution. The evaluation of the percentage of usage of dialectal items, can be undertaken once we have determined the distribution of dialectal terms. Only then could a corpus-based analysis concerning the usage of a dialectal term or its lexical equivalents be carried out.

3. Linguistic atlases

The second group of external sources that the study of ME word geography cannot dispense with are linguistic atlases. Among them we are especially concerned with *LALME* and the recently published *LAEME* and *LAOS*. The dialectal localisation of the sources is indispensable in order to be able to establish the geographical distributions of words. Nevertheless, not all the extant manuscripts of medieval works are analysed in the existing atlases, and not all the extant manuscripts are localisable. The challenge with the sources is different for each atlas. Laing/Lass (2008: ch. 3.1) state that "in the case of Early Middle English, the contingent survival of text witnesses is very patchy both spatially and temporally, and in terms of length and of genre." The paucity of surviving material for the early period has the advantage of making the analysis of the whole corpus achievable, while the Late ME material is too big a corpus to be tackled entirely. Nevertheless, this scarcity of material for the early period is problematic when attempting to establish the distribution of a word. Unfortunately, "from before about 1350 there are very few sources for northern or North Midland English" (Laing/Lass 2008: ch. 1). Most sources for the study of Early ME have been localised in *LAEME* in two main areas: the South-West Midlands and the eastern part of the country. This means that the evidence for occurrence or avoidance of lexical items in the early period has to be treated differently from that for later periods. The lack of evidence of a given lexical item in certain areas does not necessarily mean anything but that there are not extant sources for those areas.

The fact that *LAEME* is a corpus as well as an atlas offers us possibilities which are simply not available in *LALME*. As the data are not restricted to those gathered by means of a questionnaire, we can obtain the distribution of any lexical item in the corpus just by clicking some boxes.[18] Likewise, we can make concordances or we can search the tagged texts where the lexical item we are searching for occurs. The distribution maps of lexical items, based on the *LAEME* localisations of the manuscripts where they occur, are essential to our approach, not so much for giving a whole picture of the status of a lexical item in Early ME, which is an impossible task, as for providing the necessary chronological perspective to understand a possible semantic and distributional evolution of a word into the Late ME period. Some dialectal words are not geographically-restricted terms all the way through their histories. The time factor is essential for assessing the nature of a lexical item. Certain items that could have been common in the OE word-stock did eventually decay in usage in several parts of the country, and by the end of the fifteenth century they were obsolete in certain areas, and thus, became dialectal terms in places where their use was still common. For other expressions that were introduced in the English language through contact with either

---

18   So, for example, the occurrences of the item MISTER can be listed by counties and we get the following: for the form MEOSTER: SAL 272 1000; WOR 3; for MEOSTERS: SAL 272; for MEOSTer: HRF 273; for MESTERE: ESX 160; for MESTERES: KNT 291; WOR 245; for MESTER: BRK 286; CHS 118; DUR 188; ESX 160; GLO 158; HRF 1100; NFK 155 285; SAL 260; WOR 245 276; YNR 298; and for MESTer BRK 286; CHS 118; HRF 273; [-] 119 120; for MESTerES: HRF 273; for MESTerRE: HRF 246; for MESTerS: CHS 118; for MISTER: YNR 298; YWR 295; for MISTERE: YCT 296; and for MISTer: YCT 296; YER 297; YNR 298; YWR 295. The numbers are the index numbers of the corpus texts linked to information about the manuscripts where they occur, so for instance, 272 is the version in Cambridge, Corpus Christi College 402 of *Ancrene Riwle*. Besides, one gets details about the dating, script, localisation including grid reference, folios tagged, total number of words transcribed and total number of tagged words, and cross references for the other manuscripts where the same work is preserved. Likewise, there is a link to the text dictionary and to the tagged text itself.

French or Old Norse, it is also important to ascertain whether they were attested in particular areas at different times during the ME period.

Our main objective is, nevertheless, to accomplish the mapping of the distributions of lexical items in the period of ME for which a large number of sources is available. This means that we are mainly concerned in this respect with the material which was analysed for *LALME*. As stated before, the existing data for Late ME is so extensive that dealing with the entire corpus in any field of study would be unfeasible. In our approach to ME word geography we need to rely on the localisations of the manuscripts which comprise the *LALME* sources. Then, our first step in our search is to examine only those items which potentially occur in localised sources. However, on our way we encounter works preserved in multiple copies, which can be of invaluable help for our purposes, whose localisations have not been carried out in *LALME*. A clear example are the 31 extant manuscripts of the so-called 'Defective Version' of *Mandeville's Travels*, a prose work of potentially great interest for the study of lexis. Only 13 of these have been localised. Some of the copies were presumably analysed by the *LALME* authors and were probably disregarded as sources for the atlas after unfruitful attempts to fit them in the light of the features they show. Others were simply not considered at all. Thus, a second step in the process of choosing what sources to use is, to try to fit, following *LALME*, some of the texts we consider crucial for a better result in the investigation, in order to accurately map the distribution of the items.[19]

Once we have been able to establish the occurrences and avoidances of a given lexical item, we have to interpret its lack of attestation in any particular dialect area. In the late medieval period this has to be read in a different way from the interpretation made for the earlier period. In a scenario where there are records from almost everywhere in the country, not having any records for any particular item in certain very well-documented areas, with texts pertaining to different genres, has to be understood as very likely evidence for

---

19   Pursuing this line, we have produced LPs and we have fitted all the extant
      copies of the *Lay Folks' Catechism* which were not analysed in *LALME*. See
      Carrillo-Linares/Garrido-Anes (2007).

avoidance of that lexical item in that area. Obviously, the lack of attestation cannot always be considered equally in all the places because there are regions for which there are not so many existing records, and the few that have survived may not contain the term we are investigating because their subject matter may be of a completely different nature.

However, even if our criteria for mapping have to be entirely based on *LALME* evidence, we should say that localisations of texts (either in *LALME* or those done according to its criteria) cannot really be used as straightforwardly as might be thought at first sight. The occurrence of the items in certain texts is determined by multiple reasons and not all of them have to be geographical. Apart from relicts taken over from the original or from previous copies which may have been written in different dialects, there are other issues that have to do with textual family relationships. Following is an example of the non-straightforward character of the data obtained, and of the need for careful consideration of any information before it is plotted on a map.

When searching for dialectally-conditioned items in *Cursor Mundi* we analysed among others ALKIN, and we found replacements for this word in five of its manuscripts: London, British Library, Add. 36983 (olim Bedford), localised in Bedfordshire; Oxford, Bodleian Library, Fairfax 14, from Lancashire; Cambridge, Trinity College, R.3.8 (383), and London, College of Arms, 57, both from Staffordshire; and Oxford, Bodleian Library, Laud Misc. 416, a manuscript not localised in *LALME*. An approximate localisation in Staffordshire, based on some folios at the beginning of the manuscript, has been carried out following the *LALME* methodology (see Carrillo-Linares 2005-2006: 154-155). However, from these five exemplars, only one could eventually be taken into account when mapping the item, given that the textual histories of the Bedford, Trinity, Laud, and College of Arms manuscripts, and the consistency in the altered vocabulary point to the fact that the replacements were not made by their scribes, but by the scribe of a previous copy from which the four of them derive – see Carrillo-Linares (2005-2006: 155-156).

Lastly within this section, we need to mention the contribution of *LAOS* as a very useful complementary tool for the northern material. Given that the time-span covered by the first phase of *LAOS* is 1380-1500, we can benefit from its sources and use them, as they are part of the dialect continuum for Late Northern ME, since we cannot obviate the relationship between the languages of Scotland and England during a period when they were less distinct from each other than now. Many of the northern dialectal words in ME have had continuity in the Scottish dialects, and some of these terms are only in use in this part of the country, so assessing their occurrences and distribution in Older Scots is part of the necessary process to gain the farthest-reaching picture that we are capable of with the sources available.

LAOS has the same structure as *LAEME* and tasks can be performed in the same way.[20] The main difference between the two lies in the sources used for either corpus. For *LAOS* most of them are official documents and they are considerably shorter than the tagged texts in *LAEME*. The range of vocabulary found in this sort of text is more limited (Williamson 2002: 254-255). However, some more texts of the literary type, which constitute a sub-corpus for the atlas, are going to be added within the next two or three years, and this will undoubtedly increase the items in the lexicon and, with this, our chances of gaining a bigger picture of the distribution of certain lexical items in the fifteenth century. Some distribution maps are also available and this feature is in development.

---

20   The same search performed before for the item MISTER in *LAEME* gives in the *LAOS* corpus this result: for the form MISTER: AYR 40; MLO 140; PBL 917; PTH 160; for MISTERe: MLO 271; for MISTer: AGS 350; FIF 255 1856; PTH 117; for MYSTARe: WLO 61; for MYSTER: BD 364; XLC 779; for MYSTERe: MLO 263; for MYSTer: ABD 449; AGS 386; BWK 86; DMF 473; ELO 71 855; FIF 211 256 1839; PBL 48; PTH 366; ROX 145; MYSTerIS: WLO 474. Here, as well, the numbers are linked to the description of the sources, so for example number 40 is Edinburgh University Library, Laing Charters 1264, box 34, a document dated on Dec 15 1426 and sealed at Ayr. XLC stands for 'unlocalised'; the rest of the abbreviations correspond in this example to counties where these sources are localised.

4. Dictionaries

Alongside the electronic corpora and linguistic atlases mentioned above, there are several dictionaries which also constitute important external sources for the study of ME word geography. The *MED* is certainly an indispensable tool. In fact, it is probably the most useful one in the preliminary stages of the quest for actual evidence on which to base the dialectal study of a word. The electronic dictionary has basically the same contents as the printed one. However, this new format has turned the *MED* into an enormous database which, at just one click of the mouse, provides easier access to the very wide range of valuable sources on which the dictionary is based. Among these, we find works belonging to a representative variety of genres, together with a wide range of manuscripts dating from the twelfth to the sixteenth century.

The e-version of the *MED* offers multiple options for retrieving the information more quickly and effectively for our purposes. The interesting fact is that we can use it to get a good number of potential occurrences of any lexical item in the parallel manuscripts of all the ME works that this dictionary has used as sources. However, dealing with the *MED* when studying ME word geography, requires the performance of several other tasks in addition to the simple search for words and for the parallel manuscripts of the works in question. The reason is that, as will be shown, there is no automatic correlation between the raw data that we obtain from our *MED* search and the actual occurrences of words in the manuscripts of a given work. Nor can straightforward assumptions be made with regards to the dialectal value of a word in a localised manuscript, as we have suggested before.

As already pointed out, apart from displaying the meanings of any lexical item that we might want to search, the *MED* allows us to get a sample of quotations from several works where the word occurs with the meaning that we are concerned with. By doing this, we can see the word in its context, appearing for certain in, at least, one of the manuscripts of each of the different works for which the *MED* has yielded results. In the electronic *MED*, the manuscript on which the edition has been based or from which the quotation has been taken appears, in brackets, before the quotation and the page or line number where the word can be found in the chosen edition. The manuscript library reference is, in fact, a hyperlink that leads us to a useful list of manuscripts of the same work together with their *LALME* references and other dialect information, if available. The editions used as general sources for the dictionary, and the known dates for each of the manuscripts, and for the works themselves, are also provided by the *MED* below the expanded quotations.

Our *MED* searches of the lexical items in which we are interested yielded such a large amount of information, that it became essential to create an online database to organise and classify it. In our database, which is hosted by the University of Huelva server, we assign a table to each of the works of which one or more manuscripts do contain – or may contain – any of the dialectal items in question. We have over 80 tables and around 50,000 records right now, but the figures increase as our work progresses. All the potential occurrences of an item are initially entered in these tables, together with references to the works and their editions, to the manuscripts, and to their dates and dialects, when known.

At this point, it is worth noting that not all the extant manuscripts of the works obtained in our search can be assumed to contain either the word we are interested in or a lexical variant of it. As already known, not all the manuscripts of a work present exactly the same text, due either to textual variations or to the physical condition of the manuscripts. Thus, the exemplars may offer a text subject to different degrees of reworking, and they may have been preserved incomplete or damaged. This means that in the parallel manuscripts of a given work, the words in question need to be considered to be potential occurrences only, until we have personally checked the presence, absence or avoidance of each of our database records against every single manuscript of every single work.

This is not an easy task to perform. The edition references given in the *MED* preceding every quotation can certainly help us find the potential place for an occurrence of a word in a manuscript, but this is the case only to a certain extent. This is because these edition references can most often give us only an approximate idea of where-abouts in the manuscript the word should be, because line and page numbers in editions do not normally coincide with the actual manu-script folios or lines. Occurrences are easier to find in verse texts because line beginnings and endings are usually unaltered. However, the task becomes much more difficult and time-consuming when we try to spot a word in a manuscript with a prose text whose line beginnings and endings are not maintained in the editions.

The fact that we can get occurrences of a word in manuscripts precisely localised in *LALME* constitutes the main advantage of this dictionary as a point of departure for a more manageable and fruitful study of ME word geography. We should note, however, that the list of manuscripts provided by the *MED* is sometimes incomplete. Therefore, if we are aware that more manuscripts of the work have been preserved, the ones missing there will need, then, to be sought and added. The occurrence of the items in the manuscripts is determined by multiple reasons, and not all of them have to be geographical. Thus, a further step in this kind of study consists in having to distinguish the useful data from the non-useful ones. This requires making thoughtful judgments about the dialectal or non-dialectal value of the occurrences or avoidances, and taking into consideration several aspects that may have to do, among other reasons, with the manuscript textual history and with the kind of text in which the occurrence or avoidance is found.

Let us illustrate this point with the item DELVEN in *Earth upon Earth*. The *MED* supplies seventeen manuscripts for the work where the word could potentially occur.[21] Nevertheless, once the search through the manuscripts and editions was done, occurrences could only be registered for the case of the Rawlinson manuscript, given that the fragment where the word was supposed to appear was

---

21   Cambridge, Trinity College, B.15.39 (181); Lincoln, Cathedral Library, 91; Cambridge, St. John's College, E.24 (127); olim W. Yates, Manchester, sold 1893; Oxford, Bodleian Library, Laud Misc. 23; Inscription on wall at Chapel of the Trinity, Stratford-on-Avon; London, British Library, Cotton Titus A.26; London, British Library, Harley 4486; Oxford, Bodleian Library, Rawlinson C.307; Philadelphia, University of Pennsylvania Lat.33; Cambridge, University Library, Ii.4.9; London, British Library, Harley 1671; London, Lambeth Palace Library, 853; Aberystwyth, National Library of Wales, Brogyntyn 2.1; Cambridge, Trinity College, R.3.21 (601); London, British Library, Egerton 1995; Oxford, Bodleian Library, Selden Supra 53.

absent in the rest of the exemplars that are available for consultation. Thus, out of seventeen potential records for a word, we were finally left with only one actual occurrence to use in our maps.

Needless to say, the *Oxford English Dictionary*, which can also be accessed online, is another essential external source of reference. The *OED* does not only supply etymologies and make frequent allusions to the dialectal character of a word in Present-Day English, but it also traces back in time the usage and meanings of English words, for which quotations from numerous sources are provided as well. All this is useful inasmuch as it allows us to see lexical items in their broader historical context, and to widen, thus, the scope of our perspective. When dealing with a ME lexical item – e.g. the verb GRETEN – our primary sources reveal that medieval scribes from certain areas often translated this word into 'cry' or 'weep'. The study of the works and manuscripts where the word is retained or avoided, points to certain geographical restrictions in its ME usage. In order to place the results of our research within a larger temporal framework, more information about further and later developments of the history of the word can be checked against the *OED*, which, in this particular case, confirms its current dialect character, and confines its present-day use to Scots and the northern dialects of English. Any information about geographically-constrained usages of words in later periods is always useful for comparison and to keep track of both possible continuities of usage across time and space and any broadening or narrowing trajectory.

Joseph Wright's *English Dialect Dictionary* should also be mentioned for similar reasons, as it is a thorough account of 70,000 dialectal words in the eighteenth and nineteenth centuries.[22] It provides far more accurate references of the use of lexical items by listing the areas or counties where they have been recorded. Continuing with the example above, eighteenth- and nineteenth-century occurrences of GRETEN with the dialectal meaning 'to cry, to weep, to lament' are also of quite a northerly nature, as, according to

---

22   A project to digitise the *EDD* is currently being undertaken by the Innsbruck University Library. At the moment, scanned parts of the work made by the University of Toronto Library can be accessed online. See Markus/Heuberger (2007).

the *EDD*, they are restricted to Scotland, Ireland, Northumberland, Durham, Cumbria, Westmoreland, Yorkshire, Lancashire and Derbyshire.

As a reference to check the possible continuity of northern terms across time and space, we also need to consult *A Dictionary of the Older Scottish Tongue* (1931-2002), a twelve-volume work that covers the Scots language from the twelfth century to 1700. Alongside quotations from Scottish works, this dictionary also alludes to northern ME, thus complementing the sources of the *MED*. Since 2004 it is possible to search *DOST* electronically within the *Dictionary of the Scots Language*. All these dictionaries are indispensable resources that add to the historical framework of our study of ME words. Other dictionaries of Anglo-Norman, Old English, Old Norse and Latin may eventually be needed as well as further complementary tools that can add to the information gathered from the sources already mentioned.[23]

5. Concluding remarks

After this account of corpora, atlases, dictionaries and other useful electronic tools, we can conclude by emphasising the fact that until a few decades ago, the study of ME word geography was certainly possible, but it was far slower, and much more complicated and frustrating than it is today. Without the help of the (technological) resources that are available now, even small incursions into this huge field appeared condemned to be very limited, isolated, partial, and only illustrative; and trying to get a broader picture of the distribution of medieval English lexicon seemed too burdensome a task, something very difficult to achieve within a reasonable period of time.

---

23   *The Anglo-Norman Dictionary* (*AND*) is available online at <www.anglo-norman.net/>. *The Thesaurus of Old English* can be consulted at <libra.englang.arts.gla.ac.uk/oethesaurus/>, and *The Dictionary of Old English* (*DOE*) (A to F) is available on CD-ROM.

In this study we have highlighted the important contribution that external sources certainly make to the research of ME word geography. We consider that they are all necessary to be able to carry out any sort of profitable work in this line. All the sources mentioned above must be used before trying to come to any conclusive and reliable results. Nevertheless, the information extracted from them has to be very carefully scrutinised and processed, and it cannot be used without going through a slow and thoughtful process of selection and discrimination that involves working side by side with the actual manuscript sources. The need to use all these technological tools is unquestionable, as they do make the work much easier. However, we cannot expect them to do the work for us.

References

Primary sources

DOE = Cameron, Angus / Crandell Amos, Asheley / diPaolo Healey, Antoinette 2003. *Dictionary of Old English. A-F on CD-ROM.* Toronto: Pontifical Institute of Mediaeval Studies.

DOST = Craigie, William A. / Aitken, Adam Jack *et al.* 1931-2002. *Dictionary of the Older Scottish Tongue.* Chicago: University of Chicago Press; Aberdeen: Aberdeen University Press; Oxford: Oxford University Press.

Eccles, Mark 1969. *The Macro Plays.* London: Oxford University Press.

EDD = Wright, Joseph 1898-1905. *The English Dialect Dictionary.* London: Oxford University Press.

Hofland, Knut / Lindebjerg, Anne / Thunestvedt, Jorg 1999. *ICAME Collection of English Language Corpora.* Bergen: The HIT Centre, University of Bergen.

LAEME = Laing, Margaret / Lass, Roger 2008. *A Linguistic Atlas of Early Middle English, 1150-1325.* At <www.lel.ed.ac.uk/ihd/ laeme1/laeme1.html>. Edinburgh: The University of Edinburgh.

LALME = McIntosh, Angus / Samuels, Michael / Benskin, Michael [with the assistance of Margaret Laing and Keith Williamson] 1986. *A Linguistic Atlas of Late Mediaeval English*. Aberdeen: Aberdeen University Press.

LAOS = Williamson, Keith 2008. A Linguistic Atlas of Older Scots. Phase 1: 1380-1500. At <www.lel.ed.ac.uk/ihd/laos1/laos1.html>. Edinburgh: The University of Edinburgh.

Latham, Ronald Edward / Howlett, David R. 1975. *Dictionary of Medieval Latin from British Sources*. Oxford: Oxford University Press for the British Academy.

LION =*Literature online* at <http://lion.chadwyck.co.uk>.

McSparran, Frances (ed.) 2002-. *Middle English Compendium*. At <quod.lib.umich.edu/m/mec>

MED = Kurath, Hans *et al.* 1952-2001. *Middle English Dictionary*. Ann Arbor: University of Michigan Press.

Morris, R. 1863. *The Pricke of Conscience*. Berlin: A. Asher & Co.

OED = Murray, James A. H. *et al.* 1884-1933. *The Oxford English Dictionary*. Supplement, 1972-1986, 4 vols.; ed. Robert W. Burchfield. [2]1989; ed. John A. Simpson, Edmund S. C. Weiner and Michael Proffitt. Oxford: Clarendon Press. *OED online*, March 2000-, ed. John A. Simpson, <www.oed.com>.

OTA = *The Oxford Texts Archive*. <ota.ahds.ac.uk>.

Taavitsainen, Irma / Pahta, Päivi / Mäkinen, Martti 2005. *Middle English Medical Texts*. Amsterdam: Benjamins.

Secondary sources

Aarts, Jan / Meijs, Willem (eds) 1990. *Theory and Practice in Corpus Linguistics*. Amsterdam: Rodopi.

Biber, Douglas / Conrad, Susan / Reppen, Randi 1998. *Corpus Linguistics: Investigating Language Structure and Use*. Cambridge: Cambridge University Press.

Carrillo-Linares, María José 2005-2006. Lexical Dialectal Items in *Cursor Mundi*: Contexts of Occurrence and Geographical Distribution. *Selim Journal* 13, 151-178.

Carrillo-Linares, María José / Garrido-Anes, Edurne 2007. Middle English Lexical Distributions: Two Instances from the *Lay*

Folks' Catechism. In Mazzon, Gabriella (ed.), *Studies in Middle English Forms and Meanings.* Frankfurt a.M.: Peter Lang, 85-100.

Carrillo-Linares, María José / Garrido-Anes, Edurne 2008. Middle English Word Geography: Methodology and Applications Illustrated. In Dossena, Marina / Dury, Richard / Gotti, Maurizio (eds), *English Historical Linguistics 2006. Volume III: Geohistorical Variation in English.* Amsterdam: Benjamins, 67-91.

Lass, Roger 2004. Ut Custodiant Litteras: Editions, Corpora and Witnesshood. In Dossena, Marina / Lass, Roger (eds) *Methods and Data in English Historical Dialectology.* Bern: Peter Lang, 21-48.

Kennedy, Graeme 1998. *An Introduction to Corpus Linguistics.* London and New York: Longman.

Markus, Manfred 2002. The Innsbruck Prose Corpus: Its Concept and Usability in Middle English Lexicology. In Díaz Vera, Javier (ed.) *A Changing World of Words: Studies in English Historical Lexicography, Lexicology and Semantics.* Amsterdam: Rodopi, 464-483.

Markus, Manfred / Heuberger, Reinhard 2007. The Architecture of Joseph Wright's *English Dialect Dictionary:* Preparing the Computerised Version. *International Journal of Lexicography* 20/4, 355-368.

Meurman-Solin, Anneli 2001. Structured Text Corpora in the Study of Language Variation and Change. *Literary and Linguistic Computing* 16, 5-27.

Meyer, Charles F. 2002. *English Corpus Linguistics: An Introduction.* Cambridge: Cambridge University Press.

Williamson, Keith 2000. Lexico-grammatical Tags and the Phonetic and Syntactic Analysis of Medieval Texts. In Mair, Christian / Hundt, Marianne (eds) *Corpus Linguistics and Linguistic Theory: Papers from the Twentieth International Conference on English Language Research on Computerized Corpora.* Amsterdam: Rodopi, 385-395.

Williamson, Keith 2002. The Dialectology of 'English' North of the Humber, c. 1380-1500. In Fanego, Teresa / Mendez Naya, Belén / Seoane, Elena (eds) *Sounds, Words, Texts and Change.* Amsterdam: Benjamins, 253-286.

JULIA FERNÁNDEZ CUESTA / Mª NIEVES RODRÍGUEZ LEDESMA

The Northern Echo:
Continuities in Contemporary Northern English[1]

1. Introduction

Since we started our project on the history of Northern English, we have been mainly working on the OE and ME periods. Some of the results of our research have been presented at various conferences and subsequently published (see Fernández Cuesta 2004 and Fernández Cuesta/Rodríguez Ledesma 2004, 2007 and 2008). These studies demonstrated that a certain continuity can be established between Old Northumbrian and Northern ME, and that some of the most distinctive phonological and morphological features of the 'traditional' North are still attested in EModE. In the last stage of our project our aim is to determine the extent to which these features are still found in contemporary Northern English. To be able to do this, it is necessary to establish a connection between the data that we have from the past and that obtained from modern studies (*The Survey of English Dialects*, *The Computer Developed Atlas of England*, *The Linguistic Atlas of England*, and *The Newcastle Electronic Corpus of Tyneside English* – henceforth *SED*, *CLAE*, *LAE*, and *NECTE*, respectively). The present study focuses on modern English from the evidence provided by the *SED*, the most comprehensive modern dialectal survey of England,[2] although reference will also be made to other

---

1   We would like to express our gratitude to Joan Beal for her invitation to the University of Sheffield and the Spanish Ministry of Education for the grant which financed the stay at the University. We would also like to thank Derek Britton, Clive Upton and Katie Wales for comments and suggestions on a draft version of this paper.

2   Other surveys for individual areas of northern England have been compiled,

general works (Wright 1905, Luick 1914-40), monographs of individual localities (see, among others, Orton 1933, Tidholm 1979, Petyt 1985 and Shorrocks 1999) and contemporary corpora of Northern English (*NECTE*).[3]

We are aware of the risk involved in comparing evidence from different sources: so far these have consisted exclusively of written material (or studies such as *LALME*, which are based on texts), whereas for Modern English our main sources are surveys and atlases based on spoken language such as the *SED*. The *SED* offers real dialect material, although its scope is limited to the language of rural areas, where its editors Orton and Dieth assumed genuine dialect to have been better preserved. This is the reason why the informants were mainly elderly men who had had little contact with the outside world (NORMs: Non-mobile Older Rural Males). Although the *SED* is a modern survey, its authors had been educated in a philological tradition that focused on the historical development of languages, and they were interested in tracing dialect features back to ME and OE. One of the scholars associated with the project, John Widdowson, claims that an important aspect of the study of contemporary dialect is that "[it] provides fascinating insights into the history of the English language. Grammatical features from ME dialects, and even some from the OE period, have been remarkably preserved in regional speech, and many are still in use today" (2005: 12).

However, what could be regarded as a flaw from the perspective of modern sociolinguistics (the *SED* has been considered linguistic archaeology), is an asset for our purpose, since part of our study on the history of Northern English is to investigate the resilience of dialect features in contemporary varieties. On the other hand, knowledge of older stages of the language is necessary for a correct interpretation of contemporary evidence. As Upton (1997: 217) rightly argues when explaining the form *'en* for *him*:

> This could variously be taken to be a quite distinct form or, more easily, as simply the rapid articulation of *him* itself, but it is in fact a modern survival of

---

though none so far with as wide a scope as the *SED*.

3   We have also started the analysis of dialect literature from the seventeenth century onwards, including various genres: poetry, novels, plays, diaries, newspapers and broadsheets.

> the OE masculine object pronoun *hine*, and deserves to be regarded as such. Again what we are confronted with is an essentially grammatical variation, with different parts of the same pronoun system giving us both *him* and *'en*: the significance of this variation is diminished if we insist on seeing it at a simple word level.

With regard to the fact that the *SED* only records the speech of a very limited group of people, the same applies to the evidence that we have from the past. As Hogg states, "the standard language is presented to us by writers who are overwhelmingly male, upper class, literate and middle-aged" (2006: 11). The only thing that we can do in the case of both old texts and modern surveys, is to be aware of the limitations that the nature of the evidence imposes on our study and try to make the best of bad or incomplete data.

2. Methodology

For the present paper we have focused on the resilience of Northern ME features in modern English mainly from the evidence found in the *SED*. The features that we have studied are the following:

1. V+ /mb, nd, ng/ in LANG/LONG
2. Reflex of OE /a:/
3. Reflex of ME /o:/
4. Plosive vs affricate in KIRK/CHURCH, SIC/SUCH, etc.
5. /s/ vs /ʃ/ in SHALL, SHOULD
6. Demonstratives
7. Personal pronouns
8. Present indicative inflections
9. Present participle
10. Zero genitive

We have taken into consideration both the basic and the incidental material, since in some cases, e.g. the Northern Subject Rule or the uninflected genitive, the relevant information cannot be obtained from

                           Julia Fernández Cuesta / Mª Nieves Rodríguez Ledesma

the answers to the questionnaire. All the answers have been scanned, since they may contain items illustrating the features that we are studying. The heading is useful because it shows us what item and what kind of information the authors of the *SED* were trying to elicit. However, questions which did not appear to be useful for our purpose from the questionnaire heading, happened to contain answers which offer valuable information about the selected features. For example, in the case of ONE, besides the main entries (VII.1.1; IX.8.8), which were inserted for their phonological importance, additional information can also be obtained from VII.8.18 (WHICH ONE), inserted for its morphological relevance, and VII.1.12 (TWENTY-ONE), included for its syntactic importance. Although ONE does not appear in the heading of VI.2.8 (PULL EACH OTHER'S), it is recorded as a frequent answer (*one another*) and, therefore, this entry has also been considered.

Another example which shows the need to examine all the material carefully is illustrated by the 3sg. personal pronoun SHE. In order to get a complete picture of the distribution of the different variants recorded (*she, shoo, hoo*), four different entries have to be considered (cf. Appendix 1.2.), the reason being that there are cases in which two different answers are given for the same locality: for Y 22, for example, the form recorded in VIII.9.5 is *shoo* [ʃuː], whereas in IX.7.3 we find *she* [ʃiː]. In the same way, for Y 32 the form recorded in VIII.9.5 is [ʃɪ], but we find *shoo* [ʃuː] in IX.7.3.

One of the problems that we have encountered when interpreting the phonological evidence of the *SED* is the wide range of phonetic variants that are recorded for the different words. Although Brilioth (1913) and Orton (1933), among others, provide information on the development of the Northern English vowel system, it is still difficult to decide what variants should be regarded as reflexes of Northern ME, and which are the result of influence from Received Standard English. For instance, for the vowel of words such as *boot, foot, roof* (from ME /oː/) the *SED* records a wide range of variants [ʊ, uː, ui, ʊə, öu, ʏ, iʏ, ɪə, jʏ, jø, iu, iuː]. Variants such as [iʏ, ɪə, jʏ, jø, iu, iuː] are regarded as northern, whereas [ʊ, uː, ui, ʊə] have been considered as influenced by Received Standard English. If we take into account traditional isoglosses, such as the Humber-Ribble line, we can see that northern variants are generally situated to the North of this isogloss. However, reflexes such as [ʏ] which are found in Lanca-shire (especially 12 & 13), pose a problem, since the fronted vowel seems to be too far to the south to be a northern development. It would be more reasonable to suppose that this is an independent develop-ment, taking into account that there are no other 'traditional' northern features in these localities, and that this vowel is also found in areas such as West Country (Lass 1987: 252). What is more, other fronted vowels such as [ʉ:] and [y:] are "common throughout England and the Southern United States, and the norm in South Africa, New Zealand and Scotland; but none of these frontings can be shown to be historically connected" (Lass 1997: 174).

To complicate the matter further, this wide range of phonetic variation may be due to the fact that in the present-day dialect two possible phonemic systems exist side by side: one related to Received Standard, and one representative of the traditional local speech (Widdowson 1997: 135). According to Widdowson, choice is not always conditioned by the social context: the speakers may adjust their pronunciation according to circumstances, that is, whether they are speaking formally to someone they regard as superior, or informally to their family and friends.

With regard to syntax, Beal (2004a: 115) warns that the information on geographical distribution of morphosyntactic features "is obtained from questionnaire responses rather than actual utterances, and as such may reflect the speaker's passive knowledge of those features rather than actual usage". This may be true for the basic material, but is not so clear for the incidental material, which consists of extracts from the informants' conversation and so does reflect actual usage.[4]

---

4   However, we should remember that in interviews it is difficult to avoid a
     certain degree of formality.

3. Phonology

3.1. V+ /mb, nd, ng/ in LANG/LONG

One of the features which is characteristic of Northern ME is that, contrary to the other varieties of English, /a/ is not rounded to /o/ when followed by a consonantal cluster beginning with a nasal /mb, nd, ng/. As can be seen in Figure 1 (Fernández Cuesta/Rodríguez Ledesma 2008), from the evidence found in *LALME*, the distribution varies depending on the consonantal cluster following the vowel.[5]

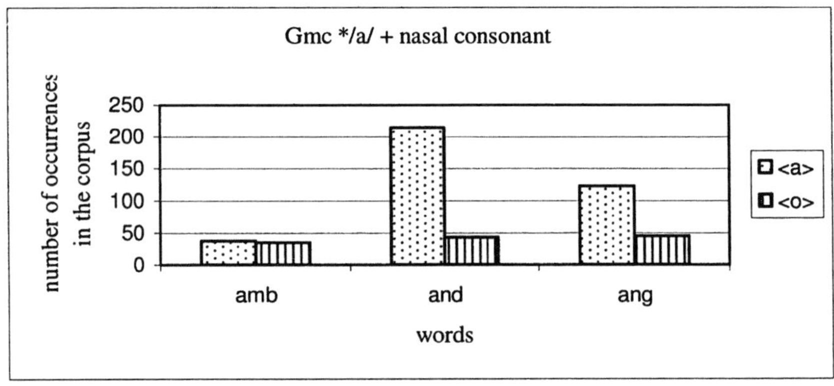

Figure 1. Gmc */a/ + nasal consonant in LME (*LALME* LPs).

The *SED* documents the resilience of this feature in mid-twentieth century Northern English in a range of phonetic contexts. In the case of [V + mb], the only word recorded is *comb*, for which there is a wide range of phonetic variation: [kjəm], [kjɛm], [kiäm], [kiam], [kɔm], [kɔːm], [kɒm], [kɒːm], [køm], [køəm], etc. As regards its distribution, the northern forms are recorded in Nb, Du and in a few localities in Y[6] (in some cases they are said to be old-fashioned or

---

5   We are very grateful to the *LALME* copyright holders for their permission to use the data.

6   Abbreviations are listed in Appendix 1.1.

rare). Standard or standard influenced forms are universal in We and La, and general in Cu and Y.

The *SED* records only two words in which the phonetic context is [V + nd]: *hand* and *land*. For HAND [a] is practically universal, but [ɒ] is found in some localities in La (4, 7, 12, 13).[7] LAND is only found in compounds (*land-horse*), and in these cases northern [a, æ] are universal in all counties. However, these data do not throw much light on the resilience of this feature, because what originally was the northern form of these two words has become the standard one.

The phonetic context which is most widely illustrated in the Survey is [V + ng]. The words recorded are: *among, long, throng, tongs* and *wrong*. In general it can be said that the northern vowel has a wide distribution: it is general in Nb, Cu, Du and We; it is recorded in North La (1-3), and in Y especially in the North and East. Although this is the general pattern, the distribution varies depending on the word. The northern form is more widely attested in the case of WRONG,[8] followed by AMONG,[9] THRONG,[10] TONGS[11] and LONG.[12]

---

7   In some of these localities, [a] is also found.

8   For WRONG the northern forms are universal in Nb, Cu, Du and We. In La they are found in the North (1-3), but also in other localities further south (6, 7 and 10). In Y they are general, except for five localities in the South-West (14, 17, 23, 27, 34).

9   For AMONG northern forms are universal in Nb, Cu, Du and We. In La they are found in the North (1-3) and in 9. In Y *amang* is dominant, but in the area south of the Humber the number of localities where standard influenced forms are recorded is much higher than elsewhere (14, 17, 18, 22-23, 27, 32-34). In some localities (4, 10, 18, 20, 25) both forms are documented.

10   As in the case of AMONG, for THRONG the northern forms are universal in Nb, Cu, Du and We. In La they are found only in the North (1-3) and in 9. In Y northern forms are general except for the area south of the river Humber (17, 23, 26, 29, 31-34).

11   In the case of TONGS the *SED* records more phonetic variants than for the previous items: northern reflexes such as [ïe, ɪe, jɛ, i, ɛ, a] and standard influenced vowels such as [ʊ, ɔ, ɒ, œ]. The distribution seems to be similar to the previous words, although besides being recorded in La and Y, standard reflexes are also found in Du (1, 4, 5) and Nb (8).

12   For LONG northern forms are dominant in Nb, Cu, Du, We, North La (1-3) and North Y. Compared to the previous items, standard influenced forms are more widely distributed in La and Y.

From the above data we can conclude that /a/ in this context has been maintained quite stable: it remains in the whole of Nb, Cu, Du and We, North La and most of Y. The main difference is that, besides being dominant in La, as was the case in ME (*LALME*), /o/ has also spread to South Yorkshire (cf Maps 1 and 2 in Appendix 2).

3.2. Reflex of OE /a:/

One of the most characteristic features of northern dialects is that OE /a:/ is not rounded to /ɔ:/ in ME. Analysis of our ME corpus reveals that, although <a> is clearly dominant, there are also instances of <o>, and that this feature seems to be lexically conditioned. From the data given in *LALME*, <a> spellings are dominant for KNOW, SOUL and OWN in all northern counties. Next come HOLY and OLD, and finally, TWO, BOTH and ONE (cf. Figure 2) – see Fernández Cuesta/Rodríguez Ledesma (2008).

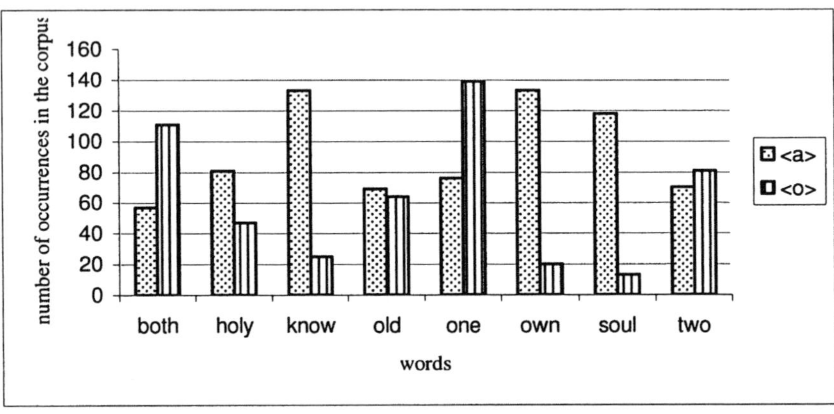

Figure 2. Reflex of OE /a:/ in LME (*LALME* LPs).

Comparison of these results with the evidence found in our EModE legal corpus from Yorkshire (Fernández Cuesta/Rodríguez Ledesma 2004) demonstrates that the words which show the highest percentage of <a> spellings in LME are precisely those which can still be found spelt with <a> in EModE (they are the most resistant to standardisation): that is the case of SOUL, OWN, KNOW and HOLY.

Most of these words are recorded in the *SED* and they all present reflexes of the ME unrounded vowel (< OE /a:/). As in the previous case, the distribution of these forms varies from word to word. Words which show the widest distribution of reflexes of the ME northern vowel are BOTH, CLOTHES, FRO, GO, HOME, MORE, NONE and ONE. For these words the northern reflexes are almost universal in Nb, Cu, Du, We, North La and North and East Y. In the case of FRO and GO, besides having northern or standard influenced realizations of the same word (*fra/fro, ga/go*), we also find two different words in competition with them, *from* and *gan*.[13]

Other words which do not present such a wide distribution of the northern reflexes are BONE, COLD,[14] LOAF, OAK, OLD,[15] ONCE, STONE, TOAD, TOES, TWO,[16] WHO, WHOSE, and WHOLE. Reflexes of OE /a:/ are widely recorded in the four northernmost counties, North La (1, 2) and North Y, although reflexes of the rounded vowel are also recorded in these areas. To this group also belong words such as MOW, OWN, SNOW and THROW, in which the vowel is followed by the semiconsonant /w/. In response to our 2008 study, Derek Britton commented that this phonetic context may have favoured the retention of <a> in ME and EModE texts. From the *SED* data, however, these words do not show the widest distribution of northern realizations. Besides, contrary to what seemed to be the case in ME, they do not present a special pattern (their distribution is similar to the others in this second group).

---

13   In the case of FRO, the standard influenced realizations [oː, u, uː] are very sparsely attested (in a few localities in La (8-12) and Y (26-27)), being *from* and *thro* the alternatives found. Similarly, in the case of GO, *gan* is the usual alternative to standard *go*: it is the general form in Nb, Du, North and East Y, whereas *ga* is mostly restricted to Cu, We and North La.

14   The distribution of COLD is rather unusual, since the standard influenced reflexes are dominant in Cu and We and very frequent in North-East Y.

15   Nb is the only county where northern reflexes are dominant. In Du both northern and standard influenced forms are found in most localities.

16   In this case standard influenced forms are very frequent in all areas and northern reflexes seem to be more recessive.

The only word which seems to be standardised in the *SED* is
ROAD, the northern realizations of which are found only in two
localities in Y (1, 19).

3.3. Reflex of ME /o:/

The change of ME /o:/ in northern dialects has been traditionally
described as a fronting of the vowel to /ø:/ and then a subsequent
raising to /y:/ (Jordan 1974: 86). According to Kristensson (1967: 93,
maps 22, 23) in the early fourteenth century ME /o:/ was fronted in
Nb, Cu and Du, with no traces of the ME fronting found in the other
northern counties.

This feature is widely recorded in the *SED* (about 40 words),
but it is not possible to compare the distribution of the reflexes of
Northern Fronting in the survey with that of *LALME*, since the *Atlas*
offers evidence for just a few items (MOON, POOR, GOOD(S)). As in the
case of reflexes of OE /a:/, the distribution of the northern forms
varies from word to word. Words which consistently show northern
reflexes are BOOTS, COOL, CROOK, MOON, NOON, ROOF, SCHOOL,
SOOT, and TOOTH. They all present a similar pattern: northern forms
are general in Nb, Cu, Du and We, in North and East Y and North
La.[17] Other words for which northern reflexes are widely distributed,
although not so frequently recorded in the four northernmost counties,
are FOOL, FOOT, GOOSEBERRIES, HOOF, LOOK, ROOT, and SPOON. On
the other hand, there are words which only occasionally present
northern variants. That is the case of FOOD (incomplete data) and
ROOM. Finally, words such as WOOL only show standard influenced
forms.

Although the study of the distribution of the different variants,
both northern and standard influenced, is beyond the scope of this

---

17   According to Derek Britton (p.c.), the La [y:] variants in ME /o:/ words almost
      certainly do not result from Northern Fronting, but are a later, post-medieval
      fronting of /u:/ resulting from GVS of /o:/. Cogent evidence for regarding this
      as late comes from the development of the diphthong [uə]. In this south La
      area [yə] comes out of this diphthong (note [uə] in adjacent areas). Notice also
      that [y] is recorded as well for the reflex of OE /a:/ (BOTH, BONE) in the same
      area of La.

paper, it seems that the various realizations recorded for the development of ME /o:/ depend on the phonetic context. For example, as stated by Orton (1933: 71), "it is highly probable that everywhere in the North ME $\bar{o}_1$ when followed by *r* regularly underwent the same changes as it usually did when medial, viz. fronting first, then diphthongization". The two words recorded in the *SED* in this context present this northern diphthongal pronunciation. In the case of FLOOR, it is universal in We, widely recorded in Cu and North and East Y, and found in some localities in Nb (3, 9), Du (6) and La (1, 2). For DOOR northern forms are recorded in Cu (4), We (2, 4), La (1, 11) and North and East Y.

In the same way, according to Orton (1933: 70-71), ME $\bar{o}_1$ becomes [ei] in final position (*do, too*). When unstressed, the development is [i]: *do* [di], *to* [ti]. In the *SED*, in the case of DO as an answer to IX.5.1 (which requires a stressed form), we find either [i:] or the diphthongs [iə], [iu(:)]. These northern reflexes are universal in Nb, Cu, Du, We, North La and North and East Y. As an answer to IX.5.5, we find in the same areas both diphthongal ([iu(:)],[iə]) and monophthongal forms ([i]). Standard influenced forms ([u(:)] are recorded in La and in South and West Y. In the case of TO, the distribution of northern reflexes ([i], [i:], [iu:], [iə]) is very similar to the previous one. The main difference is that in Cu and We TO competes with northern TILL. For TOO standard forms are recorded only in a few localities in La and Y, the usual answer being *over* in all counties. In the case of SHOE, only standard forms are recorded.

Orton (1933: 69) also stated that there were some words which were invariably pronounced with [ʊ] in the dialect of Byers Green: *broom, brother, crook, flood, glove, good, gum(boil), hood, Monday, month, mother, other, root, stood*. The *SED* shows that the short vowel for some of these words is general throughout the whole of northern England. This is the case of BROTHER, FLOOD, GOOD, MONDAY, MOTHER and OTHER. For some of these words northern forms are also recorded in some localities: BROTHER (Nb 6), FLOOD (Du 2, We 1, Cu 2, 6 and Y 10), MOTHER (Nb 4) and OTHER (Nb 4, 6). Besides those mentioned by Orton, other words which present a wide distribution of [ʊ] are: FOOT, LOOK and WOOD.

Since the fronting of ME /o:/ seems to have taken place first in the northernmost counties in the early fourteenth century, it is perhaps not surprising that we find no spelling evidence for the change in EME and very little in LME (Fernández Cuesta/Rodríguez Ledesma 2008). Although standardisation from the fifteenth century onwards makes it difficult to follow the spread of this feature to the rest of the northern counties, we have evidence of the change in our EModE corpus: <u> for GOOD and BOOK, for example, is quite frequent (cf. Figure 3).

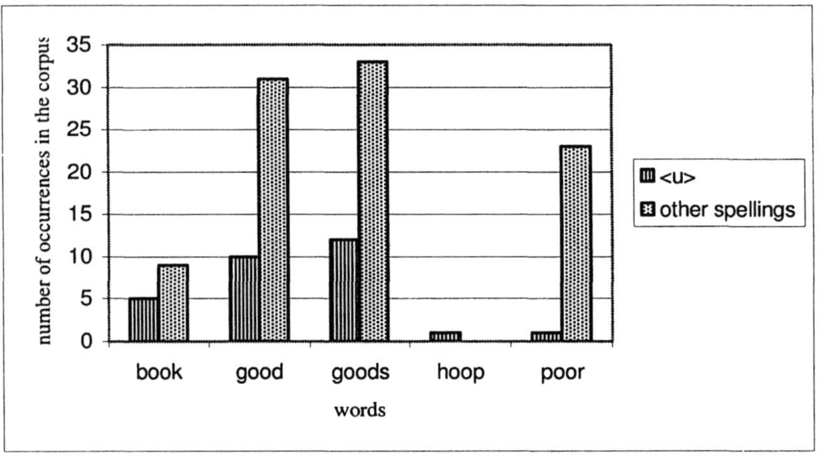

Figure 3. <u> (< ME /o:/). EModE legal corpus.

In dialect literature (Meriton's *Dialogue*, for example) spellings such as <eau> for DONE, FLOOR, LOOK and NOON illustrate the northern development.

3.4. Plosives vs. affricates

Another feature characteristic of Northern ME is the presence of <k> representing a plosive consonant in words where we find <ch> representing a palatalized affricate in Southern varieties. [18] In ME <k>

---

18   The question of whether doublets such as CHURCH/KIRK should be regarded as different words, besides showing a phonological contrast, is a rather problematic one. In *LALME* CHURCH and KIRK are mapped as *k*- and

spellings seem to be dominant for all items included in *LALME* (cf. Figure 4).

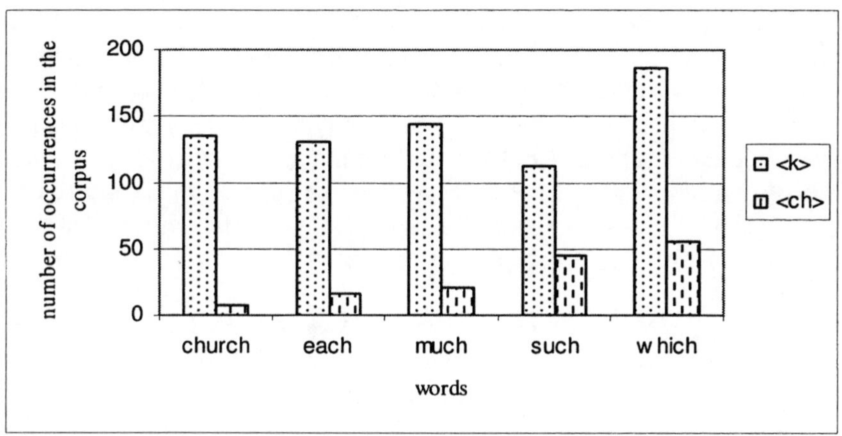

Figure 4. <k> vs. <ch> (*LALME* LPs).

The *SED* offers evidence for three of these words and they show a completely different pattern. In the case of SUCH, the northern form is widely recorded.[19] However, the few data that we have for EACH (some localities in Nb, Du and Y)[20] suggest that the standard pronunciation (with the affricate) had a somewhat wider distribution than for SUCH.[21]

---

ch- forms and in *LAEME* they are also taken as one word, $church. In the Introduction to *LAEME* (chapter 8.8.9.2) Lass discusses the status of some of these words as borrowings from Norse, and states that it does not seem very likely that a language should borrow cognates (*give, kirk*, etc.) that differed from words already existing in the language in their initial consonants, giving rise to a phonotactically inadmissible sequence. For a review of possible explanations see Lass's account in the same chapter.

19   It is universal in Cu and We, and general in Nb and Du. In La it is found in the North and in Y north of the river Humber.

20   The usual answer is 'one another'.

21   Besides Nb and Y, Wright (1898-1905) also documents northern *ilk* in Cu and La.

In the case of CHURCH, northern *kirk* is very sparsely recorded in the *SED* and is often said to be older or obsolete.[22] Wakelin (1972) tries to account for the recession of northern *kirk*, especially when compared to other words such as *beck, kirn, birk* and *sic/sike*. He argues that the reasons could be that, unlike some of the other words, *kirk* has had a standard equivalent (*church*), which would have some prestige attached to it, since it was the word used by the educated clergymen. He further states that unfamiliar words such as *kirn* retain the old pronunciation longer. However, neither of these arguments explains why words like *sic/sike,* which have a standard counterpart (*such*) and are very frequently used, have remained longer in the North.

The *SED* records other northern words with the plosive. The distribution varies greatly from word to word, but the general pattern is to find the standard word in La and South Y. The northern forms are most widely recorded for words such as CHAFF, DIKE, FLITCH and WARK. However, for words such as BIRCH and BREECHES the standard form (with the affricate) seems to be dominant in most areas.

The distribution of northern forms with /g/ for words such as YARD and BRIDGE also varies depending on the word. In the case of YARD as part of the compound CHURCHYARD, northern *garth* is very sparsely recorded and regarded as obsolete. However, in the compound STACKYARD, the northern form is widely recorded in all counties, except for La. In the same way, in the case of BRIDGE, northern *brigg* is dominant in all counties.[23] Other words that are widely recorded in the *SED* with /g/ are *rig, riggold, riggot* (RIDGEL), *lig* (LIE) and *riggs* (RIDGES).

These results show that this medieval feature was still characteristic of Northern English in the mid-twentieth century.

---

22   It is found in Nb and Cu. In the other counties *church* is almost universal.
23   In our legal corpus these words also show variation: *yard* (4x with <g>, once as part of the compound *kirkgarth*, as against 11 instances with <y>) and *bridge* (2x with <gg> and once with <dg>).

3.5. /s/ vs. /ʃ/ in SHALL, SHOULD

Another feature that is characteristic of Northern ME is the spelling
<s> in words such as SHALL and SHOULD. In ME <s> spellings are
clearly dominant for both SHALL and SHOULD in all counties, except
for Lancashire, where <s(c)h> is more frequent. Northern spellings are
still quite frequent in our EModE legal corpus.

Data from the *SED* for SHALL is incomplete, so comparison
with the ME distribution is not possible. However, it is clear that the
northern form with /s/ is frequently recorded in Y (except for the
South). In La we find /ʃal/ (besides WILL), and in the four
northernmost counties (Nb, Cu, Du, We) the form found is WILL.
Unstressed forms with /s/ (/sl, səl, sə, z/) are more widely spread and
are found in all counties. In the case of the negative form SHAN'T,
although the usual form in unstressed position is pronounced with [s],
[ʃ] is occasionally found in Du, La and Y (especially in the South).

With regard to SHOULD, northern forms are far less common,
but are recorded in Y, especially in the North and East, and
occasionally in Cu (4), and La (1, 6). As in the previous case, the
northern form is more frequent in SHOULD than in SHOULDN'T.

4. Morphosyntax

Some of the features that are characteristic of Northern ME, and even
of Old Northumbrian, still persist in modern northern dialects. This is
the case of the demonstratives, personal pronouns, present indicative
and present participle inflections, and zero genitive.

4.1. Demonstratives

In Northern ME there are various forms for plural demonstratives. For
the plural of THIS, besides *thir/ther*, we also find -*s* forms (*thise,*

these). For the plural of THAT we find (from more to less frequent, according to *LALME*) *tha, thas, tho* and *those.*

The *SED* shows that the -*s* form, which was already dominant in ME, has spread to become the general form for the plural of THIS, while *thir* is recorded only in four localities: Du 3,[24] 6 and Y 6, 21.[25] Wright (1905: 76) records this form in Nb (*thirs*), Cu (*thir'ans*) and Y (*thir*).

For THOSE, the *SED* documents *them* as the general form, *tho* and *those* being recorded only in four localities (Nb 9, Y 12, 21 and La 4 in the case of *tho,* and La 10-12, 14 in the case of *those*).[26]

Studies of the dialect of individual localities (Tidholm 1979, Petyt 1985 and Shorrocks 1999) add sociolinguistic information that is absent from the *SED*. In the case of *them* as the plural form of THAT, Tidholm (1979: 137) in his study of the dialect of Egton (North Y) states that it is almost exclusively used in age groups Old and Mid, and it is being superseded by standard *those* in age group Young. The women, for instance, only use *those.* His conclusion is that *them* will remain in Egton for a couple of generations.

In her general account of Northern English morphology, Beal (2004a: 119) does not record the forms *thir* and *tho* and gives *these* and *them* as the most common forms of the demonstratives throughout the North.

4.2. Personal pronouns

As regards personal pronouns, the characteristic northern form for the 3sg. feminine (*s(c)ho*) is practically the universal form in ME, although there are sporadic instances of *s(c)he* and *ho*. In our EModE legal corpus both *sche* (10x) and *scho* (3x) are found (cf. Fernández Cuesta/Rodríguez Ledesma 2004: 297).

In the *SED, she* [ʃi] has become the general form: it is the only variant recorded in the four nothernmost counties,[27] and it is dominant

---

24   *Thir* is also found for the singular in Du 3.
25   There is one instance of *tho* in Nb 9.
26   *Yon* is recorded for the plural in Y 24. Wright (1905: 76) records this form for the plural in Cu (*yon'ans*), Y and La.

in North and East Y (1-17, 19-20, 24-25, 27-28), and North La (1-5, 8, 12). The form *scho* [ʃuː] is restricted to West Y (18, 22, 23, 26, 29, 31, 32) and one locality in La (4). The form *hoo*, which in ME was restricted to La and WRY, is also recorded by the *SED* in these areas: it is frequent in La [28] and is also found in three localities in South-West Y, on the border with La. Maps 3 and 4 (see Appendix 2) show how the northern form, which was practically universal in ME, has receded to a small area in West Y (number 2 on Map 4) in mid-twentieth-century Northern English.

With regard to the 3ppl. pronouns, in Northern ME Scandinavian forms are general for the object, although there are sporadic instances of *h*-forms in WRY and Lancashire.

From the *SED* data, it seems that the Scandinavian form (*them*) has been superseded by the WS form *hem*, to the extent that by the time the Survey was conducted, *them* was not found at all in Y and La (the areas which had both the Scandinavian and the WS forms in ME). In the other counties (Nb 3-4, 6, 7; Du 1, 2, 5; We 3, 4), the *SED* also documents *hem* (with the exception of Cu). Wright (1905: 75) also states that in all dialects of Ireland and England the unstressed form of the pronoun is *'em*.

Analyses of individual localities, such as Tidholm (1979: 134), corroborate the data from the *SED* in the sense that *'em* is the only form used by the older speakers and is also very frequently used by middle aged (93.3%) and young people (60%).

4.3. Present indicative inflections

In ME the typical northern inflection is *-s*, although for the plural and first person singular it is restricted to contexts where the subject pronoun is not adjacent to the verb (Northern Subject Rule). This is also found in the EModE northern material.

Modern surveys and reference works record the spread of the *-s* ending to the 1sg, even when it is preceded by the personal pronoun. In the *SED* we only find information about HAVE and BE. In the case

---

27   The pronunciation [ʃə] is recorded in Nb 2, 6.
28   Cf. La 6-7, 9-11, 13-14. In 5 and 8 it is recorded as an older form.

of HAVE, there are only sporadic instances (2x in Y).[29] For the verb
BE, however, many more examples have been recorded in all
counties.[30] Wright (1905: 81) also states that in Nb, Du, Cu, We, Y,
La and North Lin, *is* is often used for *am*. According to Beal (2004:
123), however, *I's* does not occur in any of the modern corpora used
by her (*NECTE* and *Corpus of Sheffield Usage*).

Tidholm (1979: 144) states that the first person singular present
takes -*s* in age groups Old (28.7%) and Mid (9.8%), even if the
personal pronoun immediately precedes or follows the verb. This form
is generally used as a historic present, except for *is* 'am'. The women
of age group Mid use only -*s*-less tokens. Since there are few -*s* tokens
in the Mid group and none at all in the young group, this type may be
expected to die out in a generation or so (p. 144).[31]

The original northern ending for the 2sg pres. ind. has remained
in the North. Some examples taken from the *SED* are:

(1)   dɪz ðə mæind (does thou mind?) (Du 1) (p. 913)

(2)   dʊz tə ɹimɛmbə (does thou remember) (Y 5) (p. 914)

Tidholm (1979: 144) also records -*s* for the 2sg. in age-group Mid in
has (3x) and *is* (2x).

For the present indicative plural, although -*s* is the general
inflection in Northern ME, -*n* is also found in WRY and La. Wright
also notices that the plural generally ends in -*n* in Lancashire, and that
this is especially frequent with HAVE (1905: 81).

In the *SED* -*s* is found for the pres.ind.pl. in all counties except
for a few localities (We 3; La 5, 9, 10, 14; Y 14).[32] The following are
some examples of the Northern Subject Rule:

---

29   Cf. IX.6.1 (I) HAVE. (he) HAS (pp. 1045-6) and IX.6.3 (I) HAVEN'T. (he)
       HASN'T (pp. 1048-9).
30   Cf. IX.7.1 AM I (pp. 1050-1); IX.7.7 I AM. YOU ARE (2nd sg.). SHE IS.
       THEY ARE (pp. 1060-61) and IX.7.9 WE ARE. I AM. YOU ARE. SHE IS
       (pp. 1063-64).
31   Shorrocks (1999: 116) also notes the use of -*s* endings for 1sg when
       describing habitual behaviour.
32   There are several questions in the *SED* aiming to elicit semantic information
       about the noises made by animals. From these answers it is also possible to
       extract morphosyntactic information concerning the Northern Subject Rule.

(3)   people shoots them (Nb 4)

(4)   sheep bleets (Nb 1, 4, 5, 8, etc.)

(5)   the farmers wears them (Nb 8)

(6)   the barns gets holiday (Cu 5)

(7)   birds gapes for worms (Du 6)

(8)   these vets cuts them off (La 6)

(9)   the old hares gets through them (Y 1)[33]

There are also examples of *-s* ending when the verb is adjacent to a subject pronoun:

(10)   They starts clipping (Y 21, p. 270)

(11)   Farmers goes out and they *drives* them off (Y 6, 299, incidental material)

According to Beal (2004: 122), the Northern Subject Rule still operates in Tyneside English with lexical verbs, though not with BE. She states that *-s* is especially frequent after conjoined nouns and that "the constraint against using the *-s* form after pronouns was particularly strong":

(12)   Aye, and your sister and your man comes out (*NECTE*)

However, it is preferable to consider those in which the informant is asked to elaborate a whole sentence, rather than those in which s/he just must give a verbal form. For instance, in III.10.5 BLEAT the field-worker asks the informant to complete the sentence *Now tell me your words for the usual cries animals make. Sheep...* and the informant may or may not take into consideration the syntactic context, that is, use the right verbal form. However, in III.10.7 the informant is asked: *Now let's have it all together. You tell me once again*, so that s/he must construct a sentence.

33   Tidholm (1979: 144) also records *-s* in the plural in age groups Old (8x) and Mid (6x) according to the Northern Subject Rule.

As in ME, the present indicative plural is also found with the *-n* ending (mainly with HAVE) in La (10, 11, 14) and South-West Y (21, 29, 39), near La:

(13)   We han getten one (La 11)

(14)   They shearn off (ðə ʃiən ɔːf) (La 12) (p. 269)

Shorrocks (1999: 114) notes a few instances of plural *-n* in his Bolton corpus, but points out that the use of this ending (which goes back to ME) is now highly residual (Beal 2004: 123).

The Northern Subject Rule is also very frequently recorded with BE, both in the present (15) and preterite (16):

(15)   Trousers is the lang straight ones (Nb 2; incidental material, p. 298)

(16)   Shops was open while ten (Y 20; incidental material, p. 301)

4.4. Present participle

For the present participle, the inflection *-and* is generalised in Northern ME and becomes the dominant form. However, we also find examples of *-ing*, even in EME (Macaronic Sermon). Wright (1905: 81) states that in the dialects of England, the present participle ends in [ɪn] except in parts of North Nb and North Cu, where the ending is [ən]. In the dialects of Southern Scotland, and also in a few other Scottish dialects, the present participle ends in [ən], from older *-and*, and the verbal noun ends in [ɪn], from older *-ing*. In the *SED* [ən] is recorded, but it is difficult to say whether it comes from the original present participle inflection (*-and*) or from *-ing*. Tidholm (1979: 143) also states that "some /-ən/ tokens may be traces of the traditional ending (<NME *-and*, probably ON *-ande*), but most likely they are weakenings of [ɪn]."[34]

---

34   The spelling *-and* is found in Meriton's *Yorkshire Dialogue* (1633): "she leauks an Awd *farrand* Leauke" [she looks an old fashioned look] (156).

4.5. Zero genitive

Uninflected genitive has traditionally been considered characteristic of northern dialects. Klemola (1997: 351) states that this "is a feature of some antiquity, probably reaching as far back in time as the early ME period".[35] Uninflected forms seem to be more common in northern varieties and they are found in contexts for which there are no historical or phonetic explanations. Many of the examples are found with proper names. The following are some instances from our ME and EModE corpora:

(17)   Saint Iohn minstre dor [...] sain Iohn laghes [...] on sain Iohan Rike
                    (Athelstan – cf. Fernández Cuesta/Rodríguez Ledesma 2007: 129)

(18)   My husband best gown (TE1479-2)

(19)   My brother Christofer children (YW1564)

(20)   I be witt to Seynt Wilfra hede (TE1472)[36]

This feature is still found in modern Northern English. In the *SED* zero genitive is very frequently recorded throughout the northern area, as can be seen in both the basic and the incidental material.[37] With proper nouns, uninflected genitive seems to be especially frequent in La and Y:

(21)   Jack wife (La 2, 3, 9; Y 2, 7, 13, 16, 21, 24, 27, 29)

(22)   Jack Mary (Y 7)

(23)   Johnson pigs (Y11) (p.277)

Examples other than with proper nouns are also found throughout the northern area, and are also especially frequent in La and Y:[38]

---

35   There are even examples in Old Northumbrian (cf. Kirkdale runic inscription).
36   Examples (18-20) are taken from Fernández Cuesta/Rodríguez Ledesma (2004: 297).
37   Cf. VIII.1.1/18 MY DAUGHTER-IN-LAW (pp. 884-5); IX.8.6 FATHER'S BOOTS (pp. 1074-5) and IX.8.7 COW'S LEGS (p. 1076).
38   The localities investigated were more numerous in La and especially Y than in

(24)   My husband people (Cu 3)

(25)   My doctor bill (Y 4)

(26)   A lad tale (Y 4)

(27)   the old man daughter (Y 24)

(28)   a chap eyes (Y 29)

Wright (1905: 73) states that the uninflected genitive is general in all the North country dialects and occasional in the North Midlands. Tidholm (1979: 127) records its use by middle aged people.

5. Conclusions

With regard to phonology, we can conclude that all the features studied are widely recorded in the *SED* for the northern area. When comparing the ME evidence with that of the Survey, we can see that /a/ when followed by /ng/ has remained quite stable in the four northernmost counties, the North of La and most of Y. The main difference is that Southern /o/ has spread to South Yorkshire.

Concerning the reflex of OE /a:/, most of the words studied in *LALME* for this feature are recorded in the *SED* with northern variants. As in the previous case, the distribution of northern reflexes varies from word to word, but in general they present the same distribution as in ME: reflexes of the unrounded vowel tend to be dominant in the four northernmost counties, North La and North and East Y. The same applies to the distribution of plosive vs affricate consonants in words such as SUCH, EACH, CHURCH, etc. There have been attempts to account for the persistence or recession of the northern variants of some of these words, but they do not seem to be very convincing.

---

the other counties. Many of the examples given are from the incidental material.

In the case of the reflex of ME /o:/, however, it is not possible to relate the *SED* data to those of *LALME*, since we do not have enough evidence for ME. Something similar happens with SHALL and SHOULD, although in this case the lack of evidence lies on the side of the *SED*.

With regard to morphosyntactic features, it is worth remarking on the persistence of the Northern Subject Rule and zero genitive in modern Northern English. On the contrary, the traditionally northern demonstratives and the 3sg. feminine pronoun are highly recessive.

All in all, it can be said that the features studied (coming from OE and ME) have remained within the boundaries of the 'traditional North' (the Humber-Ribble line), mostly receding, although with some exceptions, such as the Northern Subject Rule. As has already been mentioned, the *SED* offers just a snapshot of mid-twentieth-century rural dialect, and therefore these results do not apply to contemporary Northern English in general. Other modern features, such as innovations taking place after ME or the retention of older features, should be studied, not only in the *SED* but also in corpora of urban Northern English, in order to get a more comprehensive picture of Northern English in modern times.

References

Primary Sources

Cawley, A. C. (ed.) 1959. *George Meriton's A Yorkshire Dialogue 1683*. Yorkshire Dialect Society Reprint II.
LAE = Orton, Harold / Sanderson, Stewart / Widdowson, John 1978. *The Linguistic Atlas of England*. London: Croom Helm.
LAEME = Laing, Margaret / Lass, Roger (compilers) 2008. *A Linguistic Atlas of Early Middle English, 1150-1325*. Edinburgh: The University of Edinburgh. At <www.lel.ed.ac.uk/ihd /laeme/ laeme.html>.

LALME = McIntosh, Angus / Samuels, Michael L. / Benskin, Michael 1986. *A Linguistic Atlas of Late Mediaeval English*. 4 vols. Aberdeen: Aberdeen University Press.

SED = Orton, Harold / Dieth, Eugen 1962. *Survey of English Dialects: An Introduction*. Leeds: Arnold.

SED = Orton, Harold / Halliday, Wilfrid J. (eds) 1962. *Survey of English Dialects: The Basic Material*. Vol.1, Parts 1, 2 &3. Leeds: Arnold.

Upton, Clive / Parry, David / Widdowson, John D. A. 1994. *Survey of English Dialects: The Dictionary and Grammar*. London: Routledge.

Upton, Clive / Widdowson, John D. A. ²1996. *An Atlas of English Dialects*. Oxford: Oxford University Press.

Viereck, Wolfgang (in collaboration with Heinrich Ramisch) 1991. *The Computer Developed Linguistic Atlas of England 1*. Tübingen: Niemeyer.

Viereck, Wolfgang / Ramisch, Heinrich 1997. *The Computer Developed Linguistic Atlas of England 2*. Tübingen: Niemeyer.

Wright, Joseph (ed.) 1898-1905. *English Dialect Dictionary*. 6 vols. Oxford: Oxford University Press.

Wright, Joseph 1905. *The English Dialect Grammar*. Oxford: Oxford University Press.

Secondary sources

Beal, Joan 2004a. English Dialects in the North of England: Morphology and Syntax. In Kortmann *et al.* (eds), II, 114-141.

Beal, Joan 2004b. English Dialects in the North of England: Phonology. In Kortmann *et al.* (eds), I, 113-143.

Brilioth, Börje 1913. *A Grammar of the Dialect of Lorton (Cumberland)*. Oxford: Oxford University Press.

Fernández Cuesta, Julia 2004. The (Dis)continuity between Old Northumbrian and Northern Middle English. *Revista Canaria de Estudios Ingleses* 49, 233-244.

Fernández Cuesta, Julia / Rodríguez Ledesma, Mª Nieves 2004. Northern Features in 15th-16th-Century Legal Documents from Yorkshire. In Dossena, Marina / Lass, Roger (eds) *Methods and*

Data in English Historical Dialectology. Bern: Peter Lang, 287-308.

Fernández Cuesta, Julia / Rodríguez Ledesma, Mª Nieves 2007. From Old Northumbrian to Northern Middle English: Bridging the Divide. In Mazzon, Gabriella (ed) *Studies in Middle English: Forms and Meanings*. Frankfurt a.M.: Peter Lang, 117-132.

Fernández Cuesta, Julia / Rodríguez Ledesma, Mª Nieves 2008. Northern Middle English: Towards Telling the Full Story. In Dossena, Marina / Dury, Richard / Gotti, Maurizio (eds) *English Historical Linguistics 2006. Volume III: Geo-historical Variation in English*. Amsterdam: Benjamins, 91-109.

Hogg, Richard M. 2006. Introduction *English Dialectology*. Online at <www.richardmhogg.me.uk>, 1-23.

Jordan, Richard 1974. *Handbook of Middle English Grammar: Phonology*. Trans. & re. Eugene J. Crook. The Hague: Mouton.

Kellet, Arnold / Dewhirst, Ian (eds) 1997. *A Century of Yorkshire Dialect. Selections from the Transactions of the Yorkshire Dialect Society*. Otley: Smith Settle.

Klemola, Juhani 1997. Dialect Evidence for the Loss of Genitive Inflection in English. *English Language and Linguistics* 1/2: 349-353.

Kortmann, Bernd *et al.* 2004. *A Handbook of Varieties of English*. 2 vols. Berlin: Mouton.

Kristensson, Gillis 1967. *A Survey of Middle English Dialects 1290-1350: The Six Northern Counties and Lincolnshire*. Lund: Lund University Press.

Lass, Roger 1987. Where do Extraterritorial Englishes Come from? Dialect Input and Recodification in Transported Englishes. In Adamson, Sylvia *et al.* (eds) *Papers from the fifth International Conference on English Historical Linguistics*. Amsterdam: Benjamins, 245-280.

Lass, Roger 1997. *Historical Linguistics and Language Change*. Cambridge: Cambridge University Press.

Luick, Karl 1914-40. *Historische Grammatik der englischen Sprache*. Leipzig: np.

Orton, Harold 1933. *The Phonology of a South Durham Dialect*. London: Kegan Paul.

Petyt, Keith M. 1985. *Dialect and Accent in Industrial West Yorkshire.* Amsterdam: Benjamins.

Shorrocks, Graham 1999. *A Grammar of the Dialect of the Bolton Area.* Frankfurt a. M.: Peter Lang.

Tidholm, Hans 1979. *The Dialect of the Parish of Egton in North Yorkshire.* Goteburg: Bokmaskinen.

Upton, Clive 1997 [1994]. Dialect Words: What Are They and What Can We Do with Them. In Kellet/Dewhirts (eds), 212-220.

Wakelin, Martyn F. 1972. Dialect and Place-names: the Distributions of Kirk. In Wakelin, Martyn F. (ed.) *Patterns in the Folk Speech of the British Isles.* London: The Athlone Press, 73-87.

Widdowson, John D. A. 1997. The Dialect of Filey. In Kellet/ Dewhirts (eds), 134-135.

Widdowson, John D. A. 2005. Time to Move on: Changing Perceptions of English Regional Dialects in the Twenty-first Century. *Transactions of the Yorkshire Dialect Society* 105/21, 9-16.

Appendix 1

1.1. County abbreviations used in this article

Nb: Northumberland
Cu: Cumberland
Du: Durham
We: Westmoreland
La: Lancashire
Y: Yorkshire

1.2. Entries from the SED listed alphabetically

Among: IX.2.12 AMONG (p. 998-9).
Birch (tree): IV.10.1 BIRCH (pp. 437-8)

Breeches: VI.14.13 TROUSERS. BREECHES (pp. 716-7); VI.14.14 SHE WEARS THE BREECHES (pp. 717-8)

Bridge: IV.1.2 BRIDGE (p. 346)

Bone: IV.6.22 WISH-BONE (p. 409); VI.9.1 HIP-BONE (p. 660); III.2.1 HIP-BONE (p. 227). Cf. also V.9.10 BROOM (p. 570) and III.1.12 SHOWS SIGNS OF CALVING (pp. 223-24).

Boots: VI.14.23 BOOTS (pp. 726-27); IX.8.6 FATHER'S BOOTS (pp. 1074-5).

Both: VII.2.11 BOTH (pp. 771-2).

Brother: VIII.1.5 BROTHER (p. 874).

Chaff: II.8.5 CHAFF (pp. 191-2); III. 5.3 CHAFF (p. 255-6)

Church: VIII.5.1 THEY GO TO CHURCH (pp. 924-5)

Clothes: VI.14.19 SUNDAY CLOTHES (p. 722); VI.14.20 ORDINARY CLOTHES (p. 723).

Cold: VI.13.18 COLD (pp. 704-5).

Comb: VI.2.4 COMB (p. 594).

Cool: V.8.11. COOL IT (pp. 555-6).

Crook: V.3.5 HOOK/CROOK (pp. 490-1). Cf. also V.3.4 CRANE (pp. 488-9) and IX.1.3 ASKEW (p. 980).

Dike: IV.2.2 DIKE (pp. 357-8); cf. also IV.2.1 (a) HEDGE (pp. 355-6) and (b) WALL (pp. 356-7).

Do: VIII.3.7 DO YOU REMEMBER? (pp. 913-4); IX.5.1 (I) DO. (he) DOES. (we) DO (pp. 1035-36); IX.5.3. DOING (pp. 1037-8); IX.5.5. DID NOT DO (pp. 1040-1).

Door: V.1.8 DOOR (pp. 465-6). Cf. also V.1.10 KEY (p. 467) and V.1.11 JAMBS (p. 468).

Each: III.13.6 FIGHT EACH OTHER (pp. 321-2); VI.2.8 PULL EACH OTHER'S (pp. 597-8).

Flitch: III.12.3 FLITCH (p. 311)

Flood: IV.1.4 FLOOD (pp. 347-8).

Floor: V.2.7 FLOOR (pp. 479-80).

Food: V.8.2 FOOD (pp. 547-8).

Fool: VII.4.10 AN APRIL FOOL (p. 803).

Foot: VI.10.1 FOOT (pp. 666-7); VI.10.2 BAREFOOT (p. 667); VI.10.5 SPLAY-FOOTED (669-70). Cf. also IV.3.10 HOOF-MARKS (pp. 374-75) and IV.3.11 PATH (pp. 375-76).

From: VIII.2.11 FROM (pp. 902-3).

Go: VIII.5.1 THEY GO TO CHURCH (pp. 924-5); VIII.6.1 GO TO SCHOOL (pp. 937-8); VIII.7.9 GO AWAY! OFF YOU GO (pp. 950-1). Cf. also V.5.9 CURDLE (pp. 508-9) and V.7.10 SPOIL (p. 532).

Good: V.8.4. SOME SWEETS (p 549);VI 5.18 PRETTY (p. 631-2).

Goose: IV.1.2 GOOSEBERRIES (pp. 447-8).

Hand: VI.7.1 (p. 640); VI.7.5 PALM (of hand) (p. 643); VI.7.13 (a) LEFT-HANDED and (b) RIGHT-HANDED (pp. 649-51).

Have: IX.6.4 (we) HAVE GOT (pp. 1049-50).

Home: VIII.5.2 STAY AT HOME (pp. 925-6).

Hoof: III.4.10 HOOF (pp. 252-3).

Land: II.3.4 (b) LAND-HORSE (FURROW-HORSE) (p. 155).

Lie: VIII.3.6 LIE DOWN. LAY (911-3); IV.2.4 TO PLASH (pp. 359-60).

Loaf: V.6.9 LOAF (pp. 518-19).

Long: IV.8.10 DADDY-LONG-LEGS (pp. 425-6). Cf. also pp. 257, 281, 286, 298.

Look: III.13.18 LOOK FOR IT (pp. 331-33); VIII.1.23 LOOK AFTER. (pp. 890-91). Cf. also VI.5.18 PRETTY (pp. 631-2).

Monday: VII.4.2 MONDAY, TUESDAY, WEDNESDAY (pp. 794-5).

Moon: VII.6.3 STARS, MOON (pp. 820-1).

More: VII.8.13 A GOOD DEAL MORE (pp. 860-1).

Mother: VIII.1.1 MOTHER (pp. 869-70).

Mow: II.9.3 TO MOW (pp. 194-5).

None: VII.1.18 NONE (pp. 761-2).

Noon: VII.3.11 AFTER-NOON (pp. 785-6); VII.3.14 THIS AFTERNOON (pp. 789-90).

Oak : V.10.2 OAK (p. 438).

Old : VIII.1.20 OLD (pp. 887-8); VII.1.21 OLDER THAN (pp. 888-89); VIII.1.22 SO OLD AS (pp. 889-90).

Once : VII.2.7 ONCE (pp. 767-8).

One: VII.1.1 ONE (pp. 747-48); VII.8.18 WHICH ONE (pp. 865-66); IX.8.8 ONE. THE OTHER (pp. 1077-78); TWENTY ONE VII.1.12 (pp. 756-7). Cf. also VI.2.8 PULL EACH OTHER'S (pp. 597-8). Cf. also VI.2.8. PULL EACH OTHER'S (pp. 597-8).

Other: IX.8.8 ONE. THE OTHER (pp. 1077-78).

Own: VIII.9.6 OWN FAULT (p. 976).

Ridge: II.7.2 RIDGE (of stack) (p. 181); V.1.2a RIDGE (of house) (p. 461); II.3.2 RIDGES (in ploughed fields) (pp.152-3)

Ridgel: III.4.7 RIDGEL (pp. 250-1)

Road: IV.3.12 ROAD (pp. 376-7).

Roof: V.1.2 ROOF (p. 460). Cf. also V.1.2a RIDGE (p. 461).

Room: V.2.4 ROOMS (p. 477); V.2.1 LIVING-ROOM (pp. 474-5); V.2.2 SITTING –ROOM (pp. 475-6); V.2.3 BEDROOM (pp. 476-7).

Root: IV.12.1 ROOT (p. 454).

School: VIII.6.1 GO TO SCHOOL (pp. 937-8)

Shall: IX.4.1 SHALL (pp. 1015-6); cf. also IX.4.3 SHALL (pp. 1017-8); IX.4.4 SHAN'T (pp. 1018-9).

She: VIII.9.5 (a) WE ARE. I AM. SHE IS. THEY ARE (pp. 973-4); IX.7.3 AREN'T YOU. ISN'T SHE. AREN'T THEY (pp. 1054-5); IX.7.7 I AM. YOU ARE. SHE IS. THEY ARE (pp. 1060-1); IX.7.9 WE ARE. I AM. YOU ARE. SHE IS (1063-4).

Shoe: VI.14.22 SHOE. SHOES (pp. 724-25). Cf. also IX.8.6. FATHER'S BOOTS (pp. 1074-75).

Should: IX.4.8 SHOULD. SHOULDN'T (pp. 1023-4); IX.4.9 SHOULDN'T
        HAVE (pp. 1024-5). Cf. also IX.4.6 OUGHT TO (pp. 1020-1) and IX.4.7
        OUGHT TO HAVE (pp. 1021-2).
Snow: VII.6.13 SNOW (p. 829).
Soot: V.4.6 SOOT (pp. 500-01).
Spoon: V.9.1 PORRIDGE STICK (pp. 561-2).
Stone: IV.2.7 GRINDSTONE (p. 361); V.3.2 HEARTHSTONE (p. 487);
        VI.13.20 STONE-NAKED (p. 706); II.9.10 WHETSTONE (pp. 200-01).
Such: VIII.9.7 SUCH A (p. 977).
Them: V.9.5 TO WASH THEM (p. 565); VI.5.12 CRUNCH THEM (pp. 625-6);
        VIII.7.5 STEAL. BURGLARS STEAL THEM. STOLE. STOLEN (pp.
        946-7). Cf. also VIII.8.15 COLLECT (pp. 967-8).
These: IX.10.5 THESE (p. 1091)
Those: IX.10.4 THOSE (p. 1090); IX.10.6 THOSE OVER THERE (pp. 1091-2).
Throng: VIII.4.11 BUSY (p. 923).
Throw: VIII.7.7 THROWING A STONE (p. 949). Cf. also I.11.5 TO
        OVERTURN (pp. 133-34).
To: VIII.6.1 GO TO SCHOOL (pp. 937-8).
Toad: IV.9.7 TOAD (p. 433). Cf. also IV.9.5 TADPOLES (p. 432).
Toes: VI.10.3 TOES (p. 668); VI.10.4 PIDGEON-TOED (pp. 668-69).
Tongs: V.3.7 TONGS (p. 492).
Too: V.6.8 TOO HOT (pp. 517-8)
Tooth: VI.5.6 TEETH. TOOTH (pp. 619-20); VI.5.8 HAVE YOU GOT
        TOOTHACHE? (pp. 621-2).
Two: VII.1.2 TWO (pp. 748-9); VII.2.14 WE TWO (p. 775).
Wark VI.1.6 A HEADACHE (p. 589); VI.5.8. HAVE YOU GOT
        TOOTHACHE? (pp. 621-22).
Who: IX.9.1 WHO (pp. 1078-9).
Whole: VII.2.12 WHOLE OF IT (pp. 772-3).
Whose: IX.9.2 WHOSE IT IS (pp. 1079-80).
Wood: V.4.2 KINDLING-WOOD (pp. 497-8).
Wool: III.7.5 WOOL (pp. 268-9).
Wrong : IX.7.1a WRONG (p. 1051).
Yard: VIII.5.5 CHURCHYARD (p. 929); I.1.3 FARMYARD (p. 49); I.1.4
        STACKYARD (pp. 49-50); I.1.9 STRAW-YARD (p. 54).

Appendix 2

Map 1. AMONG adv./prep.: '-mang(-)' type (*LALME* 1: 473, map 685).

Map 2. OE *onʒemang, -mong*. ME a + ng, o + ng (*LAE*, Ph7).

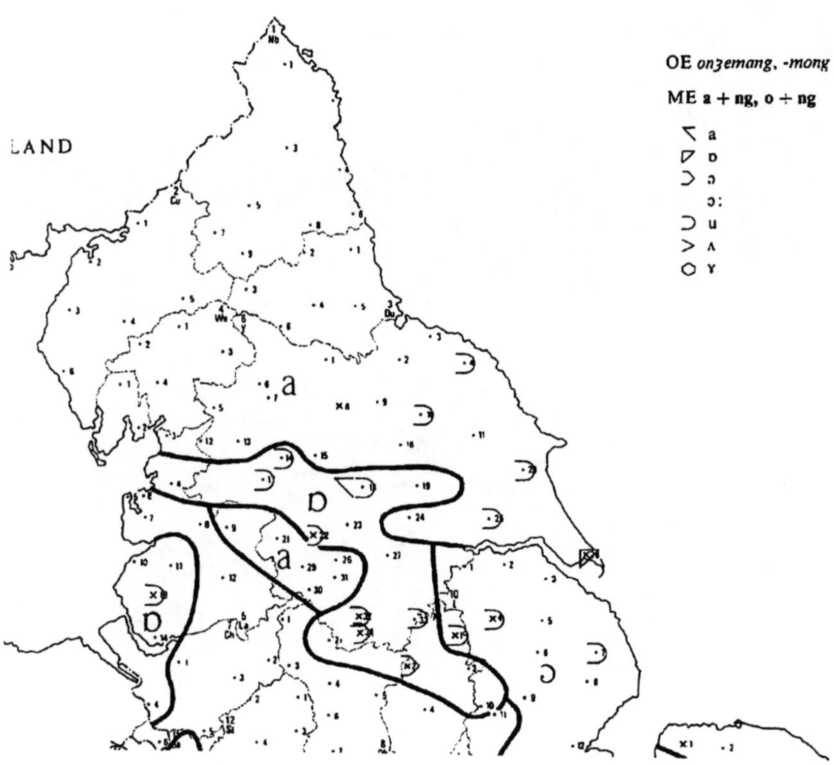

 Julia Fernández Cuesta / Mª Nieves Rodríguez Ledesma

Map 3. SHE: 'sho type' (*LALME* 1: 308, map 13).

Map 4. SHE (is) (*LAE*, M68).

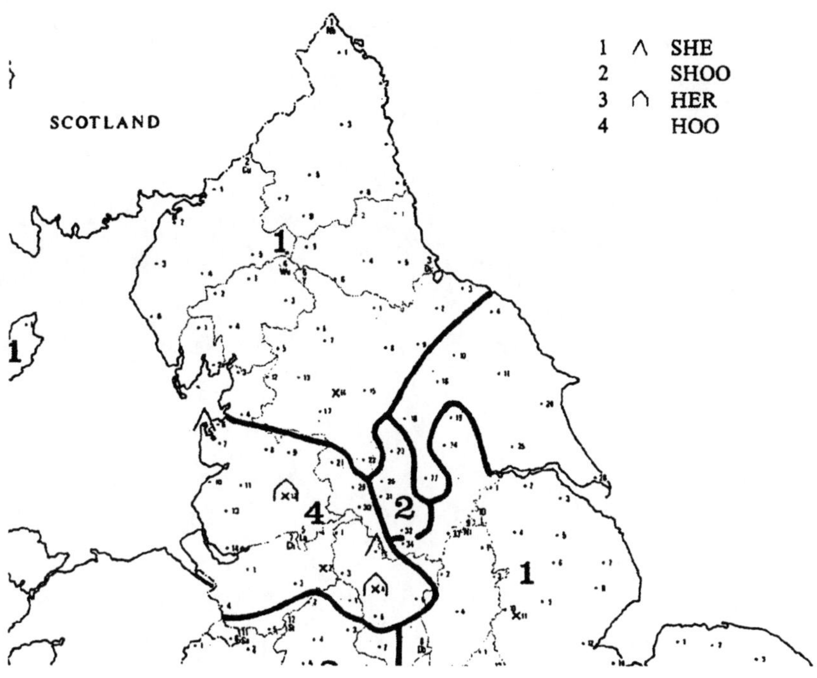

Robert McColl Millar

The Origins of the Northern Scots Dialects

1. Introduction

Northern Scotland is home to a set of Scots dialects which, while obviously closely related to each other and in some senses forming a continuum, are not always physically connected. Sometimes the varieties are divided by water or land barriers; the further north and west you travel, however, the more likely the cause for these gaps is the presence, until comparatively recently, of speakers of Gaelic.[1]

The Northern dialects are connected to the 'mainstream' Scots dialects of the Central Belt only by a narrow channel where the Grampian Mountains meet the sea just to the south of Aberdeen. The connecting dialect, South Northern, shares features with both the Mid-Northern dialects of the North-East and the northern East Central dialects and is the only truly transitional zone within the area. Ironically the truly Northern dialects of the North-East, Black Isle and Caithness are united in their diversity, in the sense that their diversity can be seen as deriving from similar sources, sources which are different from those underlying more southerly dialects. Partly this distinctiveness can be traced to the influence of Gaelic on all these varieties for much longer than on the Central and Southern dialects (in the case of Caithness dialect, further contact existed with Norn, the local North Germanic variety). As I hope to demonstrate in this study, however, something else has happened to the Northern dialects, something which bears many similarities to the new dialect formation hypotheses much discussed by historical linguists and sociolinguists in recent years.

---

1   Illustrations in this and later sections are derived from Millar (2007).

We can illustrate these tendencies in the following ways. Northern Scots uses many words and phrases not known elsewhere in the Scots-speaking world, such as *yokie* 'itchy' or *stathel* 'the main part of a cornstack; a stack in the process of building or dismantling'. North-East dialects contain words such as *teuchat* 'lapwing' and *Pace eggs* 'Easter eggs'; Caithness has *doo-docken* 'calfsfoot'; and *nask* 'chain, usually in a byre'; the Black Isle dialect contains lexical items such as *mugalees* 'to make a mess of', none of which is found elsewhere. A number of these lexical features are of Gaelic origin, as with North-East *dirken* 'fir cone' and *fuilteach* 'the weather occurring in a period at least partly in February, of varying date and duration', or Caithness *boch* 'a child's toy, a knick-knack; a contemptuous term for a person' and *buckie-failie* 'the fruit or flower of the briar; a primrose'. Caithness dialect also contains a number of Norse words not found elsewhere, such as *ingy* '(of a ewe) give birth to (a lamb)'. Phonologically, North-East and Caithness dialect both merge /f/ and /ʍ/, while, on the Black Isle, <wh> words are pronounced without the initial consonant in traditional dialect (although /f/ pronunciations are heard). North-East dialects raise /e/ to /i/ before /n/; this is only marginally acceptable in the other Northern dialects. All three dialects (along with those of the Northern Isles) use the local reflex of *this* and *that* with plural nouns.

2. New dialect formation

It has long been recognised that colonial varieties of a language, while sharing much with the standard variety of the 'homeland', have elements derived from a range of dialects, rather than merely the dominant one (although the latter may contribute the majority of features). In recent years, this understanding has been placed on a more secure (although not necessarily stable) footing, however.

Trudgill (2004) provides an excellent entrance to this debate, presenting a dynamic model of what happens when populations speaking varieties of the same language settle in a new territory.

Essentially a linguistic distinction between the first and second native generations in the colony is envisaged. The individual varieties spoken by the first native generation are accommodations both to the parental varieties and the varieties spoken in the immediate neighbourhood. These varieties are rather *ad hoc* and, interestingly, bear little resemblance to the eventual stabilised colonial variety (although they often, as a whole, carry all the features that would eventually make up the next generation's relatively mature variety). The variety of the second generation, however, represents just such a colonial- (or at least regional-) level *koiné*. Trudgill would claim that this variety is essentially a product of its sources, with features shared by as many as possible of the homeland varieties of the founding generation having a particularly good chance of survival, although social pressure and different kinds of prestige must play a part in this selection process also. Moreover, he suggests that marked characteristics of a particular dialect are unlikely to survive in the new dialect, where unmarked, but popular, variants are present.

A number of criticisms have been levelled at this model (most notably, perhaps, Hickey 2004). These have focussed in particular upon the deterministic elements inherent in it. It should be recognised, however, that when something like Trudgill's model has been applied outside of his fundamentally New Zealand material, as with Schreier's 2003 study of Tristan da Cunha English, the results appear generally to bear his findings out. Because of the nature of the dialects discussed in this essay and the time depth involved, this controversial element of the model is impossible to apply to the Northern Scots dialects.

In Schreier's study, of course, the new dialect is literally constructed on a *tabula rasa*. Very nearly the same situation applies for other situations recently studied, such as the Falkland Islands (Sudbury 2000). Even in situations such as New Zealand or French-speaking North America, where sizable native populations existed before European colonisation, scholars (such as Trudgill 2004 or the contributors to Mougeon/Beniak 1994) have generally argued that, beyond a sometimes considerable lexical presence, native influence was highly marginal (although not necessarily negligible) in the development of the new colonial vernaculars, largely due to prevailing social attitudes and behaviour at crucial moments.

Other colonial language contexts were not cast in this mould, however. Both Mufwene (in particular, in his 2001 book) and, very recently, Schneider (2007) have given some emphasis to the effects that languages other than the metropolitan one might have had upon the development of a new colonial variety under certain conditions. Mufwene in particular has described the effect which the presence of non-English vernaculars, primarily of African origin, would have had on both the developing colonial dialects of the American (and Caribbean) slave colonies as a whole, and on the evolving English dialects of the slaves and their descendants. Essentially, Mufwene proposes that these non-metropolitan inputs can have a considerable, albeit often covert, influence upon the development of new varieties which differ only in form rather than kind from the influence exerted by non-standard varieties of the colonial language.

At the same time, Mufwene proposes what might be considered a counterweight: the *founder effect*. He suggests that certain sections of a given population – whether viewed diachronically or synchron-ically – will always be considered more seminal, more proprietorial, in any society; particularly, probably, in a recently established colony. Thus, in a famous example, Anglo-Americans, although over-whelmingly outweighed in terms of actual numbers of immigrants to the United States by other groups over time (most notably, until around 1900, German-Americans), have, due to the *founder effect*, remained linguistically dominant.

But Mufwene's point is more subtle than merely this. As he points out, the founder source of a colonial variety – particularly one of a notably lower prestige type – may not be the language of the leading lights of the colony; rather, it will be those individuals who come into contact on an everyday basis with speakers of this variety. In the case of African American Vernacular English, with which Mufwene is particularly concerned, these founders would have spoken the non-standard varieties of the white indentured servants, home-steading families and lower plantation officials.

Most, but not all, of the colonial dialect formation contexts previously mentioned have been concerned with events in the eighteenth and nineteenth centuries (or, at the very outside with American English and the French of Canada, the seventeenth century). How much further back in time can we push such an analysis? I have recently demonstrated (Millar 2008) that, with Shetland Scots, we can, with some loss of definition, push this model's application some hundred to two hundred years further back. Can we analyse the formation of a new variety of Scots formed through what amounts to a colonisation seven to eight hundred years ago? Can any features of these models survive? In order to answer this, we need to consider the linguistic history of the regions where Northern Scots is spoken.

3. A history of Scots in northern Scotland

3.1. The North-East

As Macafee (2002), among others, has demonstrated, outside of its Lothian bridgehead Scots spread largely through the development in the course of the eleventh and twelfth centuries of the *burghs*, fortified markets, part of a policy on the part of the monarchy to feudalise the country and bring it into the European money-based economy. The *Inglis*-speaking inhabitants of the burghs possessed, inevitably, significantly more economic power than did the Gaelic-speakers of the hinterland. These inequalities led to relatively rapid language shift in the more prosperous and fertile areas of the south, leaving Gaelic in the marginal lands of Fife and Galloway.

The situation in the north was different. In the first place, royal power was considerably weaker north of the mountains than it was to their south, primarily because the Canmore dynasty had their power base in the latter area, while Moray (taken in its broad, medieval sense) had been the power-base of Macbeth and his ancestors. The Norman aristocracy and their burgh-building followers came as conquerors in the north in a way decidedly different from what happened in the south. The castles and defensively situated burghs of the North-East were not originally intended to be scenic; the process can be interpreted as a form of plantation on hostile territory, not dissimilar to near-contemporary developments in Ireland and Wales.

It has to be recognised that the time gap between the first significant settlement of Scots speakers and now is too great for us to pinpoint what the linguistic origin of the earliest settlers were – except, of course, that these would inevitably have been largely from central or southern Scotland. We know next to nothing about the distribution of Scots phonology and lexis in the twelfth and thirteenth centuries; extrapolating backwards from recorded usage is also well-nigh impossible. What people say now, or said in the last four to five hundred years, has little or no bearing on the linguistic reality of this first settlement.

Moreover, with the exceptions of Aberdeen and, to a lesser extent, Elgin, it cannot be said that any of the northern burghs were overwhelming successes. The soils of the North are generally wetter and often thinner, the summers are certainly shorter and the weather is more unpredictable than is the case in the south. Until the *improvement* programmes of the eighteenth and early nineteenth centuries, in addition, many areas now highly fertile were nearly impossible to farm. The prosperity upon which the burghs were based in the south just did not exist.

We can see this by focussing on Inverurie, a Royal Burgh situated on a strategic ford across the river Don, some 30 kilometres west of Aberdeen. Despite its advantageous position, the town (Milne 1947) struggled to survive, never mind grow, throughout the middle ages and beyond. Subsistence agriculture was the norm in the hinterland with the market often having little in the way of surplus to process; very strikingly, and unusual generally for this class during the period, illiteracy appears to have been common well into the modern period among the merchant class who governed the town.

What would have been the linguistic consequences of this situation? In an essay published in 2004 I suggested that the frontiers between languages so beloved of historical atlases may actually be misleading in these contexts. The margins of the dominant language would certainly be geographical, but they would be pre-eminently social and economic. I would suggest that these margins would run in our area between the citizens of the burghs, the more prosperous Scots-speaking peasantry and their poorer Gaelic-speaking neighbours and servants. Bilingualism would have been very common and was probably more equal in the burghs than was the case in the south. This rather static situation would have lasted for centuries; mass bilingualism rather than rapid change towards Scots would have been the northern route. Intermediate, heavily Gaelic-influenced, varieties would have developed and been perpetuated.

In their ongoing attempts to increase the prosperity of their burghs, the monarchy and the nobility, in the course of the middle ages, invited highly skilled immigrants into the burghs, promising lucrative cash prizes and tax breaks; many of these were speakers of Dutch and Low German. Although Scotland-wide, these effects were particularly strong in northern Scotland, primarily because of the low populations of the burghs. There are high levels of Dutch or Low German influence upon the lexis of the northern dialects, such as *loun* 'young boy', and perhaps even some prosodic transfers, such as the omnipresent diminutive *-ie*. Some of this was caused by the prosperous Hanseatic trade; its depth suggests a more extended and intimate transfer. Indeed it is highly probable that speakers of Dutch or Low German, in switching to Scots, may have emphasised the common, unmarked, features of the two languages as they changed over, creating something like a Scots-dominant *koiné*. Under these circumstances, non-native features would have been particularly likely to be prevalent.

Unfortunately, there is very little evidence for Northern Scots during the period in which it was developing. This is not altogether surprising, of course, since the non-mainstream nature of many of the features associated with this dialect can probably tell us a great deal about the social distribution of the most Northern features. What evidence we have is twofold. In the first place, literature, private correspondence and public records demonstrate largely negative evidence for the local variety. When Scots comes to be written in the North from the fifteenth century on, the language represented is largely indiscernible from Central Scots. This is particularly striking with private correspondence, which generally realises few if any Northern features before the language as a whole begins its written submersion under English from the early seventeenth century on. In the records of the various burghs of the north, however, sixteenth- and early seventeenth-century materials do occasionally evidence undoubtedly Northern features (such as <f> for <quh>) in a largely metropolitan/non-local form of Scots (Macafee 1989: 432; McClure

2002: 22). The fact that these features only occur occasionally (so that, for instance, <f> and <quh> may occur in the same text, sometimes even in the same line) suggests scribal variation with the metropolitan <quh> dominating, but the spoken <f> as an irregular presence.

We also have evidence from a variety of sources, largely but not completely literary, from the early eighteenth century onwards, most of which is in line with what we know now about Northern Scots. This is not entirely the case, however. Evidence from letters such as the early-eighteenth-century example I discussed in an essay of 1996, from an indentured servant in Maryland to his father in Culloden (near Inverness), written by another migrant, James MacCheyne, probably from Petty in Aberdeenshire, presents a different picture of what North-East Scots may have sounded like at the time. These are the first few paragraphs:

> Teer Lofen Kynt Fater:
> Dis is te lat ye ken, dat I am in quid healt, plessed be Got for dat, houpin te here de lyk frae yu, as I am yer nane Sin, I wad a bine ill, leart gin I had na latten yu ken tis, be kaptein *Rogirs* skep dat geangs te Innernes, per cunnan I dinna ket anither apertuniti dis Towmen agen. De skep dat I kam in was a lang tym o de see cumin oure heir, but plissit pi Got for a'ting wi a' kepit our Heels unco weel, pat Shonie *Magwilivray* dat hat ay sair heet. Dere was saxty o's a' kame inte te Quintry hel a lit an lim an nane o's a' dyit pat Shonie *Magwillivray* an an otter *Ross* lad dat kam oure we's an mai pe dem twa wad a dyit gin tey hed bitten at hame.
> Pi mi fait I kanna komplin for kumin te dis quintry, for mestir Nicols, Lort pliss hem, pat mi till a pra mestir, dey ca him Shon *Bayne* an hi lifes in Marylant in te rifer Potomak, he nifer gart mi wark ony ting pat fat I lykit mi sel: de meast o a' my Wark is waterin a pra stennt hors, and pringin wyn an Pread ut o de Seller te mi Mestir's Tebil.
>
> (punctuation and emphasis as in original)

There are many features in this language which would still be mainstream in North-East Scots, such as /f/ for /ʍ/. But others – the confusion of /t/ and /θ/ or /d/ and /ð/, or of voiced and unvoiced consonants – are not usual today, being associated more with the pronunciation of Gaelic-dominant Highland English speakers. In a recent essay, Macafee (2004) suggested that this document is a rare example of what she terms 'Highland Scots', a subsequently lost variety. But Petty, a small village near Fyvie in Aberdeenshire, where the scribe was from, would not normally be analysed as part of the early eighteenth century *Gaidhealtachd* (or, indeed, anywhere near it). So what does this document, representing an apparently lost variety in an area now dominated by mainstream North-East Scots tell us about the development of local varieties during this period?

Although similar examples from the seventeenth and eighteenth centuries are not common, there is literary evidence found in the works of Scott and, in particular, Hogg's *Memoirs and Confessions of a Justified Sinner*, which suggests that the actual varieties were themselves quite widespread. Again we are faced with the fact that dialects of this type do not exist today; nor have they since at least the end of the eighteenth century. It is reasonable to want to know what happened.

Taken together, we can suggest the following model for North-East Scots (and, by extension, other Northern Scots varieties). In the North-East a class-based stratification of speech was solidified from a relatively early period after the introduction of Scots into the area. The most socially elevated, and those with most means to travel regularly, would have spoken a dialectal acrolect containing few of the features specifically local with, we can predict, certain features being more markedly dispreferred than others, perhaps primarily recognisably Gaelic features.

A mesolect would also have existed, where local features were common, but mainstream Scots features were still largely privileged within the mix. This would have been the variety favoured by the burgh (lower) middle classes and by the larger farmers. The basilect would have been shared by those who were marginal socially or economically: recent immigrants and the smaller peasantry, who often regularly also spoke Gaelic.

In a manner similar to a post-creole continuum, we could represent their relationship as in Figure 1, bearing in mind, of course, that this is a schematisation of a doubtless rather more complex reality:

                                                                    Robert McColl Millar

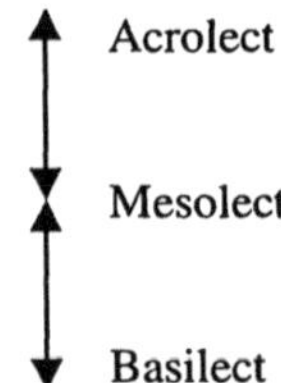

Figure 1. A post-Creole continuum.

External influences might be represented as in Figure 2:

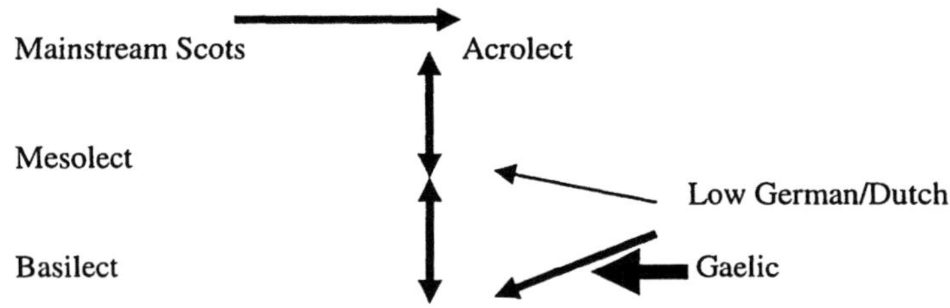

Figure 2. The linguistic ecology of North-East Scotland in the early modern period.

On this occasion, thickness of line represents level of influence. We must assume that the influence from Gaelic over the Basilect and of Mainstream Scots upon the Acrolect would have been ongoing and strong (particularly, perhaps, in the latter case), while the Low German and Dutch influence, although probably quite regular, would inevitably have a more *ad hoc* influence upon the development of the varieties in question.

Forces conspired to make North-East Scots more homogenous than this portrayal, however. Firstly, the Acrolect gradually shifted away from Scots altogether. Although it would be very surprising if the speech of the upper middle classes (and, indeed, upper classes) of the region had not continued to influence the lower middle classes in particular, the organic connection between the acrolect and mesolect was inevitably attenuated. It is more difficult to explain what happened to the basilect.

Or is it? In many studies of the language use of post-creole situations, it is commonplace for the mesolect of a particular time to correspond to the basilect of a later period, and so on, with a gradual but inexorable move towards the lexifier language ongoing. Can we see something similar here?

The basilect was gradually lost, I would suggest, in the great homogenisation of people (and language) associated with the *improvement* movement of the late eighteenth and early nineteenth centuries, although many Gaelic-influenced features had already 'seeped' up into the more mainstream dialects. Inevitably, *improvement* was at its most extreme the more marginal land became; equally inevitably, this meant that those who spoke Gaelic were regularly moved off their land and forced to seek a livelihood elsewhere, normally in circumstances where Gaelic was largely unknown.

This change would have had two effects on those who spoke the basilect of North-East Scots. In the first place, the linguistic source for many of the basilectal features was removed, meaning that, over time, the basilect would have become less basilectal. Secondly, the growing scarcity of Gaelic speakers within the North-East Scots system may have encouraged the basilectal speakers to move towards mesolectal speech in order to emphasise their North-East identity. More importantly, however, the great changes of which this forms a part encouraged homogenisation as a both conscious and unconscious search for uniformity. In this process, markedly basilectal, particularly Gaelic, features would be avoided.

A striking feature of this homogenisation was a highly localised focussing, due, it would seem, to the *feein* system, a system where periodic movement of farm labour from *fee* to *fee* was generally confined to a relatively circumscribed area around a market town. In the nineteenth century, and for a large part of the twentieth, the North-East dialect, while diverse across space, was remarkably uniform socially. This suggests that individual or small group linguistic particularities (marked both linguistically and socially) would have been less likely to survive in the new mix than were features associated with the majority culture of the region. It is also worth noting that generations of young farm servants lived in close communal quarters, generally with people from similar backgrounds to their own, from the same circumscribed area. A localised, but homogenous, *koiné* would inevitably have developed.

3.2. From North-East to Northern

The other two Northern varieties – Black Isle dialect and Caithnesian – have not, as yet, featured much in my discussion. Because of the lack of documentary evidence for the language of the Black Isle up till very recently, I will focus on Caithnesian, of which we know rather more. Many of the features noted for North-East Scots are present with these varieties, however.

Since the beginning of recorded history, there has been a fundamental split in Caithness between a Gaelic-speaking west and south and a Germanic-speaking triangle in the north-east of the county, whose boundaries lie somewhere to the west of Thurso on the north coast and around Latheron on the east coast. Within this triangle, most of the placenames are Norse; outside, practically none is. Gaelic placenames are found in the triangle, however (Millar 2007: 121-123).

It is generally agreed, although on practically non-existent evidence, that Norn, the Scandinavian dialects spoken in Caithness and the Northern Isles (and probably for a significant period in the Western Isles as well), died out in the fifteenth century (Thorsen 1954). The influence of Norn is felt in Caithnesian, although not on the same level as in the dialects of the Northern Isles. In fact, something like the gradual decay of radioactive material appears to be taking place in all of these dialects in relation to Norn influence. Studies in Shetland dialect (and to a lesser extent Orcadian) have demonstrated that the Scandinavian element in the dialects known by native speakers has decreased significantly over fifty-year intervals since the late nineteenth century (and, extrapolating backwards, from the death of Norn in these archipelagos, in the early eighteenth century in Orkney and the middle years of that century for Shetland). Since the language died out first in Caithness, therefore, we can assume that this decline has gone further there than elsewhere (although this statement does not imply steady change).

Unlike the Gaelic influence discussed for the North-East, however, the contact between Norn and Scots before the former's death was between quite close relatives. Certainly, when we look at contemporary Shetland dialect we can still find features in the dialect which are quite probably Norn. This is not possible with Caithnesian beyond lexical influence, however. It is quite likely, nevertheless, that, just as with the lexis, reinforcement of more mainstream Scots features over time gradually 'leached' them from the system.

The Gaelic influence on Caithness dialect is much more visible at all levels of the dialect – particularly lexical and phonological. This is not, of course, surprising. Gaelic remains, barely, a living presence in Caithness. You do not need to go too far back to read of widespread bilingualism, some of which continued into living memory outside Wick and Thurso, the only urban areas in the county.

Many of the particular features of Caithness dialect can be traced back to these two intense and lengthy contacts. Not all, however. Indeed, we can to a degree talk about the original sources of the Scots dialects which formed Caithness dialect.

As the Earldom of Orkney and its subordinate units gradually moved within the orbit of the Scottish crown, while Norwegian power in the North Atlantic was eclipsed, the Scots-speaking presence, both among the ruling classes and the merchant classes of the burghs of Caithness, inevitably grew. Indeed, there is much evidence of skilled workers from further south being brought into the burghs in an attempt to increase trade prospects; in particular, the growing international fishing trade. As with the North-East, some of these immigrants came from the Low Countries. In the Early Modern period Wick in particular became a cosmopolitan fishing and whaling port, acting both as a fishing centre in its own right and as an outfitter and harbour for ships from elsewhere in Scotland, England and, again, the Low Countries.

This cosmopolitan mix may explain some features of Caithness dialect. A considerable part – but by no means all – of the non-Gaelic lexis in Caithnesian is shared with that of at least some of the North-East dialects. This may be due to both dialects being quite conservative in terms of linguistic change. However, given that we know that there have been long-term and intimate contacts between the two areas, it would be very surprising if lexical transfer had not sometimes taken place.

The same goes, probably, for phonology. Alone among the Scots dialects, North-East and Caithness Scots share the change of /ʍ/ to /f/. Given that, as we have seen, this change was at least encouraged by the inability of native speakers of Gaelic to form /ʍ/, it would be easy to say that separate developments took place in both regions. I have no doubt that this happened. But there are many other Scots-speaking areas which have also come into intimate contact with Gaelic, such as the Scots-speaking enclaves of Argyll and the Black Isle, where this change did not happen (or at least where the variation of pronunciation was not picked up as a change). The pre-existing change in the North-East cannot have done the incipient change in Caithness any harm, at the very least.

But, important though it is, we cannot trace back all of the features of Caithnesian not derived from Norn or Gaelic to North-East Scots. In that dialect, the negativiser is universally *nae*, as in

(1)   A'll *nae* dee at.
        'I won't do that.'

In Caithnesian, only *no* is found, the form common to all other Scots dialects. In his work on dialect formation, Trudgill has suggested that, in the koinéisation process, unmarked forms will, all things being equal, be preferred over marked. This may well be an example of just such a process. When two sources are present, that which is least geographically specific is preferred.

4. Discussion

What, then, can we make of this historical evidence? Are we in any way capable of analysing Northern Scots as a 'colonial' variety?

One point that needs to be recognised is that, particularly in phonological terms (lexical evidence is more 'quirky'), a near-typical dialect continuum exists between the Northern and Central dialects. Since we must assume that the Northern dialects have a younger settlement history than more southerly dialects, does this mean that the continuum represents the gradual spread north of usage or, more likely, that the continuum has gradually grown over – although not fully – earlier distribution patterns? We are never likely to know.

This blind alley is not always the case with the newer dialects of Scots. In the case of Shetland dialect, I have been able to trace back (Millar 2008) lexical material in particular to a significant range of Scottish dialects. But the critical period in the creation of Shetland dialect was between the sixteenth and eighteenth centuries, a period which is quite close to our own (and therefore with distribution patterns which can be rebuilt backwards from our own through the relatively copious documentary materials). A number of assumptions certainly still have to be made, but the ideas involved *do* have substantial foundations.

Of course we would have to ask whether it is the lack of documentary evidence rather than time-depth which causes the frustrating lacuna in our understanding of the origins of Northern Scots. After all, an ongoing and vibrant discussion exists about the origins of the much earlier Anglo-Saxon dialects (Smith 2007). On this occasion, somewhat later materials can with difficulty be employed in arguments of this type.

5. Towards a conclusion

But all of this does not mean that we cannot derive anything from recent models of dialect creation when discussing the origins of Northern Scots. Elements of Trudgill's model are apparent: not least the preference for unmarked forms in the koinéisation process. The same applies for Mufwene's *founder effect*. Obviously, with Northern Scots the primary founder was Scots, in whatever form(s). But given the social situation in the medieval North-East I have outlined, with Gaelic continuing to be spoken throughout a large part of the region by a considerable part of the population, that language must have had a significant effect upon the developing language varieties. This effect must have been more fundamental, more central, than other potential influences, most notably that from the language of Low Countries immigrants, important though these probably were within the burghs. Scots remained dominant in the 'colonial' mix for social reasons;

Gaelic remained, acting in many ways like the Low variety in a di-glossic relationship. We might suggest that two founder effects were at work on the incipient variety: an overt Scots effect and a covert, and less powerful, Gaelic one.

This covert Gaelic effect, I have suggested, was at its most profound on the language of the 'lower orders', to the extent that we can speak of a social continuum rather like a post-creole continuum. Indeed, it is very likely, but not provable, that in the early years of the contact a creole-like variety was formed, but that everyday contact with more prestigious Scots varieties led eventually to its disap-pearance, or its assumption into more mesolectal forms. As we have seen, however, this level of post-colonial variation was eventually compressed by the creeping Anglicisation of the acrolect and the localised homogenisation of dialect (in itself in many ways a form of new dialect formation) during the creation of the new, 'improved', agricultural system in the course of the eighteenth and nineteenth centuries.

Caithness adds a number of complications. The dialect appears to have been directly influenced by that of the North-East, although contact with other Scots dialects seems to have created a new mixture where certain features particularly associated with the North-East were dispreferred. The contact between Norse and Scots must also be factored in there as must the intense – and ongoing – contact with Gaelic.

It can therefore be argued that many elements of the new dialect formation models put forward for relatively recent linguistic colon-isations can be employed to analyse dialects formed much earlier. When we look back seven or eight hundred years, however, any hope of precise assignment of origin is lost.

References

Hickey, Raymond 2004. Dialects of English and their Transportation. In Hickey (ed.), 33-58.

Hickey, Raymond (ed.) 2004. *Legacies of Colonial English. Studies in Transported Dialects*. Cambridge: Cambridge University Press.

Macafee, Caroline 1989. Middle Scots Dialects – Extrapolating Backwards. In McClure, J. Derrick / Spiller, Michael R.G. (eds) *Bryght Lanternis. Essays on the Language and Literature of Medieval and Renaissance Scotland*. Aberdeen: Aberdeen University Press, 429-41.

Macafee, Caroline 2002. A History of Scots to 1700. In *A Dictionary of the Older Scottish Tongue* 12. Oxford: Oxford University Press: xxi-clvi.

Macafee, Caroline 2004. Scots. In Hickey (ed.), 59-81.

McClure, J. Derrick 2002. *Doric: The Dialect of North-East Scotland*. Amsterdam: Benjamins.

Millar, Robert McColl 1996. Gaelic-influenced Scots in Pre-Revolutionary Maryland. In Ureland, P. Sture / Clarkson, Iain (eds) *Language Contact across the North Atlantic*. Tübingen: Niemeyer, 387-410.

Millar, Robert McColl 2004. Linguistic History on the Margins of the Germanic-speaking World: Some Preliminary Thoughts. In McClure, J. Derrick (ed.) *Doonsin' Emerauds: New Scrieves anent Scots and Gaelic / New Studies in Scots and Gaelic*. Belfast: Cló Ollscoil na Banríona, 3-17.

Millar, Robert McColl 2007. *Northern and Insular Scots*. Edinburgh: Edinburgh University Press.

Millar, Robert McColl 2008. The Origins and Development of Shetland Dialect in Light of Dialect Contact Theories. *English World-Wide* 29: 237-267.

Milne, James Crawford 1947. *'Twixt Ury and Don and Round About*. Inverurie: Dufton Scott and Son.

Mougeon, Raymond / Beniak, Édouard (eds) 1994. *Les origines du français québécois*. Sainte-Foy: Presses de l'Université Laval.

Mufwene, Salikoko 2001. *The Ecology of Language Evolution*. Cambridge: Cambridge University Press.

Schneider, Edgar W. 2007. *Postcolonial English. Varieties around the World*. Cambridge: Cambridge University Press.

Schreier, Daniel 2003. *Isolation and Language Change. Contemporary and Sociohistorical Evidence from Tristan da Cunha English*. Basingstoke: Palgrave Macmillan.

Smith, Jeremy J. 2007. *Sound Change and the History of English.* Oxford: Oxford University Press.
Sudbury, Andrea 2001. Falkland Islands English: A Southern Hemisphere Variety? *English World-Wide* 22: 55-80.
Trudgill, Peter 2004. *New-dialect Formation: The Inevitability of Colonial Englishes.* Edinburgh: Edinburgh University Press.

NICHOLAS BROWNLEES

Welsh English in English Civil War Pamphlets

1. Introduction

My intention in this chapter is to examine aspects of the representation of Welsh English (WE) in English pamphlets published at the outset of the English Civil War. The pamphlets in question were all published in London and in their political stance were unquestionably in support of Parliament in its struggle against the King. Given this political standpoint, it is not surprising that what we find in the pamphlets is a hostile representation of Wales and Welshness since, with the exception of Pembrokeshire, the most western of the Welsh counties, Wales had come out in favour of the royalist cause as the political standoff turned to outright warfare in the late summer of 1642.[1] In their portrayal of Wales the pamphlets attack and mock not only the Welsh counties' political support of the King but also aspects relating to Welsh character and language.

The fact that in the propaganda war between Parliament and King the anti-Welsh pamphleteers exploited the presumed non-standard language usage of the Welsh for ideological purposes was by no means extraordinary. Throughout the Civil War's battle of words we find numerous references in both the royalist and Parliamentarian press to the supposed language deficiencies of the opposition camp. For example, the main royalist pamphlet, *Mercurius Aulicus*, frequently derides the influential Parliamentarian mouthpiece, *Mercu-*

---

1   Among the myriad of works on the English Civil War (1642-1649), see Russell (1990) for a highly respected analysis of the causes of the war and Royle (2004) for a fine narrative history of these turbulent years. See instead Stoyle (2000a, 2000b) for analyses of the inherent cultural and political tensions affecting relationships between England and Wales despite the unification of the two countries a century earlier.

rius Britanicus, for its misuse of grammar, lexis and orthography.[2] In turn, the royalists were often harangued by the Parliamentarian press for their refusal to speak so-called 'plain' English, that is, an English comprehensible to ordinary English people. Instead of communicating in a language accessible to all, they were accused of either littering their speech with expressions from such papist languages as French and Spanish or speaking in metaphysical riddle.[3]

Of course, it would be reckless to believe that such comment was the result of much detailed linguistic analysis. One should presume that many of the pamphleteers were instead basing their comments on received opinion as to Parliamentarian and royalist modes of expression. Similarly it is very likely that London's anti-Welsh pamphleteers based their own representation of WE, or Welch as it was often contemptuously called at that time, on received understanding too. In fact, there is no way of knowing just how much real contact the pamphleteers had with this dialect. Had they ever been

---

2   Instances of *Mercurius Aulicus*'s condemnation of the Parliamentarian newsbook's orthography are provided later in the chapter but as an example of what the royalist pamphlet attacked in the language of *Mercurius Britanicus* one can refer to a *Mercurius Aulicus* number of 1644. At one point in this issue *Mercurius Aulicus* satirises the Parliamentarian newsbook's use of the pronoun *her*, rather than *its*, in reference to the sun. After quoting the passage in *Mercurius Britanicus*, the *Mercurius Aulicus* editor then makes his own ironic comment in brackets: "That a great quantity of fewell may be gotten against winter for the use of the City of London, by cutting Turfe, if it be done in time before the Sunne remove her beames, (Remove her beames, whether is the Sunne a maid or a widow?)" (*Mercurius Aulicus*, 30 June-6 July 1644, 1074). However, apart from *Mercurius Britanicus* there were also other Parliamentarian pamphlets that the royalist publication criticised for their bad English. For example, in referring to a short-lived Scottish pamphlet, *The Scottish Mercury*, *Mercurius Aulicus* writes, "Thus the SCOTTISH MERCURY (indeed not able to write English) falls most foully [...]" (15-21 October 1643, 583).

3   For example, *Mercurius Britanicus* responds to the royalist *Mercurius Aulicus* with the words: "I have spoke in *plain English*, not in *French*, nor *Spanish*" (*Mercurius Britanicus*, 29 July-5 August 1644, 365) and "Prethee raile at us in *English*, let us be scandalized in such language as we understand, make us hereafter capable of thy ill language, thy *profound nonsence*, thy transcendent, and metaphysicall Intelligence" (*Mercurius Britanicus*, 26 August-2 September 1644, 388). See Brownlees (2005, 2006) for an analysis of orality and polemic in English Civil War news discourse.

to Wales, or was their understanding of WE rather based on acquaintanceship with Welsh men and women who had migrated to London?[4] Or, instead, was the pamphleteers' representation of WE a mere stereotypical construct dependent on generalised notions of this regional variety? What is certain is that whatever the writers' direct contact with WE they would have been aware of the general representation of this dialect on the London stage. The stage Welshman had been a popular figure in London theatre since the late Elizabethan period, and as was the case with most dialect-speaking characters in seventeenth-century English drama WE speakers were usually figures of fun.[5] With periphery, walk-on characters this comic role was totally dominant, whilst in other more developed forms of characterisation, such as that of Fluellen in Shakespeare's *Henry V* (1599), the humour supplied by the person's use of WE was just a part, albeit important, of the greater dramatic whole.[6]

Given this literary tradition, the following analysis of WE in Parliamentarian pamphlets will need to bear in mind how far the representation of the dialect conforms to or differs from conventional characterisation of this regional variety in early modern Britain. However, apart from what the pamphlets can tell us about this, it will also be interesting to see what insights the texts provide regarding the other side to the question; that is, what the representation of WE

---

4   Bartley (1943: 285) argues that given the relative proximity of the two countries as well as their 100-year political, legislative and juridical union, and ever greater economic ties, there was a closer interrelationship between the English and the Welsh than there was, for example, between the English and Scottish or Irish. As much of this contact naturally occurred in London, Bartley says that not only would Londoners have been exposed to WE but that even "some Welsh would have been understood by an Elizabethan theatre audience" (1943: 285).

5   See Bartley (1943: 285-287) for a list of plays between 1592-1659 containing Welsh characters. In Bartley (1954) there is further analysis of the stage Welsh person in these and other early modern dramas.

6   According to Blake, Shakespeare's representation of Fluellen's WE was innovative in that "although Welshmen appeared in English before Fluellen they were not given a distinctive language. Thus Rice ap Howel in Marlowe's *Edward II* is identified as Welsh by his name and by his companions, not by his language" (1981: 84).

illustrates regarding the writer's concept of standard English, and what such a standard meant at the time of England's Civil War.[7]

2. Source materials

Six pamphlets have been examined for the present research. The pamphlets in question are respectively entitled *Newes from Wales, or, the Prittish Parliament* (1642), *The Welch-mans publike Recantation or, His hearty sorrow for taking up of Armes against her Parliament* (1642), *The Welch-Mans Warning Piece. As it was delivered in a Sermon in Shropshire* (1642), *The Welchmens Prave Resolution: in Defence of her King, her Pritish Parliament, and Her Country, gainst te malignant party* (1642), *The Welshmans Postures: or, The true manner how her doe exercise her company of Souldiers in her owne Countrey* (1642) and *The Welch-Mans Complements, or the true manner how Shinkin wooed his Sweet-heart Maudlin after his returne from Kenton Battaile* (1643). The pamphlets are all separates, that is one-off publications, and in all amount to approximately 13,000 words.[8] The longest pamphlet is *The Welch-mans publike Recantation* with about 3,000 words, whilst the shortest is *The Welchmens Prave Resolution* that runs to just less than 1,300 words.

---

7   See Porter (1999) for an interesting example of the kind of socio-historical insights that can be gained when the focus is more on the observer than the observed. In the essay in question the author's examination of the use of Scots in seventeenth-century English broadsides provides the material for considerations on contemporary English nationalism.

8   Separates can be contrasted with periodical newsbooks which at that time usually came out on a weekly basis. One such mock-Welsh periodical newsbook was *The Welch Mercury*. This newsbook, which came out between October 1643 and January 1644, provided much stylised WE, and in various respects was similar in content and language to some of the pamphlets considered in this present study. However, by virtue of the fact that it also purported to provide weekly news it lies outside the ambit of my present focus. See Raymond (1996, 2003) for an examination of separates and newsbooks during the Civil War and Interregnum.

Regarding thematic content the various pamphlets ridicule in varying degrees and at various linguistic levels particular aspects relating to Welshness generally and the Welsh royalist support in particular. Thus, *Newes from Wales* ridicules the notion that Wales could ever have its own national Parliament,[9] *The Welshmans Postures* denigrates Welsh soldiers' military training whilst *The Welchmens Prave Resolution* humorously underlines, through the format of a mock official declaration, the absurdity of the Welsh protestation of loyalty towards both King and Parliament in the Welsh struggle against the cavaliers, the King's own supporters. As for *The Welch-Mans Complements*, we find a comic contrast between the foolery of the Welsh protagonist Shinkin on the one hand and the admirable level-headedness of the English maiden that the Welshman is wooing on the other. Similarly comic in intention is *The Welch-Mans Warning Piece*, which parodies the contents and language of a Welsh sermon. Indeed, with the exception of *The Welch-mans Publike Recantation*, which more seriously illustrates the terrible mistake the Welsh made in supporting King Charles in his struggle against Parliament, what stands out in the English pamphleteers' cultural portrayal of Welshness is the emphasis placed on Welsh ignorance and stupidity. Being a region with little or no urban culture, Wales for the London-based pamphleteer remained locked in a state of semi-imbecilic rustic torpor. The risible notions entertained by the Welsh as to their illustrious ancestors, including not just classical heroes such as Aeneas and Hector, but also ancient Britain's own King Arthur, coupled with their quaint and foolish aspirations to political self-assertion cannot but be contrasted with the dire reality of their abject, semi-illiterate existence. For the pamphleteers it is this disparity between heroic aspiration and brutish, stark fact that underlies much of the parody found in their works. The ridicule the Welsh are subject to is all-embracing, and unequivocally includes their vain attempts to communicate on any satisfactory level. Thus, according to Maudlin,

---

9   For example, the pamphlet contrasts the great importance the Welsh give to the notion of establishing their own Parliament with the likelihood that in reality all such an august assembly would ever do, were it to be constituted, would be to discuss such issues as "Red-Herrings with bels about her necks" and how these fish could be put into brooks and rivers so that they would multiply (*Newes from Wales* 1642: 4).

the English maiden in *The Welch-Mans Complements*, not only is the Welsh people's own native language "mountainous [...] such as Goates would utter if they could speak" (*The Welch-Mans Complements* 1643: 2), but in an effort to speak in English her would-be Welsh suitor only manages to come up with "so much false English, and Welch wit, which is no better then [sic] English nonsence" (*The Welch-Mans Complements* 1643: 7).

3. Analysis of Welsh English

In the following examination of WE features I shall analyse in order orthography, morphology and lexis.

3.1. Orthography

Non-standard orthography is found in all six pamphlets, and its frequency oscillates from marked foregrounding in *The Welchmens Prave Resolution* to a less emphatic presence in *The Welch-mans publike Recantation*:

(1)   Since her toe understand, tat te enemy toe approach and treaten not only to cut her troat cowardly, put also to hinter te procetings of te Pritish Parliament, her tink it high time to look apout her. And tough her coms as fierce as a creat Lyon to her, and look as high as Pawls [...]
                                        (*The Welchmens Prave Resolution* 1642: 1)

(2)   [...] and Saint *Winifreds* Well could not flow in greater big streames then her saw bloud in streames mingled with vulgars and Shentlemens bloud [...]
                                        (*The Welch-mans publike Recantation* 1642: A2)

As is characteristic of fictionalised non-standard orthography, many of its occurrences are intended to reflect presumed phonological features of the speaker, who in the present case is the mock Welsh author.[10]

3.1.1. Plosive devoicing

One of the constant features in WE spelling is the substitution of *c* (or *k)* for *g*, *p* for *b*, and *t* for *d*.

(3)   *Prethren* and *Sisters*, her hope tat none of you wil pe offended at her preachment and say her speaks well put her words and actions acree not [...]
                                                (*The Welch-Mans Warning Piece* 1642: 5)

(4)   Her plood peing therefore very hot, and her head full of learned knowledges in all points and politick pusinesses, and having creat understandings, and many quick piting griefes in her posome [...] (*Newes from Wales* 1642: 1)

From a phonological point of view, the non-standard orthography indicates the substitution of the voiceless plosive for its voiced counterpart. Though there are differences in frequency, this dialectal feature is found in the utterances of all the mock WE speakers in all six pamphlets and must be regarded as one of the most stereotypical features of WE for native seventeenth-century English speakers.

The following words, whose order reflects their frequency in the corpus, exemplify the substitution process of voiceless for voiced plosive: *put*, *creat*, *pe*, *prittish*, *prave*, *kot*, *py*, *cood*, *tid*, *coot* for respectively 'but', 'great', 'be', 'brittish', 'brave', 'god', 'by', 'good', 'did', and 'good'. However, the devoicing of plosives does not occur just at the beginning of the word but also within it. Thus, instead of 'Adam' and 'about' we find *Atam* and *apout*.

That this perceived phonological trait of WE speakers had some correlation with actual WE at that time is very probable. Not only is it one of the most foregrounded WE speech markers in contemporary seventeenth-century literature but it continues to be underlined as a distinguishing phonological feature in descriptions of latter-day WE.

---

10   This is an aspect of what Chapman (1994: 2) refers to as "the ear-code of speech" being transformed into "the eye-code of writing". See Taavitsainen/ Melchers/Pahta (1999) for a general discussion of non-standard in literary and non-literary texts.

As regards the seventeenth century the plosive devoicing is a constant feature of the stage Welshman. For example, in portraying the speech patterns of Fluellen, Shakespeare in *Henry V* (1599) often resorts to the above-mentioned orthographic substitution to indicate plosive devoicing. However, as the passage below exemplifies, the devoicing process in Shakespeare's Welsh captain's speech is simply based around substituting *p* for *b*, and does not extend to the other plosives as is the case in the Civil War pamphlets.

(5)   The rascally, scald, beggarly, lousy, pragging knave, Pistol, – which you and yourself and all the 'orld know to be no petter than a fellow, – look you now, of no merits, he is come to me and prings me pread and salt yesterday, look you, and pid me eat my leek. It was in a place where I could not preed no contention with him; but I will be so pold as to wear it in my cap till I see him once again [...] (*Henry V*, Act 5, Scene 1, 5-12)[11]

The likelihood that what was a stereotypical feature of seventeenth-century WE did reflect actual speech patterns is moreover corroborated by more recent descriptions of the dialect. For example, in his eighteenth-century pronouncing dictionary Sheridan (1780: 62) writes of this aspect of WE:

(6)   The peculiarity of the Welsh pronunciation arises chiefly from their constantly substituting the three pure mutes, in the room of the three impure [...] Thus instead of *b* they use *p*; for *g* they use *k*, or hard *c*; and for *d* they employ *t*. Thus instead of *blood* they say *plut*, for *God*, *Cot*, and for *dear*, *tear*. [12]

Furthermore, regarding modern WE, Thomas says (1994: 122-123) that as "plosives in Welsh English are accompanied by a much stronger aspiration feature than are those in RP", the "aspiration which accompanies *voiced* plosives in WE is almost as strong as that which accompanies *voiceless* plosives in RP." In conclusion, the orthographically-represented plosive devoicing found in the WE pamphlets

---

11   Other examples of extensive plosive devoicing are also found in Dekker's *Patient Grissil* (1600) and Jonson's *For the Honour of Wales* (1619).

12   Regarding Sheridan's comments on WE see Beal (2004: 333-334).

recorded what since the early modern period has been regarded as one of the most salient phonological traits of WE.[13]

Although this non-standard orthography is primarily designed to reflect WE pronunciation, there are also cases where it foregrounds words of marked cultural importance. When this occurs, the deviant spelling underlines more often than not the usually comic contrast between the signified, and its high cultural status, and its non-standard signifier. Such a contrast very often leads to bathos. Thus, it is no coincidence that the plosive devoicing is found with such culturally significant terms as British and God. The WE spelling of *prittish* for 'British' is designed to underline the Welsh people's pretensions to being the original Britons. The pamphleteers are effectively saying that if the Welsh cannot even pronounce the word properly, they have no right to claim native British status. Far from being native Britons, the Welsh, in their inability to conform to the standard pronunciation, are revealing their own foreignness.

The non-standard spelling of 'kot' for 'god' is also significant. This word is above all found in *The Welch-Mans Warning Piece* which, as explained in the pamphlet's subtitle, is apparently the printed version of a WE sermon. However, as the pamphlet is anti-Welsh, the sermon is not surprisingly a spoof where what comes to the fore is the Welsh clergyman's primitive, unreformed understanding of God and religion. As illustrated in the following passage, the clergyman's warning to his congregation is fatuous in content and semi-illiterate in linguistic expression, where even the key word 'god' is misspelt.

(7)   Tus peloved her may see wat creat danger tis to pe tunkerds, horemasters, and inteet to be nought: pe cood fellows, put not tunk; love woman, put not hores; live honestly and Cot will plesse ye. So for tis time her has tone; for her tink tat Tinner is almost ready, to which Kot pring her for mercy sake, *Amen.*

Another example of plosive devoicing is *prave* as opposed to 'brave'. In this circumstance what is often being foregrounded in the

---

13   In line with Beal (2004: 333) I consider a salient pronunciation as being one that is "recognized by the speech community as being associated with a set of non-linguistic characteristics of the speaker, such as age, social class or region".

pamphlets is the comic reality behind the bombast and self-aggrand-isement of the stereotypical Welshman. For example, in *The Welch-mens Prave Resolution* we find the Welsh soldiers' so-called bravery being in fact equated to an irrational desire to fight for a cause about which they knew little or nothing. The stupidity of this innate bellicosity is then compounded by the Welsh soldiers' actual showing in battle, where at one of the first military engagements of the Civil War the Welsh contingent, according to the pamphleteer, retreated from the battlefield in abject disarray.

3.1.2. *Plosive substitution of fricative*

Non-standard orthography is also found in the words *te* and *tat*. In both cases the phonological process involves the plosivisation of the dental fricative. In some cases, as in (8), *te* and *tat* constantly replace *the* and *that*, whilst in other pamphlets (9) the substitution is irregular:

(8)   Since her toe understand, tat te enemy toe approach and treaten not only to cut
         her troat cowardly, put also to hinter te procetings of te Pritish Parliament, her
         tink it high time to look apout her [...]
                                               (*The Welchmens Prave Resolution* 1642: 1)

(9)   Her Countries of *Wales* peing te ancient Nurceries and habitations of the true
         Prittish plood, ascending from old anticke Families, having to her creat
         disgrace received many affronts, indignities, and injuries from her cunning
         enemies, especially from that Rascall [...] (*Newes from Wales* 1642: 1)

However, unlike plosive devoicing, the plosivisation of the dental fricative as seen in the non-standard forms *te* and *tat* was not regularly represented as stereotypical WE in contemporary literary texts. For example, while occasionally found in Fluellen's speeches in *Henry V* (1599) these forms very infrequently occur in Dekker's *Patient Grissil* (1600) and Jonson's *For the Honour of Wales* (1619), plays which also contain WE speakers. Rather than reflecting WE speech, it is likely that the presence of *te* and *tat* in the mock Welsh pamphlets should be seen as markers of general non-standard English, since early seventeenth-century dramatists often foregrounded the deviant pronunciation of the dental fricative *th* in their dramatisation of non-native English speakers. In most cases the dental fricative is substituted by either *d* or *t*. Thus, in Shakespeare's *Henry V* (1599), the King of France's daughter pronounces 'the' and 'that' as *dat* and *de*. Similar substitution is also found in another of Shakespeare's plays, *The Merry Wives of Windsor* (1601). The speaker, Doctor Caius, is again French, and he pronounces 'these toys' as "des-toyes" (I.iv.448). In contrast, Blake writes that the orthographic substitution of *t* for *th* was commonly adopted in the rendering of "Dutch attempts to speak English" (1981: 77). Examples of such substitution are found in Dekker's *The Shoemaker's Holiday* (1601) and Marston's *The Dutch Courtesan* (1605).[14]

3.1.3. Miscellaneous non-standard orthography

WE pronunciation is also frequently conveyed by the substitution of *sh* for *j*, *ch*, and *g*, that is, the substitution of the fricative for the affricate. This process is most frequently found with the archetypal early modern English Welsh forename Jenkin, that becomes *Shinkin*, but it also occurs with numerous other words too. These include *sheese, shildren,* and *shentleman* ('cheese', 'children' and 'gentleman'). As with the misspelt *prittish, got,* and *prave*, it is no coincidence that the non-standard orthography is found with the lexemes 'cheese' and 'gentleman'. The former, along with leeks and onions, was considered part of the Welshman's impoverished staple diet. This fact in itself was already amusing for English readers, given that it reflected the rustic backwardness of the Welsh, but the humour is further reinforced by the non-standard spelling of their principal food. Regarding 'gentleman', here the humour is centred around the clash between the Welshman's self-belief that he is indeed a gentleman, and, on the other hand, his obvious lack of education preventing him from even spelling the word correctly.

As with the previously analysed examples of non-standard orthography, the pamphleteers' use of *sh* for *j*, *ch*, and *g* was not unique in the representation of seventeenth-century WE. It is found, though not often, in Fluellen's speeches as well as in *Patient Grissil* (1600) and *For the Honour of Wales* (1619). We also see the sub-

---

14   For further information on the orthographic representation of non-native English speakers' pronunciation in seventeenth-century English drama, see Blake (1981: 80-107).

stitution of the affricate in another of Dekker's plays, *Satiromastix* (1601), though here *sh* is usually changed to *s*.[15]

Other examples of non-standard orthography comprise either the elision of initial *w* or its substitution by *v*. Thus we find *vas* for 'was' and *urld* and *hole* for 'world' and 'whole'. These changes are particularly evident in *The Welchmens Prave Resolution* (1642), the pamphlet where non-standard spelling is most obviously exploited in the representation of WE. However, not even in this pamphlet do we find the substitution of *f* for *v*, which frequently makes up the stock Welshman's speech patterns in late Elizabethan and early seventeenth-century English drama.[16]

3.1.4. 'Bad orthographies' and 'pad English'

Although, as we shall see below, WE in Civil War pamphlets is also represented at a morphological level, as well as by a few stock lexical expressions considered typical of WE discourse, what stands out in the pamphleteers' representation of this dialect is the recurrence of non-standard orthography. This is not surprising in that not only did non-standard orthography reflect non-standard pronunciation but it was also regarded by the pamphleteers as indicative of the user's generally deficient level of English. The emphasis placed on ortho-graphy, and how through its misuse, that is, "bad orthographies" (*Newes from Wales* 1642: 2), it was possible to discern a person's lack of education, comes out very clearly in *Newes from Wales* (1642: 6). In his discussion of the various measures the proposed Welsh Parliament will introduce, the mock Welsh pamphleteer says:

(10)   And because her Parishes are consisting of a few pig houses out of which a little smoak doth break forth at the top of shimneys, and that her *Schoolmasters* have put poor & peggerly *pensions, for her Instructions of her shildren*, he was therfore in intention to desire her welch *Parliament* to give her childs *Tutors and Schoolmasters* ten s. more yearly for to pay her pooks

---

15   Sir Rees ap Vaughan, the Welshman in the play, speaks in marked WE dialect in the latter part of the drama. It is worth noting that neither the substitution of the affricate by the fricative nor the above-mentioned plosivisation of dental fricatives in *3.1.2.* is a feature of modern-day WE.

16   See, for example, *Patient Grissil* (1600). It is also found in the broadside *The Welchmans Inventory* (1641).

> reparre's, and other cood necessaries, this so her children may learn to make petter *Orthographies,* then her *Fore-fathers*, and not put up [sic] derision for her pad English.

What the writer is therefore saying is that the Welsh Parliament will provide extra funds for schoolmasters so that they can teach their pupils to write "petter *Orthographies*". For the pamphleteer correct orthography is essential, and without it the future generations of Welsh children will be as rightly derided as their ancestors for their "pad English".[17]

This emphasis on orthography and the assertion that its incorrect usage resulted in contempt reflected received opinion among mid-seventeenth century pamphleteers. For example, *Mercurius Aulicus*, the royalist publication, refuted a Parliamentarian pamphlet's assertion that the King's forces, based in Oxford, should have stuck to "Lodgick", or other academic pursuits associated with that university town rather than becoming embroiled in politics by retorting: "Good Sir let *Logicke* alone till you can spell it without a D." (*Mercurius Aulicus,* 23 June-29 June 1644, 1062). Orthography provided the all-important key to understanding the value of a person or publication, and where orthography did not conform to standard practice that person was rightly ignored.[18]

---

17 *Newes from Wales* (1642: 7) also implies there are poor levels of English literacy in Wales: "And that if any of her poor cosen or country men doe through necessities, wants, and poverties, steal or porrow of her next Neighbours, any cow, sheepe, coat, or peast, and be apprehended for felonies, her shall py statutes of Parliament not pe put to her pook because her is pad reader of English Pooks and languages".

18 The exceptionally high status accorded to correct orthography did not just apply to English but also to Latin. Once again reference can be made to *Mercurius Aulicus*, which mocked the Parliamentarian newsbook *Mercurius Britanicus* for its incorrect spelling of 'Britannicus'. Regarding the Parliamentarian pamphlet, *Mercurius Aulicus* writes that "we are still resolved to take no notice, till we find him able to spell his owne name, which to this hower *Britannicus* never did" (14-20 July 1644: 1090). The royalist pamphlet reiterates the point a few weeks later when in referring to the enemy publication the editor states: "could it onely spell its owne name true (which to this day, *Britannicus* never yet did) then should your suite be granted by being taken notice of" (4-10 August 1644: 1114).

3.2. Morphology

The most foregrounded feature in the representation of WE is the use
of *her*. Throughout the corpus *her* has multiple referencing potential
in that it can refer to both the singular and plural forms of first, second
and third person pronoun, both subject and accusative, as well as to
the whole range of possessive adjectives. The following passage from
The Welch-mans publike Recantation (1642: 1) provides a typical
example of both the frequency and use of *her*:

(11)   May it please all and every one that shall cast her good and favourable eyes
        uppon this sheetes of papers, to know and beleeve that all her Country-men of
        Wales by whatsoever appellations they be called are wonderfully sorry for her
        late temerities and rashnesse, whereunto the Divill owing her a spight led her
        blind fold, for her doe <unclear> over-flowing her cheekes, and drowning her
        hearts inward and outward acknowledg and confesse, (which her will not doe
        at a Sessions, for feare of hanging) that her was very strangly deceived by
        politique jeeres, flatteries […]

The frequency of *her* in this passage illustrates the pre-eminent
position of *her* in the representation of WE throughout all the
pamphlets in the corpus. More than any other single item, be it
orthographic, morphological or lexical, it is the use of *her* that the
English Civil War pamphleteers wanted to foreground in their
representation of WE dialect. Thus, even in *The Welch-mans publike
Recantation* (1642), where the non-standard orthography characteristic of much mock WE pamphlets is far less frequent than in some
of the other separates, the use of *her* is nevertheless very high.

   In drawing upon *her* as a characterising feature of WE, the
London pamphleteers were working within the literary and cheap print
tradition of WE representation. *Her* is for example found in *Patient
Grissil* (1600), *Satiromastix* (1601), *For the Honour of Wales* (1619)
as well as in *The Welchmans Inventory* (1641).[19] However, although
the presence of *her* is found in the late sixteenth- and early seventeenth-century representation of WE it was by no means as

---

19   The inventory contains, for example, a legacy to the Welshman's wife, which
      reads: "A Note of some Legacy of a creat deale of goods bequeathed to her
      owne wife & her two shild, and all her cozens, friends and kindred, in manner
      as followeth" (*The Welchmans Inventory* 1641).

consistently foregrounded as in the Civil War pamphlets. What this means is that the London pamphleteers must have found the marked usage of *her* particularly suitable for their representation of WE and Welshness generally. Given the socio-historical context in which the pamphleteers were writing, there would seem to be two principal explanations for this emphatic usage.

The first relates to the fact that as *her* has multiple referencing potential, and is used very frequently, the text itself is often not immediately comprehensible. Of course, in comparison with the seventeenth-century reader, modern readers are at a disadvantage in that they do not possess as wide a contextual knowledge, but even accepting this I nevertheless think the Civil War reader would also have been occasionally uncertain as to who or what *her* referred to. Yet, paradoxically, this textual opaqueness served the writer's objectives in that the communicative obscurity iconically reflected the Welshman's own mental confusion. What the pamphleteer lost in ensuring immediacy of comprehension he gained in the textual representation of the comic substandard mental processes of the Welsh.[20]

The other reason why the pamphleteers may have found *her* especially suitable was because of the word's inherent femininity. Given that one of the lines of humour running throughout the Civil War pamphlets was the contrast between the Welshman's self-glorification as warrior and combatant and his actual, real-life military ignominy, the continual presence of *her* succeeds in underlining the innate femininity of the Welshman's character despite all his bombast and bluster.[21] The likelihood of this explanation would seem to be reinforced by the fact that whereas in other earlier seventeenth-century renderings of WE texts *her* had also been spelt as *hur*, in the Civil

---

20   Full comprehension becomes particularly problematic in *The Welch-Mans Complements* (1643) when it is sometimes not at all clear whether the *her* used by Shinkin refers to himself or Maudlin: "her thought with good audacities and boldnesse, to utter her mind in as good languages as her could, desiring her not to look upon her with her Welsh frowns (for frowns will spoile her beauties) but with a smiling countenance behold the dolours and griefes which *Shinkin* sustaines for her sakes [...]" (1643: 1).

21   Bowen (2004: 365) writes that "in feminizing the Welsh out of their own mouths, Parliamentary commentators maintained their satirical treatment while also impugning Welsh pretensions to military expertise."

War pamphlets only the first spelling is given, that is, the same spelling as the feminine pronoun and possessive adjective.[22]

As regards the origin of *her* in the English representation of WE there would seem to be a two-phase process. Lord (1995: 38) says that originally the use of *her* in WE may have arisen as a consequence of the Welsh word 'hi', meaning 'she' or *her*, looking and sounding similar to the English male pronoun. Therefore, originally the English understood, or, at least, amusedly took the Welsh female pronoun or possessive adjective to have both female and male referencing, and once this initial conclusion had been reached the English writers of WE extended the referencing range to all persons and cases.

The pamphleteers' massively foregrounded exploitation of *her* in their representation of WE completely dominates any other morphological, or indeed syntactic trait of WE. As regards syntax, there is little to say in that no generalised dialectal features are evident. For example, there is neither a marked use of periphrastic *do* in affirmative declaratives nor is there any foregrounded absence of subject–verb concordance. The fact that subject-verb concordance is respected is interesting in that it noticeably contrasts with the representation of WE in *The Welchmans Inventory* (1641).[23] In this pre-Civil War publication it is precisely this detail which most obviously characterises the syntax of the dialect:

---

22   For example, only *hur* is found in the few lines of WE in Thomas Nashe's play *Summers Last Will and Testament* (1600: ll. 341-343): "*Hur come to Powl* (as the Welshman sayes) *and hur pay an halfpenny for hur seat, and hur heare the Preacher talge, and a talge very well by gis* [...]". In *The Welch Man's Inventory* (1641), which was published just before the onset of the Civil War, *hur* is still the predominant form, though this one-page licensed broadside, which was "Printed by and for W.O.", can be contrasted with *The Welchmans Inventory* (1641), another version of the same story, published in the same year, but printed by "*Thomas Lambert* dwelling in Smithfield". What distinguishes this latter publication from the former is the consistent use of the pronoun *her*. It is reasonable to believe that in consistently using *her* as opposed to *hur* the author of *The Welchmans Inventory* (1641) is making a sociopolitical statement.

23   For two occurrences of a lack of subject-verb concordance in *The Welch-mans publike Recantation* (1642) see "this sheetes of papers", "led away in a fooles paradises".

(12)   *In primis* in the pantry of poultry for her owne eating, one great pigge 4.
        weeke old, one Coose, one Cock gilding, two blacke pudding, three Cowfoot.
        Item, in the pantry of plate, one Cridiron, one frypan, one trip pan, three
        woodden (sic) Cup, sixe woodden (sic) spoone, one wooden ladle, three Cann.

The presence of subject-verb concordance in the Civil War pamphlets
has two possible explanations. Either it is determined by the
pamphleteers' realisation that such a linguistic trait indeed reflected
WE, or, and in my opinion this is highly probable, the writers
preferred to represent WE deviance through other means. By focusing
their attention on non-standard orthography and the use of *her*, the
pamphleteers were already rendering their representation of WE
sufficiently opaque. Had they also characterised WE by a foregrounded lack of subject-verb concordance their texts risked
appearing little more than gibberish. This need to create a text that
generally could be easily read and enjoyed also explains why clause
structure is never so dense and non-standard that comprehension is
impeded. When sentence structure deviates from standard models, as
is the case in the following passage from *The Welch-Mans Warning
Piece* (1642: 6), it is meant to reflect the simple, often garrulous
thought processes of the stereotypical Welshman:

(13)   Tus you see good people, how tat *Atam* was fell, *Heva* was fell, *Lot* was fell,
        Taffie was fell, shust man *Shobe* was fell, ye all was fell; And how was all
        fell, all was fell from *Kot* to the *Tivell* [...].

3.3. Lexis

As is characteristic in the written representation of historical dialect,
what we find in the mock Welsh pamphlets is the foregrounded use of
certain stereotypical expressions associated with WE. These comprise
the exclamation "by Cods plutter a Nailes", or variations of this
expression, such as, "By Gods plutra nayles". Examples of the usage
of such exclamations include: "yet her have hands cods plutter a nails
and arms too" (*Newes from Wales* 1642) and "*By Gods plutra nayles*,
her had such good pay, that her desire never to be so payd againe"
(*The Welch-mans publike Recantation* 1642). However, whether these
idioms were actually found in contemporary WE is debatable since

one eighteenth-century Welsh writer described the exclamatory "by Cods plutter a Nailes" as a "Welsh oath manufactured in England" (Lord 1995: 34).

Other recurrent expressions include the discourse markers "looke you" ('you see') and "mark her that now". These expressions, and the first is also found in modern-day WE, reflect the word order of Welsh, where the verb precedes its subject:

(14)   […] and contrary (looke you) to her expectations, have to her further
         reproaches received nothing put contumelies and dirisions […]
         (*Newes from Wales, or, the Prittish Parliament* 1642: 1)

(15)   […] the Redcoats did so pay her, that her was fain to run from her pay, mark
         her that now, her could have found better occupying at home […]
         (*The Welch-mans publike Recantation* 1642: 3)

There is just one example of a word unequivocally referring to a unique aspect of Welsh life and culture. This is the term *metheglin*, derived from Welsh *meddyglyn*, and referring to a popular Welsh mead it represented one of the basic consolatory pleasures of the archetypal Welshman as personified by Shinkin:

(16)   Thus her will give away all her hath, and her selfe, and all about her, and
         make her selfe as poor as any Brittaine in Wales, that her may purchase the
         Love and affections of her dearest *Maudlin*, give her therefore her pray you
         some good answers that may comfort her despayrinng hearts as much as her
         own Country metheglin doth. (*The Welch-Mans Complements* 1643: 3)

Other WE-sounding lexemes, such as *Carriwhiblin*, and *Couf-bobby* in *The Welch-Mans Complements* (1643), could well have been invented by the English author of the mock Welsh pamphlet. As these words have neither been found in other seventeenth-century WE representations, nor exist in any Welsh or WE dictionary, it is possible they were merely intended to sound comic, thereby underlining the quintessential silliness of the Welsh language itself.

However, apart from specific WE lexis, the mock Welsh pamphlets also foreground the Welsh people's tendency to privilege particular kinds of English vocabulary. This feature is most obviously underlined in *The Welch-Mans Complements* (1643), where in her rejection of her Welsh suitor, Shinkin, the English maid, Maudlin, makes much play of Shinkin's use of language, and in particular his predilection for certain lexis. In her very first speech, Maudlin pithily tells the Welshman to avoid troubling his brain : "with studying hard words and speeches, to demonstrate your affection, Welch-men were never true". However, Maudlin's request is futile, since it is just the use of hard words that Shinklin reverts to in his attempt to win the English maiden's heart. Being stereotypically garrulous and infatuated with the sound of obscure, polysyllabic words, this Welshman cannot refrain from using such lexis in his risible declaration of love, that comically jolts from vain attempts at Ciceronian elegance to everyday expressions of common vulgarity and lust:

(17)   Sweet *Maudlin*, her do honour the very ob-umbrations of *her* shoo-ties, *her* do reverence *her* very posteriours, and would salute *her* behind and before whensoever *her* meet *her*, sweete *Maudlin* [...]

                                    (*The Welch-Mans Complements* 1643: 5)

(18)   I would *her* were any thing, so *her* might enjoy *her* corpusculum; then would *her* have about with her *Nunquam Satis*: O that sweet Angels face of thine, fair **Maudlin** hath ravelled me, I am enamelled with thy beautie [...]

                                    (*The Welch-Mans Complements* 1643: 6)

It is no wonder that Maudlin rejects the Welshman's "cotten candle eloquence [...] full of froth and emptinesse". Indeed, his amorous protestations are so vacuous that the English maiden impatiently exclaims: "I would do any thing to be rid of a foolish, idle, Welch prating parret, that loves to heare himselfe talke nothing but peddlers French" – with the reference to "French" being most likely an allusion to Shinkin's preference for grandiloquent hard words rather than the 'plain English' adopted by Maudlin.[24]

What accompanies, and renders even more absurd, the Welshman's empty rhetoric is his frequent recourse to prolonged disquisitions on aspects concerning what for English eyes was a very primitive, rustic existence. In these passages, the reader is presented with a highly detailed account of Welsh life and culture revolving around such basic goods, animals and settings as cheese, leeks, cows,

---

24   In response to one of Shinkin's speeches Maudlin proclaims: "I tel you plainly, I cannot fancy your person, nor love your conditions" (*The Welch-Mans Complements* 1643: 6).

goats, pig houses and mountains. Shinkin, for example, provides an exemplification of how the Welsh staple diet is based around an infinite number of cheeses:

> (19) *her* shall have [...] new sheeze as new as *her* moon: and old sheeze as auncient as the Creation; such sheeze as is able to go alone: besides *her* shall have raw sheeze; then *her* shall have warm or roasted sheeze; then *her* shall have baked sheeze, then fry'd sheeze, then broyled cheeze, sod cheeze, parboyl'd cheeze & stewed cheeze [...]
>
> (*The Welch-Mans Complements* 1643: 6)

Finally, whatever the vocabulary, whether it was intended as a representation of actual or mock WE, or instead a parodic exemplification of the Welsh predilection for 'hard words', it was nevertheless written by a 'taffie', the generic name the English gave to all Welshmen, who were invariably the cousin of a cousin of a cousin, and whose patronymic lineage is painstakingly referenced in the mock Welsh pamphlets by the Welsh proposition *ap* ('son of') between each given family ancestor. Thus, on the title page of *The Welchmens Prave Resolution* (1642), we read that the pamphlet was written by "Shon, ap William, ap Richard, ap Thomas, ap Meredith, ap Evans, ap Loyd, ap Price, ap Hugh, ap Rowland, ap Powel, ap Shinkin, ap Shones".

4. Conclusion

Although the anti-Welsh pamphlets examined in this chapter vary considerably as to the degree of WE they insert in the text, they all exploit the same general strategies for their representation of the dialect. In presenting WE they above all rely on non-standard orthography, the use of the multiple referential pronoun or possessive adjective *her*, and easily identifiable lexical characterization.

Regarding *her*, it is the continual use of this word that stands out in all the pamphlets and which in the eyes of the London pamphleteers at the time of the English Civil War characterizes their parodic version of WE more than any other feature. As for non-standard orthography, this is not only designed to reflect Welsh pronunciation, which – being different from standard London pronunciation – implicitly means it is comic, but also to demonstrate the Welshman's general inability to speak and write good English. This latter aspect is explicitly referred to in *Newes from Wales* (1642), the pamphlet which most emphatically expresses prescriptive meta-linguistic comment. What this pamphlet states directly, the other pamphlets are throughout implying: WE is the dialect of borderland rustics and bumpkins.

References

Primary sources

Dekker, Thomas 1600. *Patient Grissil.*
Dekker, Thomas 1601. *Satiromastix.*
Dekker, Thomas 1601. *The Shoemaker's Holiday.*
Jonson, Ben 1619. *For the Honour of Wales.*
Marston, John 1605. *The Dutch Courtesan.*
Mercurius Aulicus 15-21 October 1643; 23 June-29 June 1644; 30 June-6 July 1644; 14-20 July 1644; 4-10 August 1644.
Mercurius Britanicus 29 July-5 August 1644; 26 August-2 September 1644.
Nashe, Thomas 1600. *Summers Last Will and Testament.*
Newes from Wales, or, the Prittish Parliament 1642.
Shakespeare, William 1599. *Henry V.*
Shakespeare, William 1601. *The Merry Wives of Windsor.*
Sheridan, Thomas 1780. *A General Dictionary of the English Language.* London: J. Dodsley / C. Dilly / J. Wilkie.
The Welch Man's Inventory 1641.
The Welchmans Inventory 1641.
The Welch-Mans Complements, or the true manner how Shinkin wooed his Sweet-heart Maudlin after his returne from Kenton Battaile 1643.

The Welch-mans publike Recantation or, His hearty sorrow for taking up of Armes against her Parliament 1642.
The Welch-Mans Warning Piece. As it was delivered in a Sermon in Shropshire 1642.
The Welch Mercury / Mercurius Cambro-Britannus Oct. 1643 – Jan. 1644.
The Welchmens Prave Resolution: in Defence of her King, her Pritish Parliament, and Her Country, gainst te malignant party 1642.
The Welshmans Postures: or, The true manner how her doe exercise her company of Souldiers in her owne Countrey 1642.

Secondary sources

Bartley, James 1943. The Development of a Stock Character, iii: The Stage Welshman (to 1800). *Modern Language Review* 38, 284-288.
Bartley, James 1954. *Teague Shenkin and Sawney Being an Historical Study of the Earliest Irish Welsh and Scottish Characters in English Plays*. Cork: Cork University Press.
Beal, Joan 2004. Marks of Disgrace: Attitudes to Non-Standard Pronunciation in 18th-Century English Pronouncing Dictionaries. In Dossena, Marina / Lass, Roger (eds) *Methods and Data in English Historical Dialectology*. Bern: Peter Lang, 329-349.
Blake, Norman 1981. *Non-standard Language in English Literature*. London: André Deutsch.
Bowen, Lloyd 2004. Representations of Wales and the Welsh during the Civil Wars and Interregnum. *Historical Research* 77/197, 358-376.
Brownlees, Nicholas 2005. Spoken Discourse in Early English Newspapers. In Raymond, Joad (ed.) *News Networks in Early Modern Britain and Europe*. London: Routledge, 67-84.
Brownlees, Nicholas 2006. Polemic and Propaganda in Civil War News Discourse. In Brownlees, Nicholas (ed.) *News Discourse in Early Modern England*. Bern: Peter Lang, 19-42.
Chapman, Raymond 1994. *Forms of Speech in Victorian Fiction*. London: Longman.

Lord, Peter 1995. *Words with Pictures. Welsh Images and Images of Welsh in the Popular Press, 1640-1860*. Aberystwyth: Planet.

Porter, Gerald 1999. The Ideology of Misrepresentation: Scots in English Broadsides. In Taavitsainen/Melchers/Pahta (eds), 361-374.

Raymond, Joad 1996. *The Invention of the Newspaper. English Newsbooks 1641-1649*. Oxford: Clarendon.

Raymond, Joad 2003. *Pamphlets and Pamphleteering in Early Modern Britain*. Cambridge: Cambridge University Press.

Royle, Trevor 2004. *Civil War: the Wars of the Three Kingdoms*. London: Abacus.

Russell, Conrad 1990. *The Causes of the English Civil War*. Oxford: Clarendon.

Stoyle, Mark 2000a. English 'Nationalism', Celtic Particularism and the English Civil War. *The Historical Journal* 43/4, 1113-1128.

Stoyle, Mark 2000b. Caricaturing Cymru: Images of the Welsh in the London Press 1642-46. In Dunn, Diana (ed.) *War and Society in Medieval and Early Modern Britain*. Liverpool: Liverpool University Press, 162-179.

Taavitsainen, Irma / Melchers, Gunnel 1999. Writing in Nonstandard English: Introduction. In Taavitsainen/Melchers/Pahta (eds), 2-26.

Taavitsainen, Irma / Melchers, Gunnel / Pahta, Päivi (eds) 1999. *Writing in Nonstandard English*. Amsterdam: Benjamins.

Thomas, Alan 1994. English in Wales. In Burchfield, Robert (ed.) *The Cambridge History of the English Language*. Vol. 5. Cambridge: Cambridge University Press, 94-147.

ADRIAN PABLÉ

Reconstructing the History of Two Colonial New England Terms of Address: *Goodman* and *Goodwife*

1. Introduction

The following contribution is concerned with the titles of respect *Goodman* and *Goodwife* (and its contracted form *Goody*) as used in colonial North America, New England in particular. The titles under scrutiny have been extinct for a long time and are no longer known by Americans – except for some specialists, most likely historians, literary scholars and historical linguists. When Nathaniel Hawthorne published his *Young Goodman Brown* in 1835, however, he may still have relied on his American readers knowing that 'Goodman' and 'Goodwife' had been common titles of civility in early New England, besides the more obvious fact that he was exploiting the morphemic transparency inherent in these titles ('good + man/wife') for his criticism of Puritan ideology. Less certain is whether Hawthorne's contemporaries also realized a further parallel between the fictional piece and reality, namely that the expression *young goodman* designated a 'newly wed man' in Scotland (and in fact, Hawthorne's 'Young Goodman Brown' has only been married for three months), while *old Goodman* was a euphemistic term for the Devil (in the story, 'young Goodman Brown' meets an elderly man, who looks like his father and grandfather respectively, both known as 'old Goodman Brown': later on, this man will in fact reveal himself as the Devil). It is hardly surprising, therefore, to find modern editions of Hawthorne's *Young Goodman Brown* with a note explaining both the 'meaning' of *Goodman, Goodwife/Goody* and their status in early New England.

2. Aim and scope

The New England titles of address *Goodman* and *Goodwife* have only been treated *en passant* in the scholarly literature.[1] The present contribution, therefore, moves on unexplored grounds, and can only present preliminary findings in need of verification and further research. Some of the insights presented here are the result of written exchanges that I entertained with historians and linguists working on Early America, and whose help I gratefully acknowledge.[2]

This study considers the following themes:

- *Goodman* and *Goodwife* in Early Modern England;
- the region- and culture-specific distribution of *Goodman* and *Goodwife* in colonial America;
- possible reasons for the disappearance of *Goodman* and *Good-wife* from New England speech and culture;
- the use of *Goodman* and *Goodwife* in a late seventeenth-century New England community (i.e. Salem, Massachusetts), based on the *Salem Witchcraft Papers* (Boyer/Nissenbaum 1977), a collection of documents relating to the witchcraft episode of 1692.

Concerning the microlinguistic approach, the choice of the *Salem Witchcraft Papers* as my primary source was motivated by their suitability for the kind of investigation at issue. As the trial protocols

---

1   To my knowledge, Dawes (1949) is the only one treating early New England titles of address, among which *Goodman/Goodwife*, in more depth. Pablé (2003) also considers them, but in relation to nineteenth-century fiction. As far as the British context is concerned, there are a handful of studies dealing – in part – with the Early Modern titles under scrutiny, with respect to the fictional context, i.e. in Early Modern drama (e.g. Stoll 1989; Busse 2003) as well as based on the scrutiny of commentaries (e.g. Williams 1992) or records (e.g. Postles 2005).

2   My thanks go to Richard Brown (University of Connecticut), Loise Greene Carr (Maryland State Archives), Ava Chamberlain (Wright State University), Gloria L. Main (University of Colorado), John Murrin (Princeton University), Mary Beth Norton (Cornell University), Bernard Rosenthal (SUNY, Binghamton), Laurel Ulrich (Harvard University), and Laura Wright (Cambridge University).

contained in the *Papers* – i.e. the public examinations of people accused of witchcraft – were in part recorded by the village clerks as direct discourse, they allow us to gain an insight into late seventeenth-century 'spoken' American English.

Moreover, the witchcraft episode brought before the magistrates subjects whose voices are rarely recorded in documents of the Early Modern period, i.e. children, adolescents working as servant-girls or farm-hands, slaves, and the common folk in general. In the examination records, these people interact with both their social peers and their social superiors. These constellations are likely to advance our knowledge of the multiple ways in which forms of address were used in speech by the various groups of New England Puritans.[3]

In order to understand how *Goodman* and *Goodwife* were applied in colonial America, it is necessary to compare them with the next higher titles of address in use, i.e. the honorifics *Master* and *Mistress* (usually appearing in the records as *Mr.* and *Mrs.*). In the primary sources consulted the occurrence of *Goodman* and *Goodwife/ Goody* is confined to their use as prefixes to the names of persons.[4]

3. The English context

Obviously, the titles *Goodman* and *Goodwife* were not coined in North America, but were brought to the New World from England in the early seventeenth century, hence at a time when, according to Williams (1992), their use was already in rapid decline and subject to

---

3   Indeed, the *Salem Witchcraft Papers* are a unique source because they contain large stretches of direct discourse, whereas in other collections of seventeenth-century records from New England, e.g. the *Annals of Witchcraft in New England* or the *Suffolk Records*, the spoken interactions are chiefly rendered as indirect discourse.

4   It is noteworthy that in the *Salem Witchcraft Papers* there are no examples of *Goodman* and *Goodwife* meaning 'husband/master of the house' and 'wife/ mistress of the house', i.e. the terms are used exclusively as prefixed titles. Thus, we do not find instances where a wife refers to the husband as 'her goodman'.

high stigmatization. This statement begs the question of why the titles at issue underwent such a fate in England at all. In his article, Williams shows that already by the middle of the sixteenth century, the artisan class, which Williams compares to the 'lower middle classes' of our days, was displaying an "upwardly mobile behavior", which manifested itself in the emulation of speech and apparel associated with their social superiors (the gentility). Particularly affected seem to have been the so-called "skilled domestic artificers", i.e. those who made consumer goods (e.g. goldsmiths, tailors, shoemakers, drapers, chandlers, vintners); in fact, much to the dismay of several contemporary conservative critics, these artificers were often mistaken for members of the gentility and wrongly addressed as 'Master' and 'Sir', thus far reserved for gentlemen and affluent merchants. Writing in 1555, the poet Nicholas Grimald blamed the less well-to-do merchants for the artisans' usurpation of a title that was traditionally not theirs:

> Most men desire the title of worship, but few do worke the dedes that unto worship do apparteigne: yea the marchantman thinketh not himselfe well used unles he be called one of the worshipful sort of marchants, of whom the handicraftman hath taked example, & loketh to be called maister, whose father and grandfather were wont to be called good men. Thus through the title of maistershippe most men covet to climbe the steppes of worshippe which title, had wont to appartaine to gentlemen onely, and men of office and estimacion [...] Theyr fathers was contented to bee called goodmen, John or Thomas and now they at every assise are clepid worshipfull Esquiers
>
> (quoted by Williams 1992: 85)

Williams' scrutiny of records listing renters of several London parishes confirms that by the early seventeenth century "the prestige of *goodman* [had] fallen below no form of address at all", which explains why *Goodman Tailor* wanted to be addressed as *Master Tailor*. Williams goes on to say that "if *Mr.* was becoming the default form of address for any reasonable respectable person, then *goodman* may have been marked as affirmatively demeaning" (1992: 89). In fact, in the parish records, literate tradesmen and skilled artisans, who paid higher annual rents, were entered as 'Mr. so-and-so', whereas unskilled (and illiterate) workers, who paid lower annual rents, were entered as 'Goodman so-and-so' or without a title of address (e.g.

cloth-workers, bricklayers, porters). Williams (1992: 89) concludes as follows:

> what we do see in these data is evidence that occupation and title no longer reflected a strict social order in which birth or occupation determined who would be called what. They suggest a social order in which people were addressed in ways that reflected their economic status.

In a more recent article, Postles (2005), who looked into early to mid-seventeenth-century parish records from all over England, arrives at a different conclusion regarding the prestige attributed to *Goodman* (and *Goodwife/Goody*) in Early Modern England: Postles' choice of texts does not yield any new insights into the process described by Williams, i.e. the stigmatization of *Goodman* as a title of address, as he does not consider its use in socially asymmetrical situations (social superior addressing social inferior). Focusing on socially symmetrical usage, Postles (2005: 111) claims that, on the contrary, *Goodman* and *Goodwife* were "the most affective titles in early-modern society" and "an indication of good neighbourliness [...] usually reserved for social peers". The latter statement finds confirmation in the fact that Postles found the highest occurrence of *Goodman* and *Goodwife* in churchwardens' and constables' accounts as well as in accounts of workhouses, where they appear as titles attached to the names of people who had performed some good service (lodging poor travellers, contributing financially to the parish, engaging in voluntary labour for the workhouse, etc.). Thus, in Postles' opinion, *Goodman* had thoroughly positive connotations and

> was not applied to all males below the level of gentle folk [...] the title of *Goodman* (and *-wife*) was employed discretely and selectively; it had an almost honorific import, and demarcated a select status within a social level [i.e. the 'middling sort'], based on service and neighbourliness.

The evidence provided by Williams and Postles is not, I believe, contradictory, but rather complementary. Their findings should be kept in mind when attempting to reconstruct the history and fate of *Goodman* and *Goodwife/Goody* in the New World.

4. The colonial context

Basing his findings on a scrutiny of early colonial records, Dawes (1949) determined that *Goodman* was a 'middle class' designation among the New England colonists. My own inspection of the *Salem Witchcraft Papers* (Boyer/Nissenbaum 1977) suggests that even as late as 1692, *Goodman* and *Goodwife/Goody* were applied to highly respectable and well-to-do members of the community. As will be shown in Section 4.3, the dividing-line between 'Masters' and 'Goodmen' in New England was not a clear-cut one, and hence unlike Pre-Elizabethan England: in fact, of two New Englanders of very similar social status and economic means, one may be referred to in the records as 'Mr. so-and-so', while the other is 'Goodman so-and-so'. Before we go on to consider the cultural-geographical distribution and temporal dimension pertaining to *Goodman/Goodwife*, it is worth quoting in full length what Dawes (1949: 77-78) has to say about the New England title *Goodman*:

> Less socially significant than Mr. was the title of Goodman, also used as a designation for some members of the middle class. In fact, Goodman had the least social import of any of the general honorifics, but even Goodman had lost some of the definite social implication that was its characteristic in English society [...] Goodman in the records of the seventeenth century was used both frequently and indiscriminately as applicable to rural and urban dweller alike. [...] Goodman, save for its newly acquired characteristic of embracing the moderately prosperous townsmen along with the substantial farmers, continued to function as an indication of respectable yet not greatly elevated social station.

4.1. *The region- and culture-specific nature of* Goodman *and* Goodwife *in the early American colonies*

In the *Dictionary of American English on Historical Principles* (Craigie 1938-44: 1145), we find the following information under the entries of *Goodman* and *Goodwife*:

> *Goodman.* 'New England'. An appellation of civility prefixed to names of persons under the rank of gentlemen; similar to 'Mister'. *Obsolete.* [Then follow examples taken from records dating between 1636 and 1685].
> *Goodwife.* 'New England'. An appellation prefixed to a woman's name, equivalent to 'Mrs.'. *Obsolete.* [The examples cited as evidence are drawn from sources dating from 1622 to 1712].

On reading this, one may wonder why the two titles were confined to those colonies mainly settled by Puritans (i.e. the colonies of Massachusetts Bay, Plymouth, Connecticut and New Haven). Why would they not be attested in the Mid-Atlantic colonies (i.e. Virginia, Maryland, Delaware) as well, which were being settled at the same time? And indeed, a search on the web proves the *Dictionary of American English* wrong: for instance, among the list of names in the 1623-census of Jamestown, VA, we find four men referred to as 'Goodman + last name', five women referred to as 'Goodwife + last name' and two women referred to as 'Gody + last name'.[5] Moreover, in two articles dealing with seventeenth-century Virginia and Maryland (Beaudry 1979: 44-46; Norton 1987: 20-22), I have found examples of 'Goodwife + last name' mentioned in deposition records, dating from as late as the 1650s and 1660s. A reason why the lexicographers did not acknowledge *Goodman* and *Goodwife* as titles in use in the early southern colonies may be due to the fact that overall their presence in records from Virginia and Maryland is not as noticeable as in those from Massachusetts and Connecticut. Why is this so? In the case of Maryland, this may have to do with the fact that about three quarters of the arrivals from England were actually indentured servants, many of whom were very poor and illiterate, and who would thus not be referred to by any title. A similar argument holds for the many London deportees, mostly young homeless men and women, who were shipped in great numbers to Virginia from 1607 onwards (Wright 2003; 2004). On the other hand, this contrasts with the evidence gathered by Williams (1992) about early seventeenth-century London, where 'Goodman' was actually employed for exactly this kind of people, i.e. those who would not as a rule be able to afford to pay for the voyage. There is no way for us

---

5   See <ftp.rootsweb.ancestry.com/pub/usgenweb/va/jamestown/census/1623 cens.txt>, last accessed 3.7.08.

to know on what basis the early southern colonists were entered as 'Mr.', 'Goodman', or without a title in the lists. What we do know is that in early New England less than 25% of the immigrants were contracted labourers, i.e. there were far fewer indentured servants in the New England colonies than in Virginia and Maryland. New England and the early southern colonies thus differed in at least two ways which are pertinent to the present discussion: (i) in terms of the social and economic status of the colonists, and (ii) in terms of their denominational affiliations (i.e. Congregationalism vs. Anglicanism). I mention the latter aspect, as it may have been the case that *Goodman* and *Goodwife* already possessed indexical ('in-group') value among the Puritans in England, in which case they were taken to New England as relatively prestigious titles.

How do we know whether *Goodman* and *Goodwife* really were New England titles solely used for Puritan nonconformists? A valuable source are contemporary testimonies: for instance, in his *Magnalia Christi Americana* from 1702, Dr. Cotton Mather relates the story of Governor John Winthrop, who, while visiting Plymouth in 1632, publicly defined the term *Goodman*; allegedly, Winthrop declared that *Goodman* implied "worth as a citizen capable of serving his community in civic matters" (Dawes 1949: 78). Based on this, Dawes (1949: 78) interprets *Goodman* as an "indication of minimum civil competency" and not as indicating adherence to a particular church. We are here reminded of the positive secular connotations inherent in *Goodman/Goodwife* mentioned by Postles (2005) with respect to seventeenth-century England. According to Dawes, Governor Winthrop's metapragmatic reflection is "probably a surer guide to the New England conception of *Goodman* than is an exact history of its connotative trends prior to the era of the American migration" (1949: 78). That the 'New England conception' of the title was a somewhat controversial one in early New England is suggested by the fact that Winthrop had been asked to pronounce himself on the exact meaning (or correct usage) of *Goodman*, because two ministers maintained that it was unlawful to call any non-church member by that very title. For them, therefore, *Goodman* implied moral – rather than civic – worth. This episode suggests that 'church membership' may not have been a necessary condition for someone to be called *Goodman* or *Goodwife* in Puritan New England. At the same time, the account illustrates nicely that the titles at issue were subject to folk etymologizing, which hardly comes as a surprise given their morphological transparency.[6]

4.2. *Reasons for the disappearance of* Goodman *and* Goodwife *from New England speech and culture*

So far my scrutiny of primary sources suggests that *Goodman* and *Goodwife* remained in use until the early 1700s, mainly in New England: in fact, I have found no evidence of *Goodman* dating from the eighteenth century, and only three attestations of *Goodwife*, as a prefixed title, all dating back to not later than 1713.[7] This conclusion finds further support in the opinions expressed by some of the scholars consulted.[8] In order to argue that *Goodman* and *Goodwife* were still viable forms of address of eighteenth-century New England, it would be necessary to discover attestations dating from the latter half of that century; this, as far as I can tell, is not the case. As long as there is no counter-evidence, we may thus suppose that the titles at issue started to become disfavoured with the generation of New England Puritans born in the late seventeenth century. On the other hand, we have a statement by the linguist M. Schele De Vere, in his book on *Americanisms*, published in the early 1870s, who noted under the entry pertaining to *Goodman* and *Goody*: "continue to be used in more remote parts of [New England] and *Goody Simpkins* may be heard, without the slightest intention to speak in any but the most respectful

---

6   The etymology given by the *OED* (Volume XI: 678) is based on the same assumption, namely that *goodman* is a compound form ('good' + 'man'). For a different etymological explanation of *goodman* (and *yeoman* respectively), namely in the sense of 'countryman', see Walter Skeat's *Etymological Dictionary* (Skeat 1882 [1963]: 245/728).

7   For such late examples of 'Goodwife + name', see Upham (1867 [2000]: 627) and Murrin (2001: 27).

8   Richard Brown, professor of history at the University of Connecticut, wrote to me that he could not recollect ever encountering *Goodman* or *Goodwife* in a document after 1760 (his guess was that they were already gone by 1700). John Murrin, from Princeton University, in turn, thinks that *Goodwife* survived somewhat longer than *Goodman* – a finding that my own preliminary research corroborates.

way of *Mrs. Simpkins*" (De Vere 1872: 480). Can De Vere's statement be taken as evidence that *Goodman* and *Goody* survived unrecorded as part of the rustic dialects spoken in some forgotten corners of Maine or Vermont? If this were the case, why were these forms never used by nineteenth-century New England writers of dialect fiction, some of whom relied on stereotypical portrayals of Yankee speech and culture?

What factors, then, caused *Goodman* and *Goodwife* to disappear altogether as titles of address? At this stage, I can only offer some speculations as far as New England is concerned. With the decline of Puritan orthodoxy, those addressed as *Goodman* or *Goodwife* may have felt these titles to be 'patronizing'; to this we could add the fact that the discard of *Goodman* from New England speech was contemporaneous with the replacement of *Master* by *Mister*. On the latter phenomenon, Dawes (1949: 76-77) writes:

> with the etymological change [i.e. from *Master* to *Mister*] its impact of social dignity was lessened [...] *Mister* became the more generalized title and progressively less important as a socially dignifying agency.

Overall, thus, the trend in eighteenth-century New England was towards further democratizing society and secularizing the legal system, based upon the English model. The claim to moral superiority by 'the better sort' came into popular dispute. Hence, it seems that a similar process to what occurred in mid-sixteenth century England affected the New England colonies a century and a half later: there was a reaction to social differences among the middling sorts, and those formerly addressed as *Goodman/Goodwife* began referring to themselves (were referred to by others) as *Mister/Mistress*.[9] Furthermore, there was a growing 'Anglicization' of New England society, i.e. its alignment with English culture and values, starting in the late seventeenth century: thus, as *Goodman* and *Goodwife* had disappeared altogether as titles of address from London by 1700, they too became

---

9   Laurel Ulrich, from Harvard University, pointed out to me that this process of levelling triggered further socio-pragmatic changes: thus, by the 1780s, as nearly everybody had become a 'Master/Mister' and a 'Miss(tress)', high-status women, e.g. the wives of the ministers, were referred to as 'Lady so-and-so'.

less frequent in the New England towns and, later, in the more rural areas as well. As *Goodman* and *Goodwife* were also linked to 'church membership' (at least in the minds of some New Englanders), we may assume that the introduction of the *1691 Charter of Massachusetts Bay*, which granted freedom of worship to dissenters from Congregationalism, also contributed to their disappearance. With 'church membership' no longer being an important marker of Massachusetts society, there was thus no need to distinguish those who were 'good men' (in the literal sense) from those who supposedly were not; New Englanders whose (grand)fathers once thought the title *Goodman* to be a sign of respectability, no longer did so and preferred to call themselves by the next higher title, i.e. 'Master/Mister'. It is sensible to assume that no single factor of those mentioned above but rather all of them were responsible for the ultimate demise of *Goodman* and *Goodwife* as markers of New England culture.

4.3. Social variables involved in the use of Goodman *and* Goodwife
in late seventeenth-century Salem, Massachusetts

My scrutiny of the *Salem Witchcraft Papers* (Boyer/Nissenbaum 1977) suggests that the social variables determining whether Salemites were addressed/referred to respectively as *Goodman* and *Goodwife* or *Master* and *Mistress* were the following ones: (i) family background, (ii) holding an office of dignity and/or a higher military rank, (iii) employing labourers, and (iv) affluence, whereas (v) occupation and (vi) moral character do not seem to have exerted particular influence. As far as (vii) church membership is concerned, the Salem records suggest that while all the 'Goodmen' (and 'Goodwives') and the 'Masters' (and 'Mistresses') must have adhered to a form of radical Protestantism, not everybody was admitted to the communion table. Let us take Sarah Good, who was tried and executed for witchcraft, as a counterexample: Good was *not* a church member, and still she is occasionally referred to as 'Goody Good' in the Salem records. Sarah Good hardly represented the Puritan ideal of a 'good wife' (in the literal sense): in fact, she was divorced from her husband, homeless and therefore not the female head of a household;[10] together with her two children she wandered from door to door begging for food.[11] On the other hand, it is not difficult to ascertain 'Goodmen' and 'Goodwives' of Salem who had an impeccable reputation (which, however, roused jealousies among their neighbours and sometimes led to accusations of witchcraft). In fact, some of the 'Goodmen' of Salem were householders owning considerable estates, whose opinion, moreover, counted in public matters. A prime example of this type is 'Goodman Francis Nurse', about whom Charles W. Upham (1867 [2000]: 53-55) relates the following:

> On the 29th of April, 1678, Allen sold the Bishop farm to Francis Nurse [aged fifty-eight], of the town of Salem, for four hundred pounds. Nurse was an early settler [...] he is described as a "tray-maker". The making of these articles, and similar objects of domestic use, was an important employment in a new country remote from foreign supply. He appears to have been a very respectable person, of great stability and energy of character, whose judgment was much relied on by his neighbors. No one is mentioned more frequently as umpire to settle disputes, or arbitrator to adjust boundaries or estimate valuations, or on local juries to lay out highways and assess damages. [...] the venerable couple [i.e. Francis and Rebecca Nurse] were living in truly patriarchal style, occupying the "mansion" of Townsend Bishop.

Let us now consider the occupational status of those Salemites who bore the title of *Goodman/Goodwife*, as opposed to those who were entitled to *Master/Mistress*. Among the 'Goodmen' of Salem we indeed find artisans, mechanics, seafaring people and landowning farmers (the latter usually identified as 'husbandman' or, less frequently, as 'yeoman'):[12]

---

10   In fact, women referred to as 'Goodwife/Goody so-and-so' were as a rule either married or widows, and the female heads of a household to boot. A 'Mistress', in turn, was not necessarily married.

11   In light of this, *Goodwife/Goody* seem to have been applied to women of a wide range of life-styles. This is not acknowledged by the biographer and historian Charles W. Upham (1867 [2000]: 145), who described the title under scrutiny in purely positive terms: "Surely no better terms were ever used to characterize a worthy person [...] and the whole catalogue of pretentious titles ever given by flatterers or courtiers to a married lady cannot, all combined, convey a higher encomium than the term *Goodwife*".

12   My data confirm what Dawes (1949: 77) noticed in his primary sources with respect to *yeoman*: in fact, the latter does not seem to have been used as a title

(1a)   Being desired by *goodman Buckly* to give my testimony to his wives
        conversation before this great Calamity befell her
                        (Revs. John Higginson and Samuel Cheever for Sarah Buckley)

(1b)   *W'm Buckley* of Salem Village *Cord wayner* (Complaint v. George Jacobs, Jr.,
        Daniel Andrew, Rebecca Jacobs, Sarah Buckley, Mary Witheridge, Elizabeth
        Hart, Thomas Farrer, Elizabeth Colson, and Bethia Carter, Jr.)

(2a)   Mattha Corie kiled him because he told her she did not doe weel by *Goodman
        parkers* Childringe (Elizabeth Booth v. Martha Corey)

(2b)   *John parker* of Salem *seaman*
                        (Preparation for the Court of Oyer and Terminer, May – August 1692)

(3a)   We whose nams Are heareunto subscribed being desired by *goodman
        Nurse* to declare what we knewe concerning his wives conversation for
        time past (Petition for Rebecca Nurse)

(3b)   Rebecka Nurse the wife of *francs Nurce* of Salem Village *husbandman*
                                            (Mittimus for Martha Corey *et al.*)

(4a)   Then *Hen: Kenny* rose up to speak Q[uestion]: *Goodm: Kenny* what do you
        say? (Examination of Rebecca Nurse)

(4b)   Edward putnam and *Henery Keney Yeoman* both of Salem Village
                                            (Warrant for Arrest of Martha Corey)

The wives of these men are as a rule referred to as *Goodwife* or
Goody:

(5a)   *Goodwife Tyler* did say, that, when she was first apprehended, she had no
        fears upon her
        (Rev. Increase Mather's Report of his Conversation in Prison with Mary Tyler)

(5b)   *Mary Tyler* wife of *hopestill Tyler* of Andover, *Blacksmith*
                                            (Case of Mary Tyler)

(6a)   Likewise *Goodwife Pease* and Hobs and her daughter Abigail doth Afflict him
        and thretten the same (John DeRich v. George Jacobs, Sr. *et al.*)

---

of social status in New England but rather as an occupational designation,
whereas *Goodman* never appears as such. Thus, someone whose occupational
status was indicated as 'yeoman' may have been addressed as 'Goodman so-
and-so' or 'Mr. so-and-so', depending on other factors.

(6b)   *Sarah pease* the wife of *Robert pease* of Salem *Weaver* who stands charged
        with sundry acts of Witchcraft (Warrant for arrest of Sarah Pease)

(7a)   Joseph Fullers apparicon the Same day also came to me & told me that *Goody*
        Corey had Killd him
                (Ann Putnam, Sr. v. John Willard, William Hobbs, and Martha Corey)

(7b)   *Martha Corey* Wife of *Gyles Corey* of Salem *husbandman*
                                              (Indictment v. Martha Corey, No. 1)

It is noteworthy, however, that other male Salemites engaging in the
very same professional activities are referred to in the records as 'Mr.
so-and-so'. Among them, we thus find artisans and farmers, the latter
as a rule identified as 'yeoman' (and *not* as 'husbandman'):

(8a)   on this 20th Instante of may: 92 about an hour by sun I went to *mr John*
        Putnams to see mersey Lueis (Mary Walcott v. Mary Easty)

(8b)   The Deposistion of *John putnam weaver*: and Hannah his wife
                (John Putnam, Jr. and Hannah Putnam v. Rebecca Nurse, Mary Easty,
                                                              and Sarah Cloyce)

(9a)   Here is the wife of *Mr Tho: Putman* who accuseth you by credible
        information (Examination of Rebecca Nurse)

(9b)   according to Complaint of Capt Jonathan Walcot and *Serj't Thomas putnam* of
        Salem Village *Yeoman*
        (Mittimus for Susannah Martin, Lydia Dustin, Dorcas Hoar, and Sarah Morey)

How should we account for the discrimination between 'Mr. John
Putnam' and 'Goodman Robert Pease' (both weavers by profession),
and 'Mr. Thomas Putnam' and 'Goodman Henry Kenny' (both of
them entered as 'yeomen')? The Putnams were the richest people of
Salem, well educated, and of ancient stock; its male members,
moreover, were all holders of an office of dignity and/or had an
impressive military record. Thomas Putnam, for instance, had been a
sergeant in the army and a war veteran, who acted as a clerk during
the witchcraft episode, while John Putnam was a constable. Generally
speaking, it can be claimed that those Salem men performing
important official tasks in the community consistently appear in the
records, provided that a title is mentioned at all, as 'Mr. so-and-so'
(and never as 'Goodman so-and-so'). Ezekiel Cheever, sheriff, and

Edward Putnam, deacon, are further specimens illustrating the point made above:

(10)   *Mr Edward Putnam* affirmd the same to the jury of inquest that *Mr Cheevers* doth (Edward Putnam & Ezekiel Cheever v. Martha Corey)

Furthermore, particularly affluent businessmen are also entered as 'Mr.': this was the case with George Carr, an enterprising and prosperous person, who was engaged in ship-building and who owned the ferry across the Merrimac, and Phillip English, who is classified as a 'merchant' in the records: the English family owned 21 vessels, a wharf, and 14 buildings in Salem by 1692, the year when English was made a selectman:

(11)   and was present with *mr George Carr* and mr Richard Carr and I also saw a blue bore dart out of mr Brdbery gate to *Mr George Carrs* horses
                    (Richard Carr and Zerubable Endicot t v. Mary Bradbury)

(12)   & *Mr English* then run a pin into Maryes hand as she attested
                    (Abigail Hobbs and Mary Warren v. George Burroughs *et al.*)

It is of significance on that score that people like Carr and English, but also the members of the Putnam family mentioned above, could all afford to employ labourers, i.e. had authority over others. Evidently, the highest functionaries were also bearers of the title *Mr.*, such as Judge Hawthorne and the minister Deodat Lawson. The special status of magistrates and the clergy would often be indicated by an adjectival epithet (e.g. 'the worshipful/the reverend Mr. so-and-so'):

(13)   Then *Mr. Hathorn* read farther of Croslys evidence
                    (Examination of Martha Corey)

(14)   they were sat down at the Table, *Mr Lawson* & his wife & severall more
                    (Bray Wilkins v. John Willard)

The wives of Salem men referred to as 'Mr.', in turn, are generally mentioned as 'Mrs./Mis(t.)', and *not* as 'Goodwife/Goody':

(15)   and that he kiled *Mist. Lawson* because she was so unwilling to goe from the village (Ann Putnam, Jr. v. George Burroughs)

(16)   then their Came a streked snake creeping over her shoulder and crep into her
        bosom *mrs. English* had a yelo bird in her bosom
                                              (Susannah Sheldon v. Mary English *et al.*)

(17)   between my Hon'rd father mr George Carr: and *Mis Bradbery* [...] as we ware
        riding hom by the house of *Capt Tho: Bradbery* [...] I also saw a blue bore
        dart out of *mr Brdbery* gate
                                              (Richard Carr and Zerubable Endicott v. Mary Bradbury)

However, Ann Putnam, wife of the richest man in Salem village, 'Mr.
Thomas Putnam' (see 9 above), is spoken of twice in the same record
as 'Goody Putnam' (rather than 'Mrs. Putnam'). This is noteworthy
because (i) Ann Putnam is addressed like the 'Goodwives' of men
who are never referred to as 'Mr.', and (ii) because it is Ann Putnam's
servant-maid, Mercy Lewis, who allegedly referred to her as 'Goody
Putnam':

(18)   mercy lewes said it was *goody putnam* that said it was goody nurse: *goody
        putnam* said it was mercy lewes that told her
                                              (John Tarbell and Samuel Nurse for Rebecca Nurse)

This is in stark contrast with (19), which concerns another servant-
girl, Mary Warren, speaking about her employer, Elizabeth Proctor,
who appears throughout the records as 'Goodwife/Goody Proctor', but
never as 'Mrs. Proctor'. This is what we would expect, as John
Proctor's profession is indicated as 'husbandman', which is why he is
referred to / addressed as 'Goodman Proctor'. In spite of this, the maid
Mary Warren speaks of Elizabeth Proctor as 'Mistress Proctor' on one
occasion, which can hardly be taken as evidence of the maid's
admiration for her mistress; after all, Mary Warren is accusing her and
her husband of witchcraft:

(19)   Q. Did you ever see any poppetts? An. yes once I saw one made of cloth in
        Mistris procters hand. (Examination of Mary Warren, May 12, 1692)

The last two examples suggest that the titles of address appearing in
the official records may not always have been the ones used in the
more intimate everyday situations. Ann Putnam was undoubtedly
entitled to being addressed as 'Mistress Putnam' – and indeed she is
once referred to as such in *A Brief and True Narrative*, written in 1692

by her contemporary, the minister Deodat Lawson – but may have been called 'Goody Putnam' by her friends and neighbours, or even by Mercy Lewis, her servant-girl. In turn, it is possible that linguistically insecure people like the servant-girl Mary Warren called her master and mistress 'Master Proctor' and 'Mistress Proctor' in the courtroom, even though she daily heard them spoken of as 'Goodman Proctor' and 'Goody Proctor'.[13] A different explanation for Mary Warren's hypercorrection, supported by the records, could be that Mary was used to addressing the Proctors as 'Master' and 'Mistress' and spoke of them as 'my master/mistress (Proctor)' in their absence:

(20)   Noe sir, but when I was afflicted *my master Procter* was in the Roome & said if ye are Afflicted I wish ye were more Afflicted & you and all: I said *Master*, w't make you say soe (Examination of Mary Warren, May 12, 1692)

5. Concluding remarks

In this study I have argued that the titles of respect *Goodman* and *Goodwife* were not exclusively a New England phenomenon, as commoly assumed by historians and linguists, but also occurred in the Mid-Atlantic colonies. However, they were much more frequent in the Puritan colonies than in Virginia or Maryland and remained in New England for a longer period, in fact until the early decades of the eighteenth century. It may be that *Goodman* and *Goodwife* were already popular with the Puritan dissenters in England because their literal meaning (a 'good man/wife') epitomized the Puritan creed; if that was the case, they would have been taken to the North Atlantic

---

13   However, Mary Warren's use of 'Mistress Proctor' contrasts with her intimate address towards her employer in the very same record, namely 'Betty Proctor'. Moreover, Mary Warren addresses the Proctors repeatedly by means of the second person singular pronoun in emotional discourse (see examination of April 21). As pointed out by several scholars (e.g. Hope 1998; Finkenstaedt 1963), the *thou* pronoun is not exactly a marker of respect when used in conjunction with a negatively connoted term (thus Mary Warren uses expressions like 'thou wicked creature', 'thou wretch').

colonies as positively connoted forms. With the secularization of New England in the early 1700s, however, *Goodman* started to become stigmatized and the socially neutral form *Mister* (rather than *Master*) began to gain the upper hand; the same is true for *Goodwife*, which was replaced by *Miss(tress)*. The reasons for the disappearance of *Goodman* and *Goodwife* from colonial North America were similar to those which led to their extinction in Early Modern England: ambitious members of the 'middle classes' aspired to the social prestige reserved for those above them (in Old England the gentility, in New England the 'better citizens', i.e. the economic and political elite), and therefore also to the titles of address associated with the higher social segments.

A close scrutiny of the *Salem Witchcraft Papers* suggests that among the social variables relevant to the assignment of the title 'Mr.' (as opposed to 'Goodman') occupational status did not play an important role, while family reputation, office-holding, military record and wealth certainly did. Contrary to what is commonly assumed, church membership (in the sense of 'publicly professed converts admitted to the communion table') was not a prerequisite for being addressed as 'Goodman' or 'Goodwife'; on the contrary, some of the *Goodmen* and *Goodwives* of colonial New England, though supporters of Protestantism, must have been renegades in the eyes of the authorities.

Taking into consideration 'close-to-oral' records, such as the Salem examination protocols mostly written down in direct discourse, allows the researcher to study – however imperfectly – the micro-pragmatic level of discourse. Thus, we have seen that clear-cut divisions as reflected in official records, e.g. the one between 'Goodman/Goodwife' and 'Master/Mistress' in seventeenth-century New England, may not always have regulated everyday usage in informal situations; what is more, the rather formal courtroom situation may have led to hypercorrective usage on the part of people unaccustomed to bearing witness before the highest authorities. The examples mentioned above concerning the address forms used for Ann Putnam and Elizabeth Proctor are cases in point.

References

Primary sources

Boyer, Paul / Nissenbaum, Stephen (eds) 1977. *The Salem Witchcraft Papers. Verbatim Transcriptions of the Court Records.* 3 Vols. New York: Da Capo Press. At <etext.virginia.edu/salem/witchcraft/texts/transcripts.html>.

Secondary sources

Beaudry, Mary C. 1979. Insult and Slander in Seventeenth-Century Virginia. *Journal of the Virginia Folklore Society* 1, 42-51.

Busse, Ulrich 2003. The Co-Occurrence of Nominal and Pronominal Address Forms in the Shakespeare Corpus: Who Says *thou* or *you* to Whom? In Taavitsainen, Irma / Jucker, Andreas H. (eds) *Diachronic Perspectives on Address Term Systems.* Amsterdam: Benjamins, 193-221.

Craigie, William A. *et al.* (eds) 1938-44. *A Dictionary of American English on Historical Principles.* 4 Vols. Chicago: University of Chicago Press.

Dawes, Norman H. 1949. Titles as Symbols of Prestige in Seventeenth-Century New England. *William and Mary Quarterly* 6/1, 69-83.

De Vere Schele M. 1872. *Americanisms. The English of the New World.* New York.

Finkenstaedt, Thomas 1963. You *and* Thou. *Studien zur Anrede im Englischen (Mit einem Exkurs über die Anrede im Deutschen).* Berlin: De Gruyter.

Hope, Jonathan 1998. Second Person Singular Pronouns in Records of Early Modern 'Spoken' English. In Rydén, Mats *et al.* (eds) *A Reader in Early Modern English.* Frankfurt a. M.: Peter Lang, 377-396.

Murray, James *et al.* (eds) [2]1989. *The Oxford English Dictionary.* 27 Vols. Oxford: Oxford University Press.

Murrin, John 2001. Things Fearful to Name: Bestiality in Early America. In Reis, Elizabeth (ed.) *American Sexual Histories*. Boston: Blackwell, 14-35.

Norton, Mary Beth 1987. Gender and Defamation in Seventeenth-Century Maryland. *The William and Mary Quarterly* 44/1, 3-39.

Pablé, Adrian 2003. The Goodman and his *Faith*: Signals of Local Colour in Nathaniel Hawthorne's Historical Fiction with Reference to Cultural Translation. *Babel* 49/2, 97-130.

Postles, Dave 2005. The Politics of Address in Early Modern England. *Journal of Historical Sociology* 18/2, 100-121.

Skeat, Walter [1882] 1963. *An Etymological Dictionary of the English Language*. New York: Capricorn.

Stoll, Rita 1989. *Die Nicht-Pronominale Anrede bei Shakespeare*. Frankfurt a.M.: Peter Lang.

Upham, Charles W. [1867] 2000. *Salem Witchcraft. With an Account of Salem Village and a History of Opinions on Witchcraft and Kindred Subjects*. Mineola: Dover Publications.

Williams, Joseph M. 1992. When Degree is Shak'd: Sixteenth-Century Anticipations of Some Modern Attitudes Toward Usage. In Machan, Tim W. / Scott, Charles T. (eds) *English in Its Social Contexts*. Oxford: Oxford University Press, 69-101.

Wright, Laura 2003. Eight Grammatical Features of Southern United States Speech Present in Early Modern London Prison Narratives. In Nagle, Stephen / Sanders, Sara (eds) *English in the Southern United States*. Cambridge: Cambridge University Press, 36-63.

Wright, Laura 2004. The Language of Transported Londoners: Third-person-singular Present-tense Markers in Depositions from Virginia and the Bermudas, 1607-1624. In Hickey, Raymond (ed.) *Legacies of Colonial English. Studies in Transplanted Dialects*. Cambridge: Cambridge University Press, 157-171.

Notes on Contributors

NICHOLAS BROWNLEES is Associate Professor of English Language at the University of Florence. His main research interests focus on language and discourse in 17th-century English news publications and pamphlets. He is the author of *Corantos and Newsbooks: Language and Discourse in the First English Newspapers* (Pisa ETS 1999) and editor of *News Discourse in Early Modern Britain* (Peter Lang 2006). He is the coordinator of the Florence Early English Newspapers (FEEN) Corpus consisting of news pamphlets of the English Civil War and Interregnum. He is presently engaged in a major research project focusing on the transmission of news in Early Modern Europe.

MARÍA JOSÉ CARRILLO-LINARES is Associate Professor in the Dept. of English Philology at the University of Huelva. She graduated from the University of Seville in 1991 and obtained her PhD in 1997. Her main field is Middle English and her research interests include the study of Middle English medical and scientific literature and Middle English dialectology. She is currently engaged on a project on Middle English word geography in collaboration with Edurne Garrido-Anes.

MARINA DOSSENA is Professor of English Language and Head of the Department of Comparative Languages, Literatures and Cultures at the University of Bergamo. Her research interests focus on the features and origins of British varieties of English and the history of specialized discourse. Recent publications include the proceedings of ICEHL 14 (3 vols., edited with Maurizio Gotti and Richard Dury; Benjamins 2008), and *Studies in Late Modern English Correspondence: Methodology and Data* (edited with Ingrid Tieken-Boon van Ostade; Peter Lang 2008). She is also the author of *Scotticisms in Grammar and Vocabulary* (Birlinn 2005), and is currently compiling a corpus of 19th-century Scottish correspondence in co-operation with Richard Dury.

JULIA FERNÁNDEZ CUESTA is Associate Professor in the English Dept. at the University of Seville, Spain. She obtained a BA and PhD in English from the University of Salamanca, specializing in History of English and Old English. Her research interests centre on English historical linguistics, historical dialectology and language contact. Since 2001 she has coordinated a research project on the history of Northern varieties of British English in collaboration with Nieves Rodríguez Ledesma. Their publications in this area include 'Northern Features in 15th-16th-Century Legal Documents from Yorkshire' (2004), 'From Old Northumbrian to Northern Middle English: Bridging the Divide' (2007), 'Northern Middle English: Towards Telling the Full Story' (2008), 'Towards a History of Northern English: Early and Late Northumbrian' (forthcoming). They are currently compiling a corpus of Northern English from the 8th to the 16th century.

EDURNE GARRIDO-ANES is a lecturer in the English Department at the University of Huelva. She obtained a BA and a PhD in English Philology, specializing in the study of Middle English scientific manuscripts. Her research interests include English historical dialectology, language contact and the editing of Middle English texts. Along with María José Carrillo Linares, she is currently working on a project on Middle English word geography.

MARGARET LAING is currently Research Fellow in the Institute for Historical Dialectology, English Language, University of Edinburgh. As a member of the Middle English Dialect Project, under the direction of Angus McIntosh, she contributed to the production of *A Linguistic Atlas of Late Mediaeval English* (AUP/Mercat Press 1986). Since then she has been engaged in a major research project, in collaboration with Keith Williamson and more recently with Roger Lass, to create *A Linguistic Atlas of Early Middle English*. She has written on late Middle English, most notably with Michael Benskin – 'Translations and *Mischsprachen* in Middle English Manuscripts' (1981). She has published extensively on early Middle English, including *A Catalogue of Sources for a Linguistic Atlas of Early Medieval English* (Brewer 1993) and many articles arising out of the investigation of early Middle English dialects and scribal systems.

Since September 2007 she has been working, in collaboration with Keith Williamson and Michael Benskin, towards the creation of an electronic, web-based version of *LALME* (e-LALME).

ROGER LASS, Professor Emeritus of Linguistics and Honorary Research Associate in English at the University of Cape Town, is a Collaborating Scholar of the Institute for Historical Dialectology at the University of Edinburgh. His special interests are the history of English, historical linguistic theory, and its interface with evolutionary biology. His most recent publications include *Historical Linguistics and Language Change* (CUP 1997), volume III of *The Cambridge History of the English Language* (editor and contributor: CUP 1999) and (with Margaret Laing) 'Tales of the 1001 Nists: the phonological implications of litteral substitution sets in some thirteenth-century South-West Midland texts' (*English Language and Linguistics* 2003). He is currently working on the *Linguistic Atlas of Early Middle English* with Margaret Laing and Keith Williamson.

ROBERT MCCOLL MILLAR is Senior Lecturer in Linguistics at the University of Aberdeen. His most recent books are *Language, Nation and Power* (Palgrave Macmillan 2005), *Northern and Insular Scots* (Edinburgh University Press 2007) and *Trask's Historical Linguistics* (Hodder Arnold 2007). He has recently embarked on an Arts and Humanities Research Council funded project on lexical change in the Scottish fishing communities; he is also completing a monograph on the linguistic history of Europe in antique and medieval Europe.

HERMANN MOISL is a Senior Lecturer in computational linguists in the School of English and Linguistics at the University of Newcastle, UK. His research interests are in natural language processing, formal language and automata theory, artificial neural networks, dynamical systems, and multivariate statistical analysis of linguistic corpora. From an earlier life he also retains an interest and some research activity in the development and cultural role of literacy, and in early Germanic and Celtic languages and history.

ADRIAN PABLÉ is Junior Assistant Professor of linguistics in the English Department at the University of Lausanne, Switzerland. He has a PhD from Zurich University. His dissertation focused on the language and sources of Arthur Miller's *The Crucible*. His main research interests include Integrational Linguistics, Historical Dialectology, Linguistic Historiography and Translation Studies. He is currently involved in two research projects, one concerning the history of the New England dialect, the other on language and identity in Swiss bilingual communities.

PIETER VAN REENEN is Professor Emeritus of Computer Linguistics at the VU University Amsterdam and Honorary Research Associate in Dutch at the Meertens Instituut Amsterdam. His special interests are language variation and change in Old French, Middle Dutch and Modern Dutch dialects. He is one of the authors of a database of Modern Dutch dialects: the Goeman-Taeldeman-Van Reenen-Project (GTRP), and of a corpus of 14th-century Dutch charters: the Van Reenen-Mulder Corpus (CRM). His most recent publications include *Chartes de Champagne en français conservées aux Archives de l'Aube 1270-1300* (Orléans: Paradigme 2007), and (with others) volume II of *The Morphological Atlas of Dutch Dialects* (Amsterdam: AUP 2008), which is based on GTRP.

MARGIT REM is Associate Professor in the Dept. of Dutch Language and Culture at the Radboud University Nijmegen. She graduated from the University of Amsterdam and obtained a PhD at the VU University Amsterdam in 2003 (*De taal van de klerken uit de Hollandse grafelijke kanselarij*). She is involved in the completion of the Van Reenen-Mulder Corpus (CRM) of 14th-century Dutch dialects and published on the basis of this corpus. Her special interests are Middle Dutch, the standardization of Dutch, historical linguistics and historical text corpora.

Mª NIEVES RODRÍGUEZ LEDESMA is Associate Professor in the English Dept. at the University of Seville, Spain. She obtained a BA and a PhD in English from the University of Seville, specializing in History of the English language and Middle Scots. Her research interests centre on English historical dialectology, Scots and language contact. She has been working with Julia Fernández Cuesta on a project on the development of the Northern varieties of English. Their publications in this area include 'Northern Features in 15th-16th-Century Legal Documents from Yorkshire' (2004), 'From Old Northumbrian to Northern Middle English: Bridging the Divide' (2007), 'Northern Middle English: Towards Telling the Full Story' (2008), 'Towards a history of Northern English: Early and Late Northumbrian' (forthcoming). They are currently compiling a corpus of Northern English from the 8th to the 16th century.

EVERT WATTEL is Associate Professor Emeritus in the Department of Mathematics, Geometry section, of the VU University of Amsterdam. In 1968 he got a doctors degree in Topology from Amsterdam University. His main interest is the application of mathematics to language and sciences studies. Among several other topics in mathematics he has been working on map construction, extrapolation, geodesics and stemmatology for medieval manuscripts.

Linguistic Insights

Studies in Language and Communication

This series aims to promote specialist language studies in the fields of linguistic theory and applied linguistics, by publishing volumes that focus on specific aspects of language use in one or several languages and provide valuable insights into language and communication research. A cross-disciplinary approach is favoured and most European languages are accepted.

The series includes two types of books:

- **Monographs** – featuring in-depth studies on special aspects of language theory, language analysis or language teaching.
- **Collected papers** – assembling papers from workshops, conferences or symposia.

Each volume of the series is subjected to a double peer-reviewing process.

Vol. 1   Maurizio Gotti & Marina Dossena (eds)
          Modality in Specialized Texts. Selected Papers of the 1st CERLIS Conference.
          421 pages. 2001. ISBN 3-906767-10-8. US-ISBN 0-8204-5340-4

Vol. 2   Giuseppina Cortese & Philip Riley (eds)
          Domain-specific English. Textual Practices across Communities
          and Classrooms.
          420 pages. 2002. ISBN 3-906768-98-8. US-ISBN 0-8204-5884-8

Vol. 3   Maurizio Gotti, Dorothee Heller & Marina Dossena (eds)
          Conflict and Negotiation in Specialized Texts. Selected Papers of
          the 2nd CERLIS Conference.
          470 pages. 2002. ISBN 3-906769-12-7. US-ISBN 0-8204-5887-2

Editorial address:

Prof. Maurizio Gotti   Università di Bergamo, Facoltà di Lingue e Letterature Straniere,
                       Via Salvecchio 19, 24129 Bergamo, Italy
                       Fax: 0039 035 2052789, E-Mail: m.gotti@unibg.it